CW01648728

Real Families

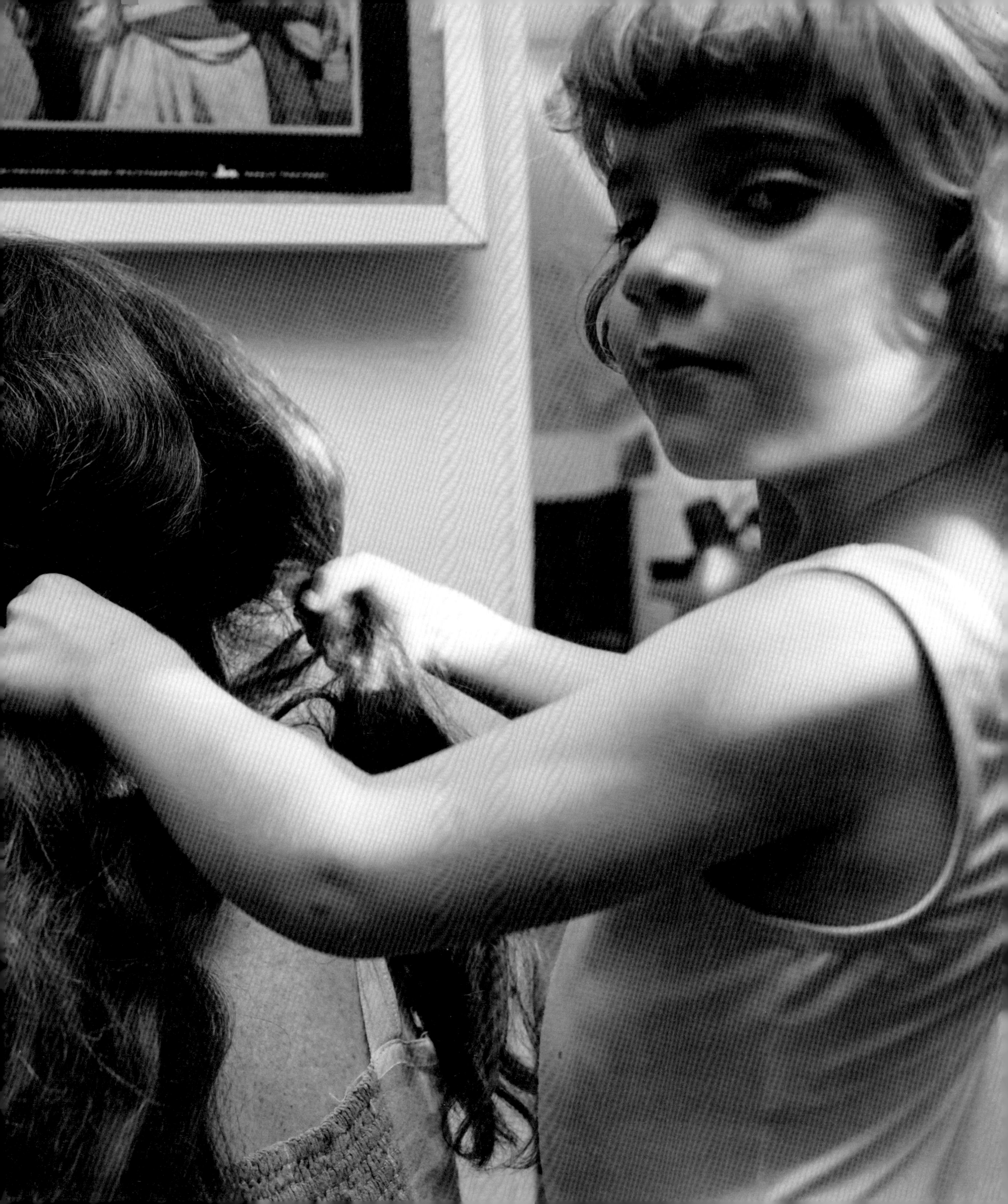

Stories of Change

The Fitzwilliam Museum,
University of Cambridge
in association with
Paul Holberton Publishing

Real Families

Susan Golombok

First published in 2023 to accompany the exhibition
Real Families: Stories of Change at the Fitzwilliam Museum,
University of Cambridge, 6 October 2023 – 7 January 2024

ISBN 978-1-913645-51-9
British Library Cataloguing in Publication Data
A catalogue record for this book is available from the British Library
Produced by Paul Holberton Publishing
1 Burwood Place
London W2 2UT
www.paulholberton.com

Designed by Paul Sloman
Printing by E-graphic Srl, Verona, Italy
Front cover: Chantal Joffe, *Me, Em and Nat* (p. 158)
Back cover: Thomas Holton, *Bored* (p. 106)
Frontispiece: Nicholas Nixon, *Bebe and Clementine, Cambridge, Massachusetts* (p. 106)

This publication has been generously supported by The Marlay Group Fund

Details: page 24: cat. 22; page 64: cat. 59;
page 116: cat. 79; page 142: cat. 117

MIX
Paper from responsible sources
FSC® C133174

This edition has been printed on certified
FSC® GardaMatt Ultra paper and other controlled sources

Foreword
Luke Syson 6

Stories of Change
Susan Golombok 9

What is a Family? 25

A Sunday Kind of Love
Jackie Kay 27

Annunciations: Three Women Talk Back to Tradition
Rebecca Birrell 35

Everyday Madonnas
Rosie Millard 45

Family Transitions 65

Legitimising Motherhood
Katy Hessel 67

Attachment and Human Experience
Pasco Fearon 73

Siblings: A Love–Hate Relationship
Claire Hughes 81

Roman Charity and Modern Families
Mary Beard 97

Family Dynamics 117

Much to Give Thanks For
Andrew Solomon 119

The Visitation
Dorothy Byrne 129

Family Legacies 143

Who You Think You Are
Alex Graham 145

There Will Be Blood
Olivia Laing 153

Timeline 172
Further reading 173
Acknowledgements 174
Index 175
Picture credits 176

Foreword

We are not always as aware as we might be of the ways images shape our opinions and beliefs. As a result, written texts or organised encounters and their records are often regarded as solid evidence, data to be collected and analysed. But pictures, sculptures, photographs and so on, for all that they can be both highly personal – equal to any in-person interview – and still proclaim broader values and assumptions, are not usually included in research projects or academic disciplines that fall outside those directly and traditionally concerned with the study of art and material culture. That is one of the reasons why this collaboration between the Fitzwilliam Museum and the Centre for Family Research in the Psychology Department within Cambridge's School of Biological Sciences has an experimental aspect.

Many of us record our family lives and loves through image-making, more usually a holiday snap or casually assembled group shot than a formal portrait, though we make those too, at weddings and the like. These declare our affections, identities and allegiances. They mark important moments. And they can reveal, sometimes inadvertently, tensions or happiness. The kinds of historical grand portrait – like the picture by Sir Joshua Reynolds that begins this exhibition (**15**) – that we encounter in art galleries assert a view of family which focuses on a unit of father, mother and offspring, with sons often positioned more importantly than daughters. Some of this patriarchal propaganda has been challenged since – roughly – the latter part of the nineteenth century, when artists, often women, painted pictures about their own lives and relationships, set frequently within the domestic arena. Susan Golombok has realised that the ways of creating and nurturing families that have come to the fore in the fifty or so years of the Centre's existence have become the subject matter in the same period for artists in many media, who have recorded their own places in their own families and sensitively observed the family lives and structures of others. Their language is often, unsurprisingly, figurative. The photograph looms large, narrowing the space between these potentially universalising images and our own photographic stashes. Use is also made by artists of the material culture of childhood, of family rituals, and the exhibition juxtaposes these pieces with some of the historic objects that inspired them.

Susan's courage in using these works of art as evidence is really admirable, a model for future collaborative work within our university museum. It's not easy to curate an exhibition for the first time, and our understanding of the images, both recent and historic, that are analysed here is, I believe, profoundly enriched by their investigation from an unexpected, but crucial, academic point of view. Susan and her colleagues at the Centre see things in these works that others might miss. As a result, we are presented with an array of images that may well resonate with our own experiences, familiar in both senses of the word. I find many of them moving – some distinctly upsetting, others joyous – and that's to do with what they set out to do, but also my own life experiences. Not every kind of family structure or interaction is investigated; the show would be too big and it has seemed important to focus on those areas that are specifically the remit of the Centre. But the narrow view of family promoted by Reynolds is hugely broadened here and I hope that many will see their experiences and decisions reflected.

All of us at the Fitzwilliam have enjoyed our collaboration with colleagues at the Centre, and we are especially grateful to Susan Golombok not just for bringing us this idea but also for her extraordinary and sustained effort in seeing it through. Like Susan, I would also like to acknowledge the fundamental support of Coralie Malissard and Capucine Poncet, who both worked for two years seeking out the modern and contemporary artists whose work speaks so vividly to the research strands of the Centre. Rebecca Birrell and Rebecca Virag did the same for the historic works. I'd like to thank those living artists who gave so much time to conversations about their lives and art, and to all the private and institutional lenders, and, often unsung in this context, the many gallerists who were excited by this project and got behind it. The gallery of writers assembled in this catalogue is surprising and remarkable; I would like to thank them all for writing so expertly and personally. I am also extremely grateful to The Marlay Group Fund for their contribution towards such a high-quality publication. Finally, and crucially, the Fitzwilliam Museum joins the Centre for Family Research in thanking the Wellcome Trust for its support of this project. The Wellcome has long ensured that research on health and well-being breaks down disciplinary barriers to arrive somewhere new, beneficial and exciting. I think that is what has happened here.

Luke Syson
Director and Marlay Curator

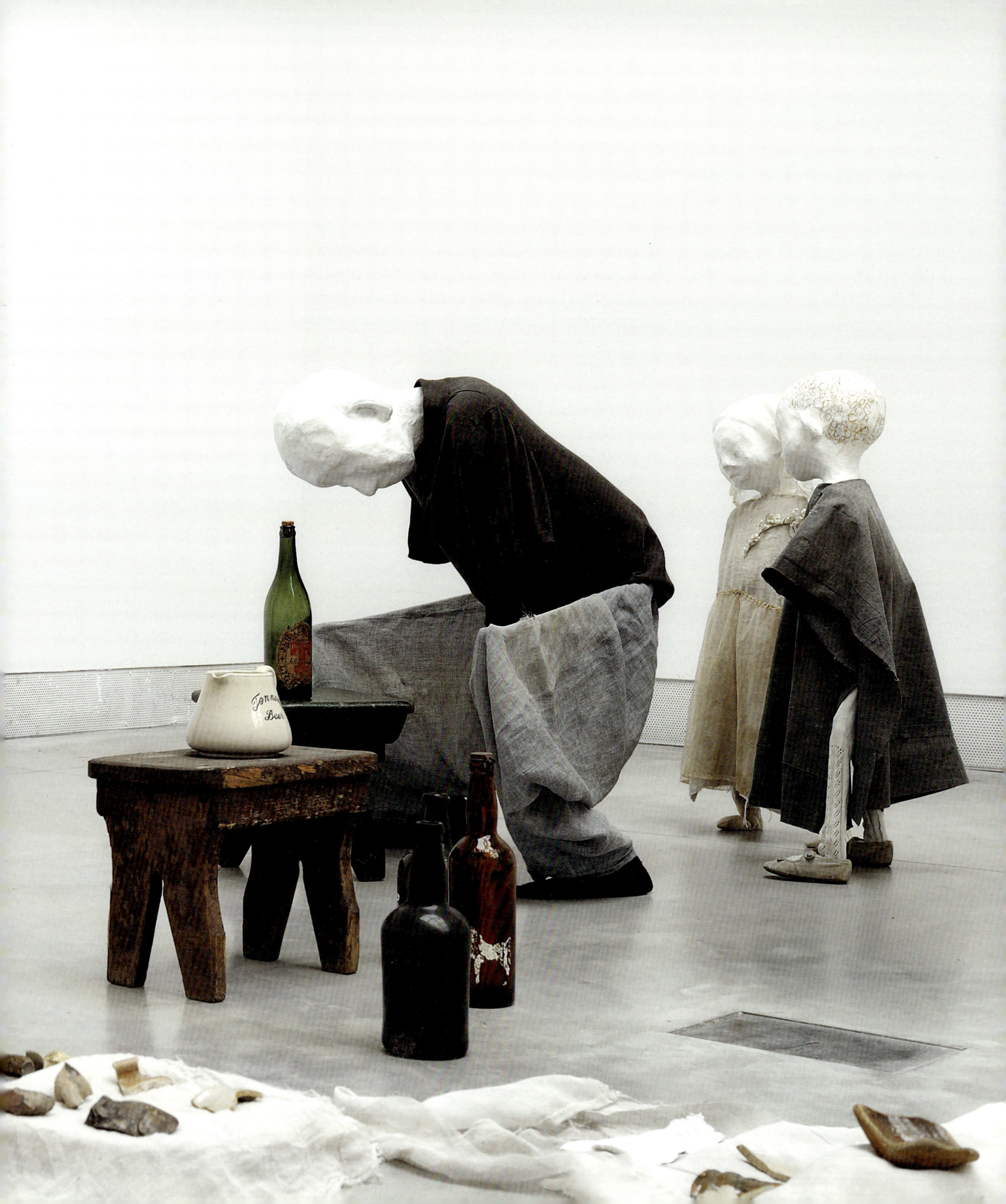

Stories of Change

1.
Cathy Wilkes
Untitled (Possil, At Last)
2013, mixed media
470 × 435 cm (detail)
Tate: Presented by
Tate Members 2014
T14119

Susan Golombok

In the spring of 2015, the artist Cathy Wilkes had a solo exhibition at Tate Liverpool. Among the spectacular installations, there was one that broke my heart (1). At the centre, a despairing man, who I took to be a father, was hunched over a beer bottle from Tennent's Brewery in Glasgow. Behind him, dressed in delicate cloth, stood two small children, who I presumed to be his own. To me, the desolate father and vulnerable children standing apprehensively yet stoically behind him summed up decades of psychological research on the effects of parents' adversity on their children. But unlike academic research, it went straight to the heart.

At the time, I was director of the Centre for Family Research at the University of Cambridge, and I had been studying family relationships and how they affect children all my working life. I was in Liverpool for a psychology conference, and I had slipped out to the Tate next door in the break. When I returned to the conference, the plight of this small family played on my mind. I felt strangely drawn to them. In the afternoon, I paid them another visit. Moving backwards and forwards that day from the world of academic research and its dedication to scientific principles, complex theories and empirical evidence, to the world of art where stories are told in different ways, the idea of an exhibition on the family – something I had been thinking about for some time – began to take shape.

One challenge for researchers is how to transmit their findings beyond their immediate academic circle. For me, this had always been important as I work in a controversial area of family research; I study the impact on children of growing up in new family forms, where prejudice and assumption often trump the reality of family life. I began this research in 1976, after reading an article in the feminist magazine *Spare Rib* on the predicament of lesbian mothers who fought their ex-husbands for custody of their children. At that time, not a single mother had won. In every case, the children had been forcibly removed from her on the grounds that they would be psychologically harmed by remaining with a lesbian mother. The article included a request from a group of women in Cambridge, who called themselves *Action for Lesbian Parents*, for a volunteer to carry out an objective study of what actually happens to children who grow up with lesbian mothers. At the time, I was studying for a master's degree in child development and I became that volunteer.

Not long afterwards, in January 1978, a feature in the London *Evening News* with the headline 'Dr Strange Love' exposed a Harley Street doctor who was helping lesbian women become pregnant through donor insemination. This was the first time the British public learned of the existence of lesbian mother families. It triggered a national outcry. Questions were raised in the House of Commons and the House of Lords, and there was a call by MPs to 'Ban these Babies' (**2**). Later that year, in July, Louise Brown was born through *in vitro* fertilisation (IVF) in Oldham, Lancashire – the first baby in the world conceived outside the human body (**3**). This became possible through the scientific work of Robert Edwards at the University of Cambridge in collaboration with the obstetrician Patrick Steptoe. Again, there was bitter opposition to this new way of creating families, with allusions made to 'Frankenstein' babies and scientists accused of 'playing God'. Looking back, 1978 was a watershed year for the family.

Today, same-sex marriage is enshrined in law in more than 30 countries and more than eight million IVF babies have been born around the world. In the intervening years, we have witnessed a profusion of new family forms; some had previously been hidden from view because of fear of stigmatisation, and others became possible through advances in reproductive technologies following the introduction of IVF. We now have families formed through egg donation, sperm donation, embryo donation and surrogacy, and families with lesbian mothers, gay fathers, transgender parents and single parents by choice. Parenthood today is accessible in ways we could never have imagined when lesbian mothers and 'test-tube' babies hit the headlines in 1978.

The Centre for Family Research has been at the forefront of research on these families, especially on the impact on parents and children. Our research has shown that new family forms are just as likely to flourish as traditional families, and sometimes more so. What matters most for children is not the make-up of their family. Instead, it is the quality of relationships within it, the support of their wider community and the attitudes and governance of the society in which they live. Just because people become parents in new ways does not make them less capable or love their children less.

By the time I encountered Cathy Wilkes's mesmerising exhibition in 2015, much had changed. In the United Kingdom, the Adoption and Children Act, passed in 2002, which enabled children to be adopted jointly by same-sex couples, came into force in 2005, and in 2008 the Human Fertilisation and Embryology Act removed the requirement for fertility clinics to consider the child's 'need for a father' in the decision to offer fertility treatment. It also enabled the non-biological parent of a child born through assisted reproduction to same-sex couples to be a legal parent of the child. In 2018, the Act was amended to permit single parents to become the legal parents of children born through surrogacy. In 2023, a draft Bill was submitted to government recommending reforms to make surrogacy work better for children, surrogates and intended parents, and the first donor-conceived children became legally entitled to request the identity of their donors.

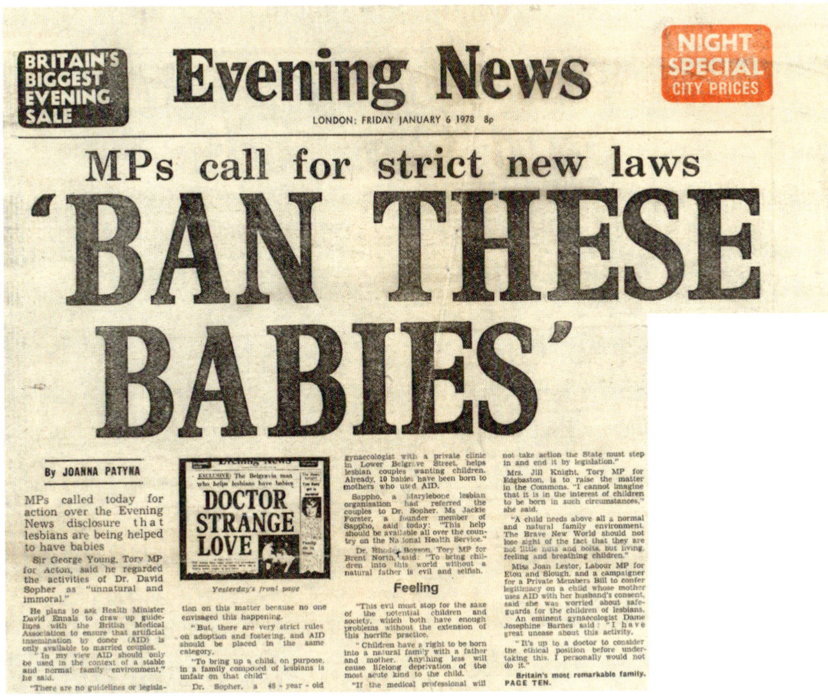

BRITAIN'S BIGGEST EVENING SALE

Evening News

NIGHT SPECIAL CITY PRICES

LONDON: FRIDAY JANUARY 6 1978 8p

MPs call for strict new laws

'BAN THESE BABIES'

By JOANNA PATYNA

MPs called today for action over the Evening News disclosure that lesbians are being helped to have babies

Sir George Young, Tory MP for Acton, said he regarded the activities of Dr. David Sopher as "unnatural and immoral."

He plans to ask Health Minister David Ennals to draw up guidelines with the British Medical Association to ensure that artificial insemination by donor (AID) is only available to married couples.

"In my view AID should only be used in the context of a stable and normal family environment," he said.

"There are no guidelines or legislation on this matter because no one envisaged this happening.

"But, there are very strict rules on adoption and fostering, and AID should be placed in the same category.

"To bring up a child, on purpose, in a family composed of lesbians is unfair on that child"

Dr. Sopher, a 48-year-old gynaecologist with a private clinic in Lower Belgrave Street, helps lesbian couples wanting children. Already, 10 babies have been born to mothers who used AID.

Sappho, a Marylebone lesbian organisation had referred the couples to Dr. Sopher. Ms Jackie Forster, a founder member of Sappho, said today: "This help should be available all over the country on the National Health Service."

Dr. Rhodes Boyson, Tory MP for Brent North, said: "To bring children into this world without a natural father is evil and selfish.

Feeling

"This evil must stop for the sake of the potential children and society, which both have enough problems without the extension of this horrific practice.

"Children have a right to be born into a natural family with a father and mother. Anything less will cause lifelong deprivation of the most acute kind to the child.

"If the medical professional will not take action the State must step in and end it by legislation."

Mrs. Jill Knight, Tory MP for Edgbaston, is to raise the matter in the Commons. "I cannot imagine that it is in the interest of children to be born in such circumstances," she said.

"A child needs above all a normal and natural family environment. The Brave New World should not lose sight of the fact that they are not little nuts and bolts, but living, feeling and breathing children."

Miss Joan Lestor, Labour MP for Eton and Slough, and a campaigner for a Private Members Bill to confer legitimacy on a child whose mother uses AID with her husband's consent, said she was worried about safeguards for the children of lesbians.

An eminent gynaecologist Dame Josephine Barnes said: "I have great unease about this activity.

"It's up to a doctor to consider the ethical position before undertaking this. I personally would not do it."

Britain's most remarkable family. PAGE TEN.

Yesterday's front page

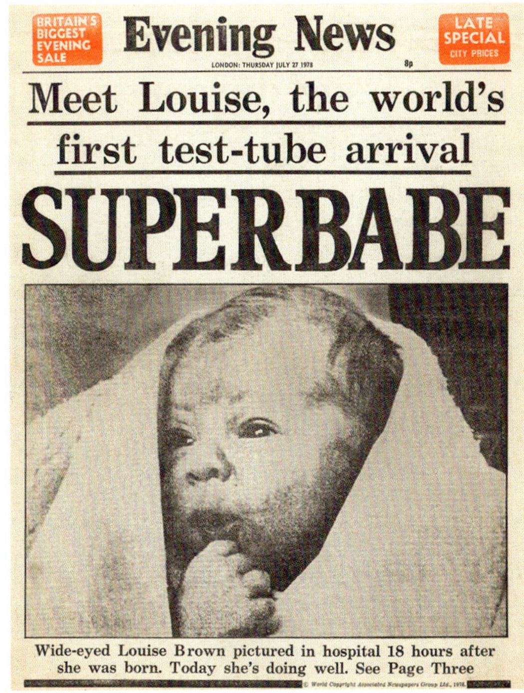

BRITAIN'S BIGGEST EVENING SALE

Evening News

LATE SPECIAL CITY PRICES

LONDON: THURSDAY JULY 27 1978 8p

Meet Louise, the world's first test-tube arrival

SUPERBABE

Wide-eyed Louise Brown pictured in hospital 18 hours after she was born. Today she's doing well. See Page Three

2.

'Ban these babies', *Evening News* front page, Friday 6 January 1978

3.

'Superbabe: Meet Louise, the world's first test-tube arrival', *Evening News* front page, Thursday 27 July 1978

Internationally, laws have also been introduced that give greater security to new family forms. Examples include same-sex marriage, passed by the United States Supreme Court in 2015, and a new law in France in 2020 allowing lesbian couples and single women to access assisted reproduction, which was previously only available to heterosexual couples. The findings of studies carried out at the Centre for Family Research, and by our colleagues around the world, contributed to these legislative changes.

But it wasn't the end of the story. Speaking to children about their thoughts, feelings and experiences has always been an important part of our research. Many of the children we spoke to told us they had faced stigmatisation and lack of understanding of their family in school, outside their home and even from wider family. In a study of the school experiences of children with same-sex parents that we carried out with Stonewall, we spoke to children as young as four right up to those finishing secondary school. They told us that their classmates sometimes made negative comments about their family which upset them. Some were rejected because of their family. And others didn't feel able to be open about their family because they saw children being picked on because they had lesbian or gay parents.

A special aspect of this study was that the children themselves came up with a set of recommendations on ways in which schools could do things better. They said that teachers shouldn't assume that everyone has a mum and dad; that different kinds of families should be talked about in school;

that it shouldn't be left up to the children to explain their family to others; and that families like theirs should appear in the books they read, the films they see and the pictures on the walls of their classrooms. In our more recent study of children with transgender parents, the message was the same. The children wanted people to understand that having LGBTQ+ parents isn't a problem – it's other people's reactions that can be the problem. As Julie, age twelve, put it, 'Queer families aren't that unusual from any other family really. Apart from the way we get treated, there's not really a big difference.'

From what the children told us, it was clear that the solutions lie in better understanding and greater acceptance of diverse families. But how to get the message out? It was the stark contrast between the dry, but important, research findings presented at the psychology conference and the vibrancy of Cathy Wilkes's show next door that crystalised the idea of an exhibition in my mind as a means of conveying different experiences of family through art. Artists' representations of family – both of their own and other people's – give insights into family relationships in ways that research reports cannot. Artworks can convey the emotional tone of family relationships more directly: the love of a parent for their child; the anger of a partner who feels betrayed; the ambivalence of an adult towards a mother or father dependent on them. From infancy, we build up representations of our experiences of family relationships in our minds, especially those with our parents. Artists are uniquely placed to translate their own internal representations of family to the outside world, and so increase understanding of family relationships by others. Artworks also provide alternative ways of thinking about family, including cultural and political perspectives, and have the potential to contest preconceived ideas of what a family is, what a family is not and how a family should be.

When we study families at the Centre for Family Research, we examine different family structures, different family dynamics, and how each affects the other. Much of our research is longitudinal, sometimes following families from the birth of a child, or even pregnancy, through to adolescence and sometimes adulthood. We are also interested in intergenerational aspects of family life. There is a long history of engagement between art and psychoanalysis. This exhibition is different. The point of contact is between art and psychological research.

Real Families: Stories of Change reflects four key threads of the centre's work. 'What is a Family?' explores what we mean by family, and questions the widely held assumption that the traditional family is best. It begins with new family forms, followed by non-traditional families that are not so new, and ends with works on infertility and the experience of childlessness, both voluntary and involuntary.

'Family Transitions' examines the family life-cycle, beginning with artists' representations of motherhood and fatherhood from early infancy onwards, highlighting the process of bonding, as well as the feelings of ambivalence that can accompany this role. A thread running through this section relates to changes in children's development from early childhood to adolescence, the role of parents, siblings and grandparents in their lives and the influence of children on their parents. As children become adults, they are often faced with the expectation that they will care for their own parents, something that can produce mixed emotions, including feelings of obligation and resentment as well as closeness. This section ends with artists' depictions of their ageing parents.

'Family Dynamics' focuses on emotional bonds and tensions between family members. Families are often portrayed as extremely happy or deeply dysfunctional, but the reality usually lies somewhere between the two. A particular interest of the Centre for Family Research is in how family relationships influence children's development and well-being. This section explores positive and negative family dynamics – acceptance, rejection, comfort and conflict – and wider social, cultural and political influences on family relationships.

'Family Legacies' explores the transmission of family from one generation to the next through genetic inheritance, social and cultural practices, language and objects, which can forge emotional connections and elicit family memories. The huge popularity of television shows such as *Who Do You Think You Are?* and the enormous number of people who are signed up to databases such as Ancestry.com and 23andMe to search their family tree highlight the importance to many people of a sense of connection and belonging. This section ends with a spotlight on Chantal Joffe, whose works focus on her own family. From her childhood, through to the birth of her daughter, Esme, and her adult relationships with her sister, her ageing mother, Esme as a teenager and her new partner, the artist reflects changes in relationships between family members over time in a deeply psychological way.

In the essays that follow, the authors were asked to choose one or more artworks in the exhibition and to write about the artist's work from the perspective of family, whether in terms of the artist's experience of their own family, or what their work says about family more generally, and/or why the work is meaningful to the author. They include acclaimed writers on the family, art historians and academics involved in family research. Each has looked at artworks in the exhibition from a different perspective, giving unique and diverse insights into the show.

In setting myself the same task as the other authors, I found myself returning again and again to Stuart Pearson Wright and Mary Husted. Although these two artists have had very different experiences of family life, they both explore what it means to have lost and found close biological relatives. The question of whether social bonds in families are more important for children's psychological well-being than biological ties is central to my research on new family forms. Our studies have repeatedly shown that the quality of family relationships matters more than biological relatedness. We have also found that donor-conceived people who search for information about their donors do so out of curiosity; they wish to construct a more complete narrative of their lives and, consequently, a more coherent sense of identity. And yet, a small minority of people born though donor conception express an overwhelming desire to find out about and meet their unknown donor, just as some adopted people are compelled to search for their birth parents and some birth parents pine for the children they gave up for adoption. I wondered whether the works of Stuart Pearson Wright and Mary Husted might shed light on the meaning of biological relationships through art.

In January 1975, Stuart Pearson Wright was conceived by anonymous sperm donation in the treatment room of a fertility clinic on the fourth floor of a busy London hospital. Earlier that day, his biological father had made his donation in a dreary room across the hall. Forty-four years on, in 2019, Stuart found his donor, a man he now refers to as his father. For Stuart, not knowing his biological father had a profound effect on how he saw himself and on his work as an artist: 'It's really my life's work, trying to come to terms with my story. The story I want to tell is about my conception. About how someone in my position feels about the fact that they were conceived in that way. The fact that my parents have never met each other.'

Stuart visited the hospital in 2017. He spoke to the doctor who had inseminated his mother and he took photographs of the 'specimen room', as it was euphemistically called, and of the room where he had been conceived. As he put it, 'I wanted to be in at least one room where I knew for a fact that my father had been. I was so desperate to feel a connection with this unknown man. To feel a sense of closeness.' Visiting the clinic was a devastating experience for him: 'I really felt my world was unravelling. I can't tell you how sad I was.' It wasn't possible for Stuart to find out the identity of his biological father. Sperm donors were anonymous in these days. To be doubly sure, the clinic had destroyed the records.

Stuart describes his childhood as chaotic and nomadic. He had a half-sister and a half-brother from his mother's first marriage, both much older than him, who lived with their father, his mother's ex-husband. He explained, 'I was always, in my own mind, an only child, because my brother and sister had a separate father. They had a connection that I didn't have. They were separate and I didn't really know them.' His mother then married Bob, Stuart's legal father; it was Bob's infertility that had led them to the clinic. Stuart was around five years old when his parents separated. He remembers little about Bob. His predominant memories are of being on the move with his mother from one temporary home to another in the aftermath of the separation.

When his mother left Bob, she lost all the family photographs, something that still plays on Stuart's mind, 'There's only one photograph of me as a baby, and I found it about seven years ago. My cousin had it in a photo album and we recognised it as me. It was the first time I'd seen a photograph of me as a baby.' Family photographs are something that most of us take for granted. They tell the story of our childhood, help us understand how we fit into our families and how we reached the place we came to be. For Stuart, that window into his early years was missing, and it disturbed him deeply. Perhaps it's no surprise that he turned his artistic talent to portraiture, swimming against the prevailing tide of conceptual art.

Some years later, Stuart's mother married for the third time. Her new husband, Stuart's stepfather, was an ex-neighbour who Stuart knew as Uncle Cyril. It started well. As Stuart described it, 'He was a jolly chap. He was a great guy with young kids. He was very kind to me when I was a young boy.' But when Stuart became a teenager, the relationship between them began to sour. Stuart was critical of Cyril's laziness and lack of ambition: 'I was yearning for the kind of father who would take me hiking and teach me things and talk to me. And we would go out and we would do things and we would travel.' Stuart wanted a father figure who he could learn from, and Cyril did not match up. 'I realised I was quite good at drawing,' Stuart recounted. 'That became my thing. And then that became everything because that was what I could do. I could immerse myself in that and I could create my own worlds there, and that became my safe place.'

Art school was a revelation for Stuart: 'All of a sudden, I met other art students and I connected with people like me. I met another guy who didn't know who his father was. He was a brilliant figurative painter. Everyone was making conceptual art. He and I were painting pictures with people. We went out to draw together. We were working against all the trends.'

Cyril died when Stuart was in his early twenties. 'I found this photograph of me in my Cubs uniform standing with him, and I didn't know what I felt about it, but I thought that I wanted to make a painting of it, because that's one way of remembering him,' said Stuart. 'I didn't want to make photorealist paintings. I wanted to use the photograph as a starting point for making something that was part of my aesthetic world, where I might play with perspective, and light, and all those technical elements.' For Stuart, the painting, *Stepdad* (**4**), was a way of thinking about his relationship with Cyril and trying to come to terms with it. Today, he is very fond of the painting, but he's still not sure about his feelings for Cyril.

Around 2014, when he was approaching 40, Stuart began to dwell on the fact that he didn't know his biological father. He became increasingly upset and angry towards the doctors who had destroyed the records. 'I needed to know it and I couldn't know it, and I wouldn't accept that,' he said. 'It was the blackest hole of despair I've ever experienced. It was so bleak and so dark

4.
Stuart Pearson Wright
Stepdad

2015, oil on linen, protective cardboard on the back
35.1 × 45.2 × 2.8 cm
Private collection, Bonn

and so terrifying and so sad. I couldn't know who my father was. It tore me apart.' The *Halfboy* paintings, exhibited at the Heong Gallery in Cambridge in 2018, were the result. As Stuart put it, 'Making the *Halfboy* paintings was about trying to understand my childhood – trying to understand where the sadness and anger in my life came from and to what extent it came from not knowing who my father was. I was an anomaly in my family. And I always put this down to the fact that I had a sperm donor father. I knew there was something different about me. I knew there was something that made me stick out like a sore thumb from all my extended family.' As a child, Stuart didn't want to feel different and didn't like feeling insecure. In *Halfboy and Halfsister* (5), he poignantly depicts his feelings of distance and separateness from his sister when he was a boy: 'I was yearning for a solid family with a mother and a father. I mean, a real father, not a stepfather with whom I had

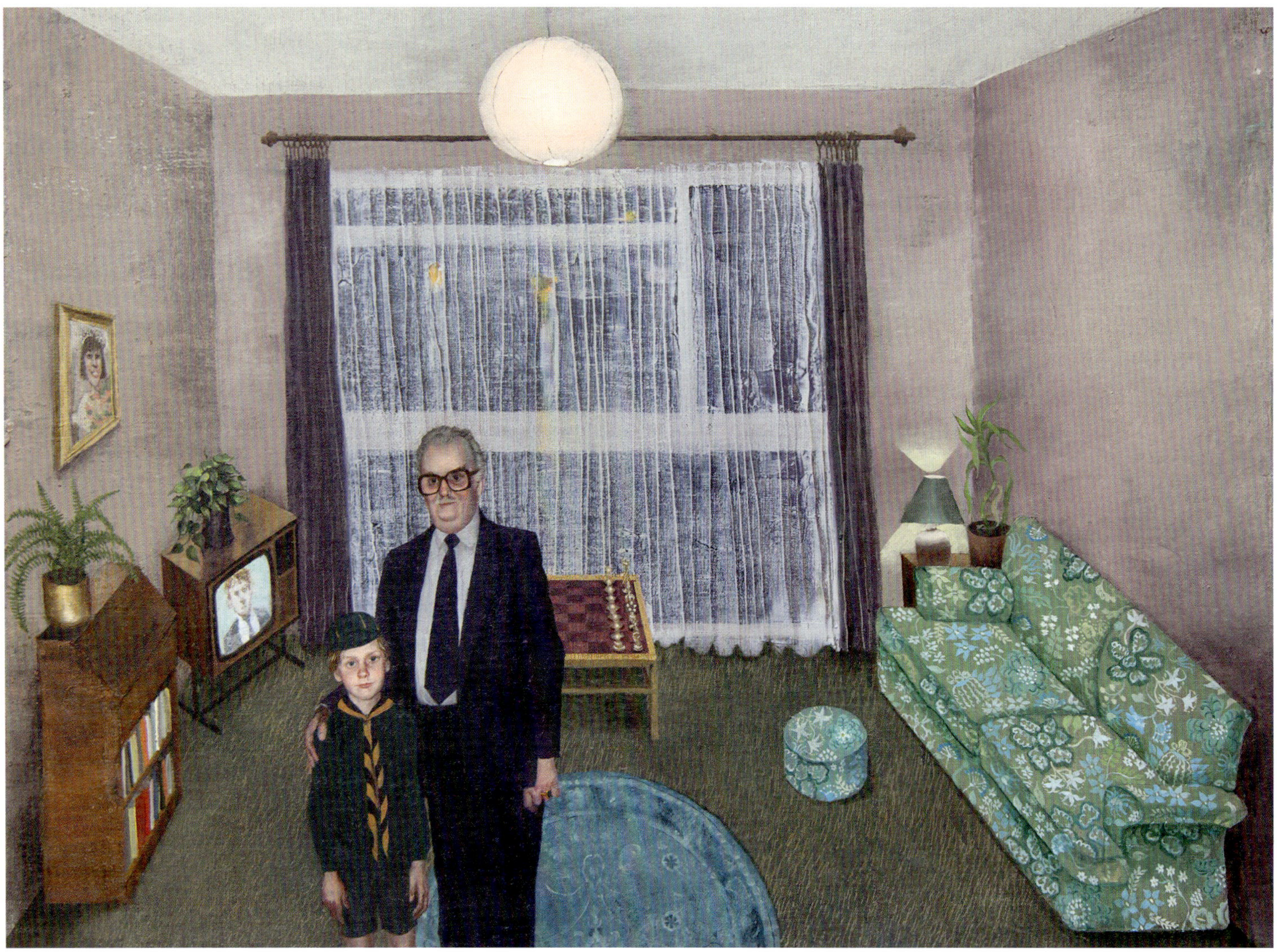

5.
Stuart Pearson Wright
Halfboy and Halfsister
2018, oil, sheep's wool, zebrawood, wire and mixed media on linen
120.4 × 100.4 cm
Courtesy Stuart Pearson Wright

no connection, and siblings of my own age, and a secure environment at home.' It is impossible to know what would have happened had Bob been a dad to Stuart, but, as Stuart himself acknowledges, it's likely that his feelings about his biological father would have been less distressing and intense.

Stuart began the process of searching for his biological father in the run-up to the *Halfboy* exhibition. He requested a DNA testing kit from the website Ancestry.com, but he didn't have the courage to send it back. It remained in a cupboard for more than a year. It was only when the *Halfboy* show was over that he decided to do the test, and it took over his life. As Stuart described it, 'I was on the computer the whole time, constructing family trees. I almost completely stopped working. It was a process of many

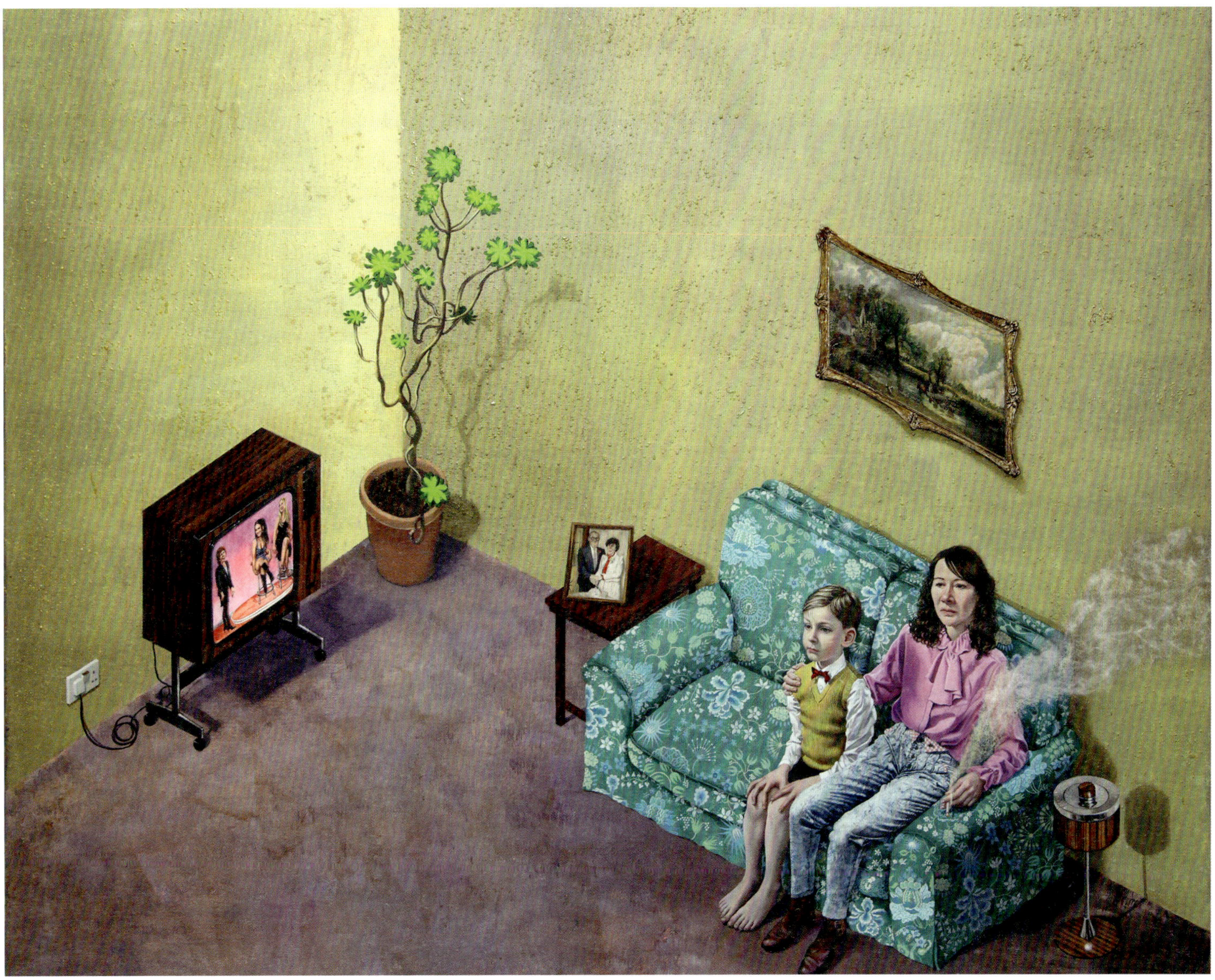

months.' But it was not in vain. The news came on his 44th birthday. He had found his biological father. Within days, he had met him: 'When I first met my real father, the first thing we did is we went on a walk up a hill. He saw some mushrooms, he picked one. He knew its Latin name, he chopped it in half, and he said, "You can eat it, but it tastes like shit." So, in a nutshell, that was the dad I wanted, with the education, with the get-up-and-go, but with a sense of humour.'

But Stuart found not only the man he saw as his father; he found a half-brother and a half-sister too. He also discovered a half-brother who had died two years earlier of motor neurone disease. That half-brother, who turned out to be like him in so many ways, was also a portrait artist. By a curious twist of fate, Stuart had seen his photograph on the London Underground. 'When he was dying, he was actively raising money for the Motor Neurone Disease Association. He launched a campaign called 100 Portraits. He wanted to paint 100 portraits before he died,' Stuart told me. 'I had seen the poster on the Underground in 2005. I remembered it when I saw a photo of him with the poster. I remember seeing that it was about portraits, and I'd been looking at a photo of my brother.'

Today, Stuart lives deep in the countryside with his wife and two children – the family he had always dreamed of. And he has connected with biological relatives who he hadn't previously known, but who he also sees as family. 'Everything I have now is everything I wanted for myself as a child,' he told me. 'And my father is really helping me to understand who I am.' But there is one last step for Stuart to take: 'I still don't know what to call him. I want to call him "dad", but I haven't quite had the bottle to call him "dad" to his face. So, I've still not said it when I when I ask him something. I've never said "dad".'

For Mary Husted, it was not her biological father, but her son who she yearned for. In 1962, as a seventeen-year-old art student, Mary found herself pregnant. The father was her boyfriend, who she loved, but he was not in a position to raise a child and neither was Mary. Back then, unmarried mothers were scorned by society, often cast out by their families, or sent away to have their babies in secret. Reflecting on that period in her life she said: 'I was terrified. I didn't know how I could tell my parents. I went for as long as possible without saying anything.' It was a close family friend who realised what Mary was hiding. But it was her dragon aunt who decided what she should do. Mary would be sent to live in Reading with her aunt's old schoolfriend Joan, who had been a midwife and could tell her what to expect and prepare her for all that lay ahead. Unlike her forbidding aunt, Joan was Mary's saviour: 'She talked to me, and she listened to me, and she supported me in what I was going to have to do. And she was there for the birth holding my hand. She told me that I had a son. I called him Luke.' But Mary was not allowed to keep her son. All through her pregnancy she knew that she would have to put him up for adoption. It was her family's decision. Mary had no say.

In the winter of Mary's pregnancy, the snow began on Boxing Day and didn't stop. From her room, she watched it fall outside her window as her time with Luke ran out. Mary had just ten days with her new-born son: 'During those days, when I was holding and feeding him, I watched him. I learned the shape of his head, the curve of the nape of his neck, the pattern of his hairline, the layout of his features. I marked the recognitions of myself and of his father in his small frame. And I drew him: small pencil drawings. I knew they were all I would have of him.' The tiny drawings came from her heart. She drew him at three days old, eight days old and, finally, at ten days old, when he was taken from her (**6–8**).

On the day she lost her son, a social worker and a foster mother came to collect him. Mary held Luke in her arms for one last time, as the older women looked on, unsure of what she would do. But they needn't have worried. As Mary described it, 'I had little real choice but to do as I was told. The whole of society was against me. It had been drummed into me that to bring a child into the world with the stigma of illegitimacy was an act of gross irresponsibility and selfishness. The only way I could make reparation to my child was to give it up for adoption so that it could "grow up in a proper family", become legitimate.' Mary breathed in Luke's scent, wrapped him in a shawl and handed him to the foster mother, who immediately turned and walked out of the door.

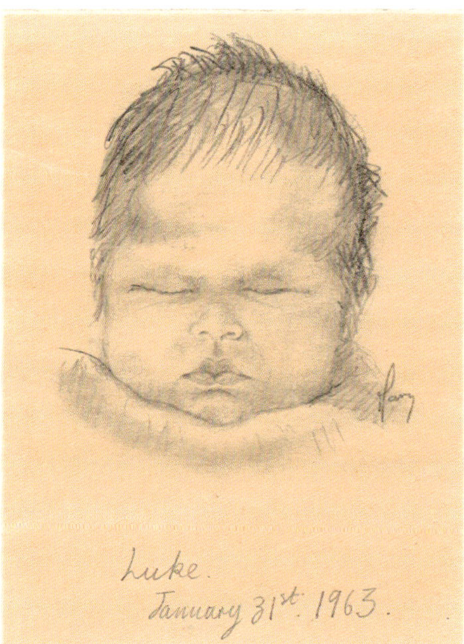

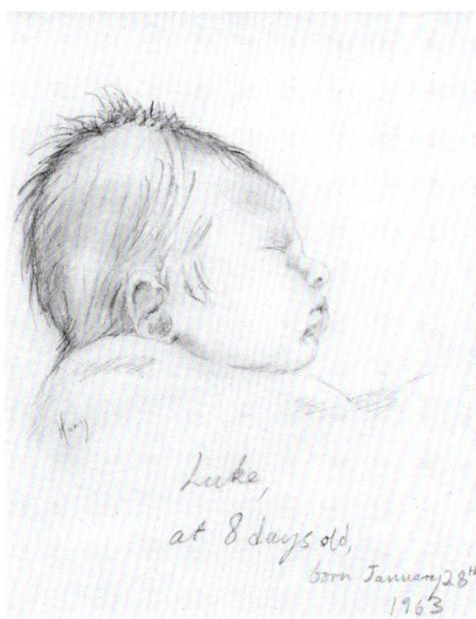

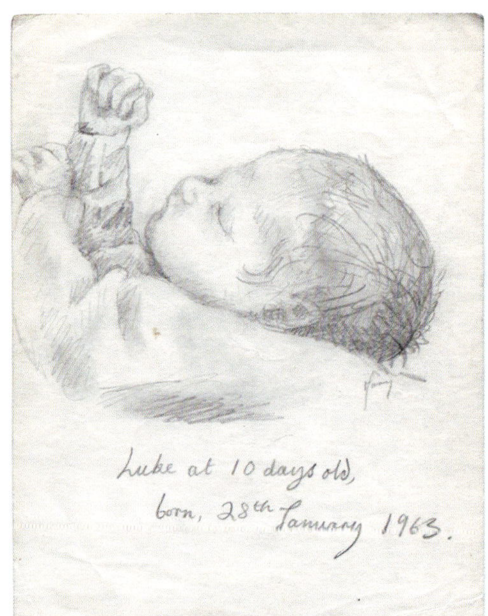

6–8.
Mary Husted
Luke [at 3 Days Old]
31 January 1963

1963, pencil on paper
42.7 × 34 cm (framed)
Private collection

Luke at 8 Days Old,
Born 28 January 1963

Re-drawn in 2011 after a copy of the lost original, pencil on paper
42.7 × 34 cm (framed)
Private collection

Luke at 10 Days Old,
Born 28 January 1963

1963, pencil on paper
42.7 × 34 cm (framed)
Private collection

9.
Mary Husted
Dreams, Oracles, Icons . . .

1991, collage
92 × 92 × 6 cm
The Women's Art Collection,
Murray Edwards College,
University of Cambridge

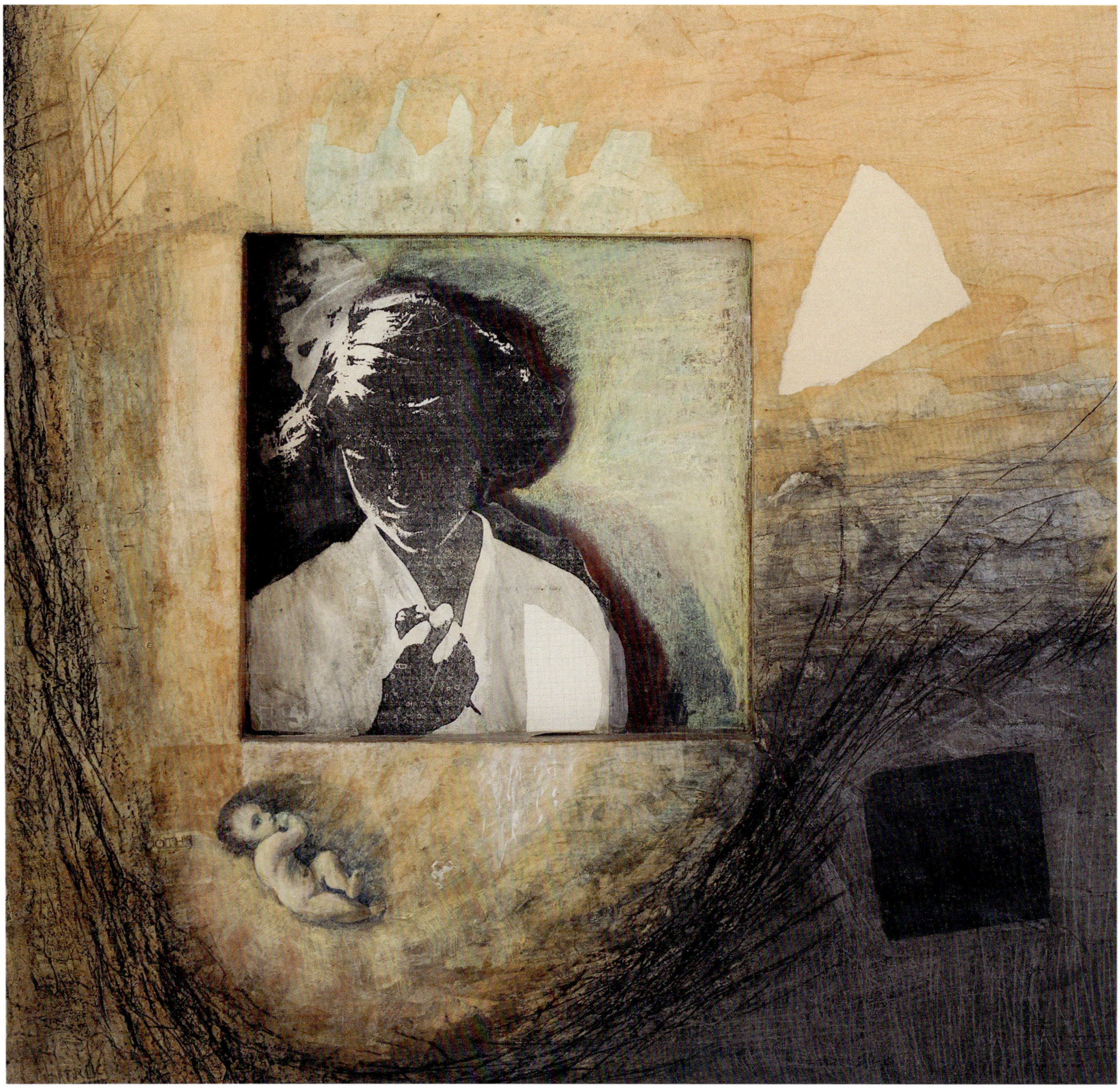

For the next two weeks, the precious drawings were Mary's solace. She spent the days alone, gazing at the lines of grey pencil on white paper. She asked to see Luke once more, to say a final goodbye: 'My father lent me his camera, and the social worker took one photograph of us together. I bent down to my baby and placed my cheek next to his. There we were for posterity, two children side by side. That's the only photograph I had of him. That was saying goodbye.'

But there was one last duty to perform. When he was two months old, Luke was placed with an adoptive family, and Mary was required to go before a magistrate to sign the adoption papers. This meant that she would lose him permanently. 'I sat with the magistrate for well over an hour and I couldn't sign the papers. I knew that I would be giving up all my rights to him. I wouldn't ever be able to find him. I would never see him again,' she recollected. 'But then I realised that he would have come to love the woman he was with. She would have come to love him. And I couldn't do it to him or to her. So, I signed. I gave him away.'

'They say to you, "Go and live your life. It never happened." They think it's a kindness, but it's not,' Mary told me. 'But in a way, you do. I got married. We had three children. But it didn't last. Then I met my current husband. He was a student at the time, and his parents were horrified about my three children. Against all odds, it worked. We met in 1970 and we're still together. We had another child. So that's four children we raised together.'

It was only when Mary entered her forties and her children began to leave home that she allowed herself to think about her past. She found the drawings of her infant son, hidden away for all those years, and old memories and feelings began to surface. In 1986, at the age of 42, Mary went back to art school. After she graduated, hints of her lost child began to appear in her work: 'Mostly these references were hidden within the texture of the work, but in one piece, *Dreams, Oracles, Icons…* made in 1991 (**9**), it was more explicit. In the recessed square at its centre is a photocopied image of myself as a young teenage girl, holding an injured greenfinch in my hand. Around this is an abstracted coloured space with partly hidden words woven into it, and in the bottom left-hand corner is a small painted infant, falling away.' Little did Mary know that this work would reunite her with her long-lost son.

In 1992, Mary was approached by a curator who was helping to establish the Women's Art Collection at New Hall, now Murray Edwards College, in Cambridge. When the curator visited Mary to look at her work, *Dreams, Oracles, Icons…* was hanging in the hallway: 'As soon as she saw it, she felt it was a good piece for the collection,' said Mary. 'My heart gave a lurch, as it was such a personal work, but then I had this notion that maybe, if it went into a public collection, one day my son might see it and recognise that I was open to contact. It was a daydream of him walking, by chance, into a gallery. This was purely fanciful, but it helped me part with it. For me, *Dreams, Oracles, Icons*… became a flag out there in the world, saying "I am here".'

Mary had begun to search for her son in the mid-1990s. She contacted After Adoption Wales, who tried to access the records on her behalf, but with no success. It turned out that her family had falsified the name of the adoption society to prevent her from finding him. But she did manage to obtain a copy of his birth certificate: 'I remember clearly the day it came through the post and I held it in my hands. At last, I had tangible proof that he had existed, that he was not some fiction of my imagination. There had been moments when I almost doubted it had happened. After so long a time it sometimes felt as if it were a story that I had told myself to explain why I was subject to such sadness.' Mary put her name on the Adoption Contact Register in case her son ever wished to find her.

It was not until January 2007, after the law had changed to give birth parents the right to find out more about the children they had given up for adoption, that Mary embarked on a further attempt to find her son. In September, she received the information she had longed for; her son was alive and well and living in the UK. Not knowing how long it would take to find him, or whether he would wish to have contact with her, Mary settled down to wait. But events took an unexpected turn: 'Exactly a week later I found a message in my Hotmail junk box, titled "Family Tree". It read: "I am putting together a family tree and related family information with a friend of mine and we are looking for a Mary Vivienne Husted who may have lived in the Reading area of England in the 1960s. If this is not you then I would be grateful if you could let me know so that we can eliminate that possibility."' I knew at once who it was: my son, looking for me! I answered, 'Is your search connected to Luke Husted?' At once there came a reply: 'Yes, it's me.' Luke, renamed Ian by his adoptive parents, had found Mary through the Murray Edwards Art Collection. When he saw *Dreams, Oracles, Icons*… he recognised that it was about him. As Mary put it, 'He had seen and recognised my flag.' Two weeks later, on their first meeting, Mary handed the tiny drawings of her lost infant to the adult son she had found 44 years later saying, 'Here are the drawings I did of you those first (and only) ten days. They are yours.'

Stuart Pearson Wright's depictions of not belonging in his family, and Mary Husted's tender drawings of her infant, convey a profound sense of loss and longing for someone they felt closely connected to and saw as family, but didn't know. Through their works, these artists illuminate the heartache that can come from fractured family relationships, reflecting not only their own experiences, but also the experiences of others in situations like their own, and how deeply felt and all-consuming these feelings of loss can be. Their stories also highlight the considerable changes that have taken place in social attitudes and the law in recent years. In 2023, the first donor-conceived people in the UK who are legally entitled to request the identity of their donor come of age. Also in 2023, Nicola Sturgeon, the First Minister, apologised for the forced adoptions that took place between the 1950s and the 1970s in Scotland. (The UK government declined to do so despite the recommendations of the Joint Committee on Human Rights.) These changes will help prevent the anguish experienced by Stuart Pearson Wright and Mary Husted in future generations. But new technologies have also had a part to play in ways that these artists, in their earlier years, could never have imagined. For Stuart Pearson Wright and Mary Husted, it was through the internet that those who they had lost were found.

My research on different family structures has led me to the conclusion that the quality of family relationships and prevailing social attitudes generally matter more for children than whether they are biologically related to their parents. Children born with the help of an egg, sperm or embryo donor, or a surrogate, or who are adopted as infants, usually do well. But there are always differences between families whatever their structure. Stuart Pearson Wright and Mary Husted show that, for some, biological connections can matter very much. These artists express the profound psychological consequences that can result from severed biological relationships under difficult family circumstances. I was intrigued by these artists for that very reason. They show the power of art in conveying individual family stories in deeply compelling and affective ways.

Real Families was chosen as a title for the exhibition for several reasons. By making us think about what a real family is, it questions stereotypes and assumptions about both the traditional family and the happy family. Also, adopted and donor-conceived children are asked about their 'real' – meaning biological – parents, even if they have never met them, and gay fathers and lesbian mothers are asked which parent is the child's 'real' parent. *Real Families* is also a foil to the Thatcher government's definition of families with same-sex parents as 'pretend' families. On top of all these reasons is a very simple one – many of the artworks in the exhibition portray real families, often the artist's own.

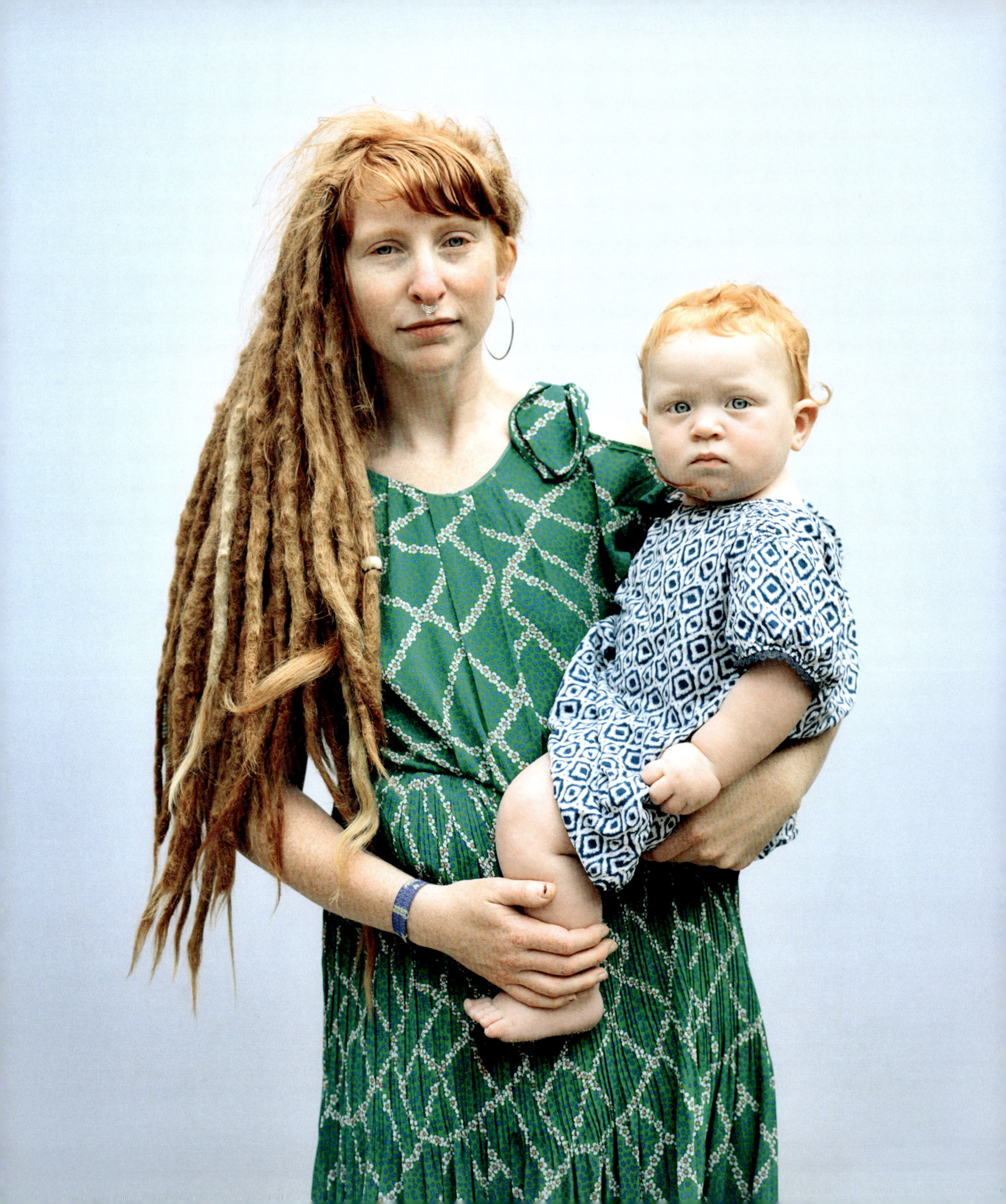

New forms of family, such as those with LGBTQ+ parents and those formed by assisted reproduction, have been portrayed by artists in recent years. These families have become possible through breakthroughs in reproductive technologies, alongside changes in social attitudes and the law from the 1970s onwards. Artists have also grappled with the difficult experience of separation and of not having children, whether by choice or not. All the artists here prompt us to consider our understanding of what makes a family.

The Centre for Family Research, founded in 1966, has pioneered the study of new family forms. The psychologists, sociologists, anthropologists and bioethicists who have worked at the centre investigate families created by IVF, egg donation, sperm donation and surrogacy. They also study families with lesbian mothers, gay fathers, single parents by choice and transgender parents. This research has contributed to greater legal rights and fairer, more representative policies and legislation for new families in the UK and around the world.

What is a Family?

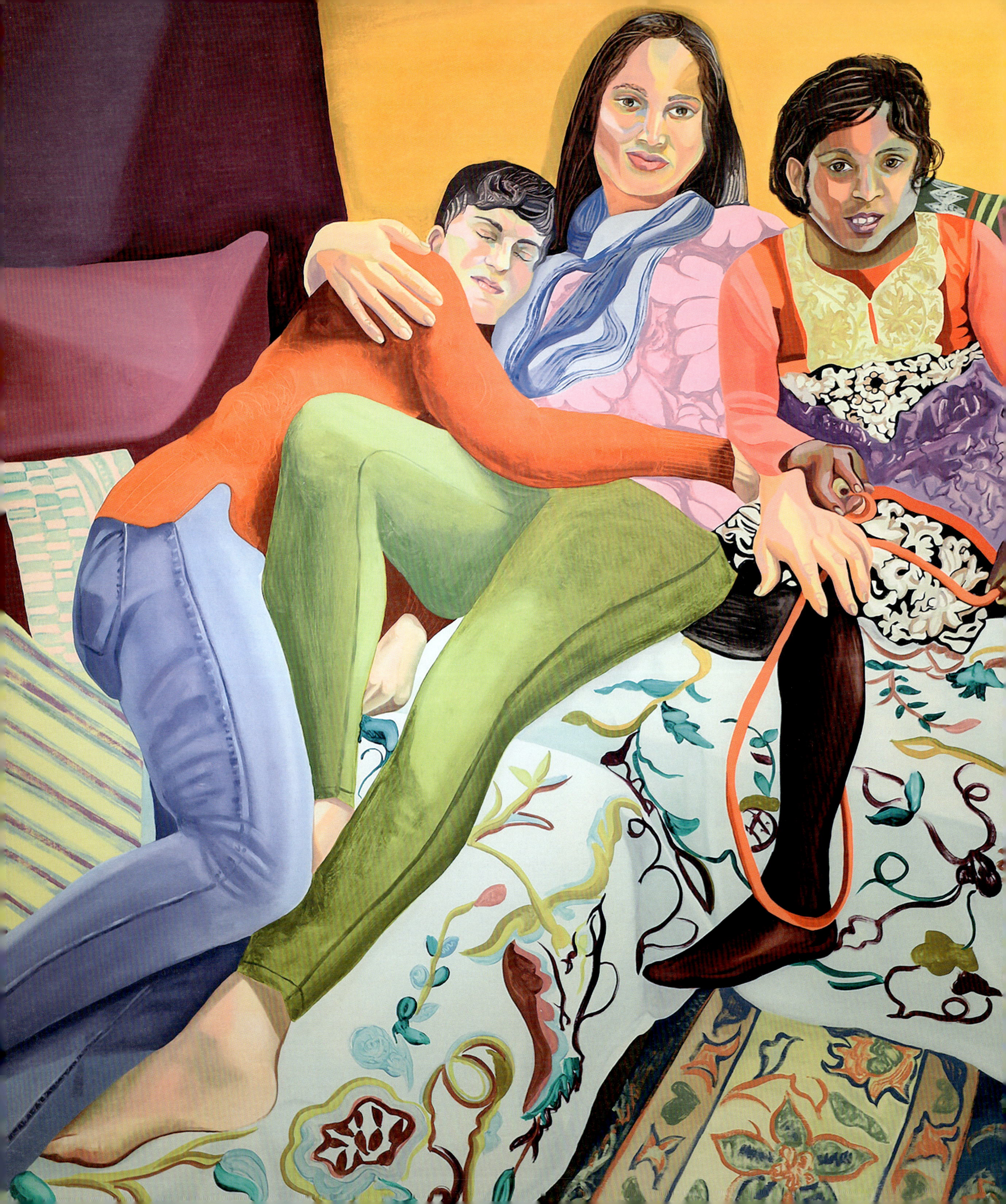

A Sunday Kind of Love

Detail of **10**, Aliza Nisenbaum, *Susan, Aarti, Keerthana and Princess, Sunday in Brooklyn*, 2018

Art finds a way to tell the time. Aliza Nisenbaum's extraordinary *Taking Care* exhibition (at the Tate in Liverpool, 2021) showed us the people, in all their diversity and variety, that helped get us through the pandemic. The NHS Frontline. In this exhibition, we saw a different side to the nurses and doctors, physicians, porters and hospital chaplains. Although these workers were from hospitals in and around Liverpool, they could have been from just about any hospital anywhere in the world. Nisenbaum's paintings have that complex quality; her sitters are strangers and familiars. Looking at them, we feel we might already know them. Her paintings are of real ordinary-extraordinary people. They are at once public and private; she brings the invisible to high visibility status. She brings the unseen people to the canvas, the ones whose stories we don't usually get to hear. For her, painting is a political act.

Large group paintings of hospital workers or art gallery workers interest Aliza Nisenbaum and so does the institution of the family. She's curious about the dual roles people play, as individuals and as part of groups. She's interested in people and their lives – in what makes their life difficult or what eases their pain. Aliza asked members of the staff at Alder Hey Children's Hospital to draw their thoughts and feelings around the pandemic and their feelings about their working life. Each person's portrait also shows personal drawings. Each person is painted individually and then assembled in the group. Here, in this exhibition, the sitters tell the stories. Just like Paula Rego before her, Nisenbaum finds stories fascinating. (Paula Rego said, 'We interpret the world through stories ... everybody makes in their own way, sense of things, but if you have stories it helps.') The fabric of our lives. Life's rich tapestry. When we look at Aliza Nisenbaum's paintings, we automatically think about what has been missing from the galleries, the lives we've not been seeing. There's a freshness, a vitality to her work which comes partly from the stories she chooses to tell and partly from Mexico. Nisenbaum was born there and her palette, her intuitive sense of colour, her candour feels very Mexican. I was reminded of Aliza looking at Diego Rivera's murals in Mexico City, last winter. I was reminded of her visiting the house of Frida Kahlo and hanging out in Frida's neighbourhood. 'Color is my favourite thing about painting,' Aliza has said. 'Color relationships almost define the effect of a painting. You can't cheat with it. It's somewhat subjective but we try to find a common language.'

Jackie Kay

In *Taking Care*, Aliza recreates the strange and spacey time we have all just been through, a time that feels as if it already belongs to another time, both to the past and to the tentative future. Time has a way of swivelling like this, turning on its back and propelling forward. Art has a way of looking forward and back at the same time. Her work, from *Kayhan Reading the New York Times* in 2017, to *Stephanie and Christina* in 2014, to *Friday Night in Brooklyn* in 2019 and *Neena dreams of DJing* in 2021 captures people at a precise moment in time, an intimate moment, and yet lifts us out of time too. Aliza Nisenbaum brings, just like Alice Neel did before her, different people to the canvas. Bringing them into the centre of her world also means placing them in the centre of ours. 'The painting must capture the absolute truth of an individual,' Cézanne said – Cézanne, who Picasso called the father of us all. (It would be an interesting exercise to think of the relationship artists have with each other, what they hand down to each other, a creative blend of DNA.) Alice Neel painted her first self-portrait in 1980, naked, except for her spectacles, with a paintbrush in her hand. Her genius had been to excavate the characters of her Harlem neighbourhood, to see beneath their surface. And now, late in life, she revealed what was beneath her own surface. The artist, with her blank canvas, is naked too.

I'd like to think of Aliza Nisenbaum as a granddaughter of Alice Neel. I can see the line she comes down. The artistic family lines. Nisenbaum's *Las Talaveritas* belongs to a series of portraits of undocumented immigrants from Mexico and Central America. The painting shows a mother and daughter. The daughter is shown twice to repeat two moments in time.

Aliza's paintings shine the light on the people she has chosen to inhabit her canvas, but they also, paradoxically, afford those people some kind of privacy. We see them inside their own world, getting on with their world. The gaze isn't at us. They are looking out from inside their own world, and yet we are invited in. 'I paint my time using the people as evidence,' said Alice Neel. Painting is a cumulative register of time spent with someone, Nisenbaum said. She sees her work as a collaboration between herself and her sitter.

In this painting, *Susan, Aarti, Keerthana and Princess, Sunday in Brooklyn* (**10**), a colourful family rests on a sofa. The two girls and one of the mums appear to be watching something, perhaps TV, whilst the other mum dozes with her arms round her partner. The colours on the throw on the sofa half echo the carpet's colours and chime with the palette of the whole family's clothes. It is as if to say that not only is the fabric part of the family's lives; but also that the fabric *is* their lives. They form the fabric; they fabricate themselves into real life. 'I'm interested in giving a backstory or a dream space to the subjects I'm depicting,' Aliza has said. In this painting one of the mothers appears to be dreaming, as if she has just dreamed up her life, or found herself fully formed in her dream life, her dream of a life that perhaps once included being in a family like this one.

A Sunday, an ordinary Sunday. A day of rest for this ordinary family. They are so real, so down to earth, so unquestionably themselves, you can almost hear them breathing. And that day, that Sunday, is a single moment and a lifetime – ephemeral and everlasting. The difference between life and art is that art can keep on telling the time. Lives are time limited. Art has no limit on its time.

Aliza's work doesn't come with all kinds of philosophical or political justification. In fact, when I asked her about the harmonious palette in this painting and whether it was intentional, she replied that it wasn't, but she loved the interpretation! That's the joy of looking into the heart of a painting and thinking about what it means. Paintings are like poems in this respect; a poem is a wee canvas. The thing that's glorious about this painting is the ease of the family it portrays; it makes you imagine the artist's ease, the ease of her easel! A kind of call and response between artist and sitter. Gone are the likes of the stuffy *Washington Family* by Edward Savage, the famous family portraits of kings and queens and earls, dressed in formal clothing. The take-us-seriously family portraits; we-are-a-serious family paintings. This family here on *Sunday in Brooklyn* is not asking to be taken seriously. This family is just getting on with the serious business of chilling out on a Sunday!

'My work starts from looking and attention, and what can come from that. It's what it means to look carefully, rather than coming with all kinds of ideological baggage. It's just sitting with people,' Aliza Nisenbaum has said. It's as if Aliza Nisenbaum has even found a co-operative practice: she sits with her sitters; her sitters are accompanied. The line between subject and object is blurred. In each of her paintings, it's almost possible to hear her saying, I'm with you. The artist who paints people thinking *I sit with you* is an artist who wants to move away from the old divisions.

And just as this is a new look at a new family, the artist is showing us a different family to the ones we are used to seeing hanging in the art galleries. It is enough to see them here. Just the art of inclusion makes a bold and vivid statement. Beyond that, the artist seems to be saying, no statement needs to be made. To redefine perhaps requires no more than inclusion. When people are given a chance to sit alongside, they will sit alongside. When the definition of a family is visually broadened, all kinds of families can sit at the table (or on the sofa). We live in a world where the family is changing all the time, the notion of what makes a family constantly evolving, expanding, renewing. We live in a world where the family must be reimagined and re-presented (**11**).

It's a joy to see Susan, Aarti, Keerthana and Princess so at home in each other's skins, so separately together. What is it in the painting that makes them appear so at ease? Is it their shared palette? Their shared love of a Sunday? Their love? It feels as if it is all these things at once. Each person

10.

Aliza Nisenbaum

Susan, Aarti, Keerthana and Princess, Sunday in Brooklyn

2018, oil on linen
145 × 162.6 cm
Norwich Castle Museum & Art Gallery (Norfolk Museums Service)
Commissioned by the Contemporary Art Society for Norwich Castle Museum & Art Gallery through the Valeria Napoleone XX Contemporary Art Society initiative
NWHCM: 2018.39

in this painting is an individual and yet each is part of the group we call family. In this case the family doesn't look uncomfortable or threatening or morose or anxious or grieving. This family looks like it celebrates and appreciates itself. This family is comfortable in its own skin.

Their lives, though they might have taken some invention, some waiting for laws to come into being, some waiting for technology to catch up with the imagination, are not fabricated. They are not made up. These are real lives and in front of us is a real family – one that perhaps you have not seen before. The artist is at pains to show how ordinary they are, how relaxed, how at ease, in the comfort of their own home, woven into the fabric of their lives. This is a Sunday, a Sunday like the Sundays in songs and musicals. A Sunday, a moment out of their lives to show us their lived lives. A blissful doze, a daydream perhaps, a smiling contented face. A dream of a family, a dream family that happens to be real.

Alice Neel said that portraits are documents created out of the immediacy of experience and their effect changes with the passage of time and that they thereby record time. Bringing people to the centre of a canvas that have been excluded from it feels also like a political act. When have we seen this family before? How many lesbian families hang in art galleries in the cities around the world?

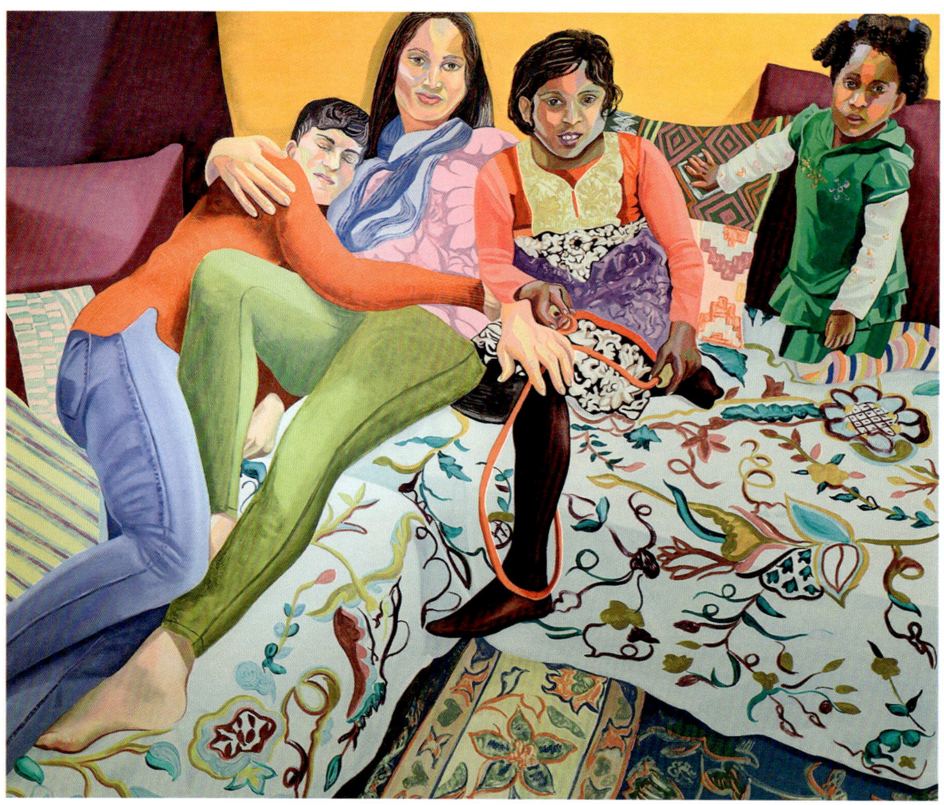

Those of us from unusual remarkable families never perhaps saw ourselves as all that unusual until we stepped outside to a series of questions. I remember people would often question whether my mother was my mother and whether I was her daughter. To ourselves, our family was solid, close, thick. 'Closer than blood,' my mum liked to say. To the outside world, we seemed like a fiction. 'Is that lady your daughter,' a woman once asked my mother. 'Your daughter is awful tanned. Is she that colour every day?'

Once, when about to leave my mum, after visiting her in the hospital, she called me back to her hospital bed. 'Here. Do you know where you're from?' she asked. I was surprised, wondering what might come from her mouth next. 'My womb!' she said triumphantly. She wasn't smiling. Her face looked serious, as if this sudden brainwave had just occurred. As if somehow, between us, love had pulled off the greatest feat yet. We'd changed our story – adoptive mum and daughter – into a reality. We'd bypassed all the other stuff, conception, DNA, to create this marvellous immaculate conception; we'd made up our own family, invented ourselves and now, for good measure, at nearly ninety, my mum was telling nearly sixty-year-old me that I came from her womb. When I went back home that night, I told my dad what she had said. I expected him to be a little surprised or to roar with laughter. But he just nodded in agreement. 'She's quite bloody right,' he said.

Tolstoy famously wrote, 'All happy families resemble one another, each unhappy family is unhappy in its own way'. But my family was different and happy. I was different to both my parents in so many ways. I was a different colour. I had a different sexuality. When I was sixteen, I said to my mum, 'How would you feel if I were to tell you that I am a lesbian?' I had to ask the question in the conditional, it seemed more cautious, more circumspect. She replied in the conditional too. She said, 'I would be very upset, because you would be becoming someone I don't know or understand. You wouldn't be Jackie any more.' This last remark stung and filled me with a deep unease. Perhaps she was right? I had an image in my head of what lesbians looked like and they didn't look like me. I had an image created from goodness knows where because there were no images on television or on records, or in Kelvingrove Art Gallery, and you had to scour things to find the smallest of mentions.

The notion of the 'real mother' was always a complex one for me. My real mother was my mum, the woman I knew and loved, the one who was there, real, tangibly real, physically real in my life. The other mother, the birth mother, was less tangible, more imagined, more invented. When I wrote about them in *The Adoption Papers*, I gave the adoptive mother the earthy voice; the birth mother the more ethereal one. If I had painted them, I would have painted a more realistic painting for my adoptive mother and I might have tried Cubism or something Picasso-like for my birth mother. My birth

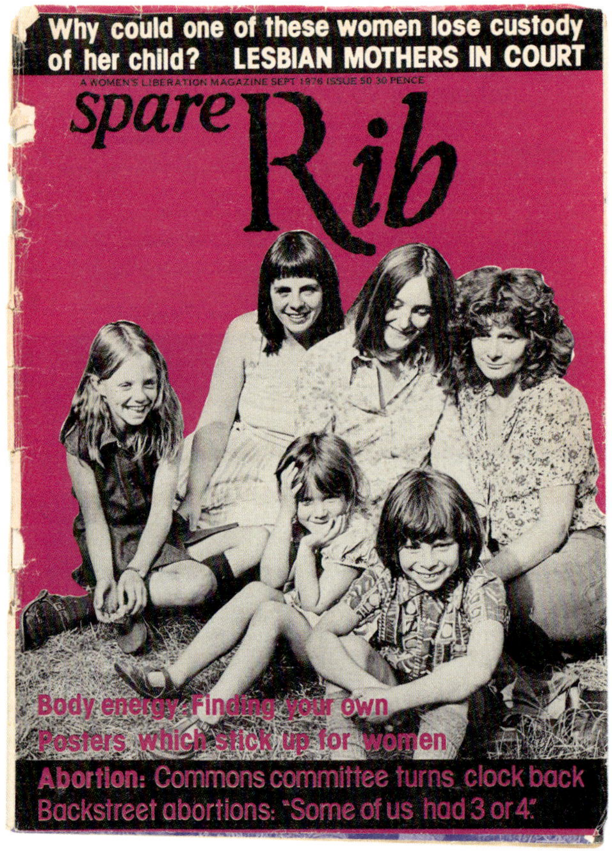

11.
Spare Rib, issue no. 50, September 1976

mother would have been a surreal painting. Totally fabricated and invented, with a lot of feeling in the choice of colours. It's funny – just thinking about painting both of my mothers takes me back to my art class aged sixteen and a girl, the class bully, saying 'Miss, Miss, Jackie's a lezzie', and the art teacher turning to me and saying, 'Well are you, Jacqueline? Are you a lesbian?' 'I don't know, I really don't know,' I said.

We change within our families and expect the family to hold us – to change with us, to love us through all our changes. Years later, my mum, aged 85, said, out of the blue, one ordinary Sunday: 'Jackie, I must apologise to you'. I asked, 'What for?' 'When you first told me you were a lesbian, I didn't support you enough,' she said. 'None of my friends had lesbian daughters and I didn't know what to do.' 'You don't have to apologise,' I said, moved and close to tears. 'Did you feel guilty?' I asked my dad. 'Naw,' he said categorically. 'What else were we supposed to do?'

I remember my son, when he was around fourteen, feeling a little uncomfortable having a lesbian mum and being part of a lesbian family. I remember saying to him, 'Matt, it's quite cool to have a lesbian mum' and him replying, 'It's not cool at all. It would be cool to have a lesbian gran.' I remember calling my mum up that night and telling her what Matt had said. And her laughing and saying, 'What am I supposed to do at this late stage, change my sexuality?' And we all laughed at that. And my son, now a brilliant documentary maker, who brings to his screen people who have been left out in some way or another, is totally comfortable with his family, with what his grandfather once called his 'esoteric household'.

The family is magic if it can keep changing, keep adapting to the time that art holds up, keep changing the reflections in the mirror, keep reflecting. So: Aliza Nisenbaum's painting made me think of all these stories. Made me think of artists I admire. Of Lubaina Himid, who said, 'We were using art to change things'. Of Maud Sulter, who said, 'The whole notion of the disappeared is something that runs through my work'. Of Frida Kahlo, who said, 'I used to think I was the strangest person in the world but then I thought there are so many people in the world, there must be someone just like me who feels bizarre and flawed in the same ways I do. I would imagine her, and imagine that she must be out there thinking of me, too . . . .' Of Audre Lorde, who said, 'Art is not Living. It is the use of living.' Of Julia Margaret Cameron, who once wrote to a friend, 'The history of the human face is a book we don't tire of, if we can get to its grand truths and learn them by heart'. Every painting tells a story. *Sunday in Brooklyn* reminded me of the expression 'a month of Sundays', of how much my mum liked to begin a sentence, 'never in a month of Sundays'. Our lives, though they might have taken some invention, some waiting for laws to come into being, some waiting for technology to catch up with the imagination, some waiting for the people we love to change, are not fabricated and yet they are made up. They are real and yet they are fictional. They transgress and they defy. Our different real lives. This is what makes the work of Aliza Nisenbaum so very welcome. The real lives that hum and buzz and throng on her canvas.

Belonging can be a contested state, for the immigrant, for the lesbian mum, for the queer daughter, for the black girl or boy. It's a fine thing when belonging is taken for granted or has a natural grace, an unstuffy, unfixed quality. It's a fine thing when your family can sit down at the table. To be imagined is to be seen. It is a fine thing to be seen on a sunny Sunday. Not a gloomy Sunday. A Sunday kind of love.

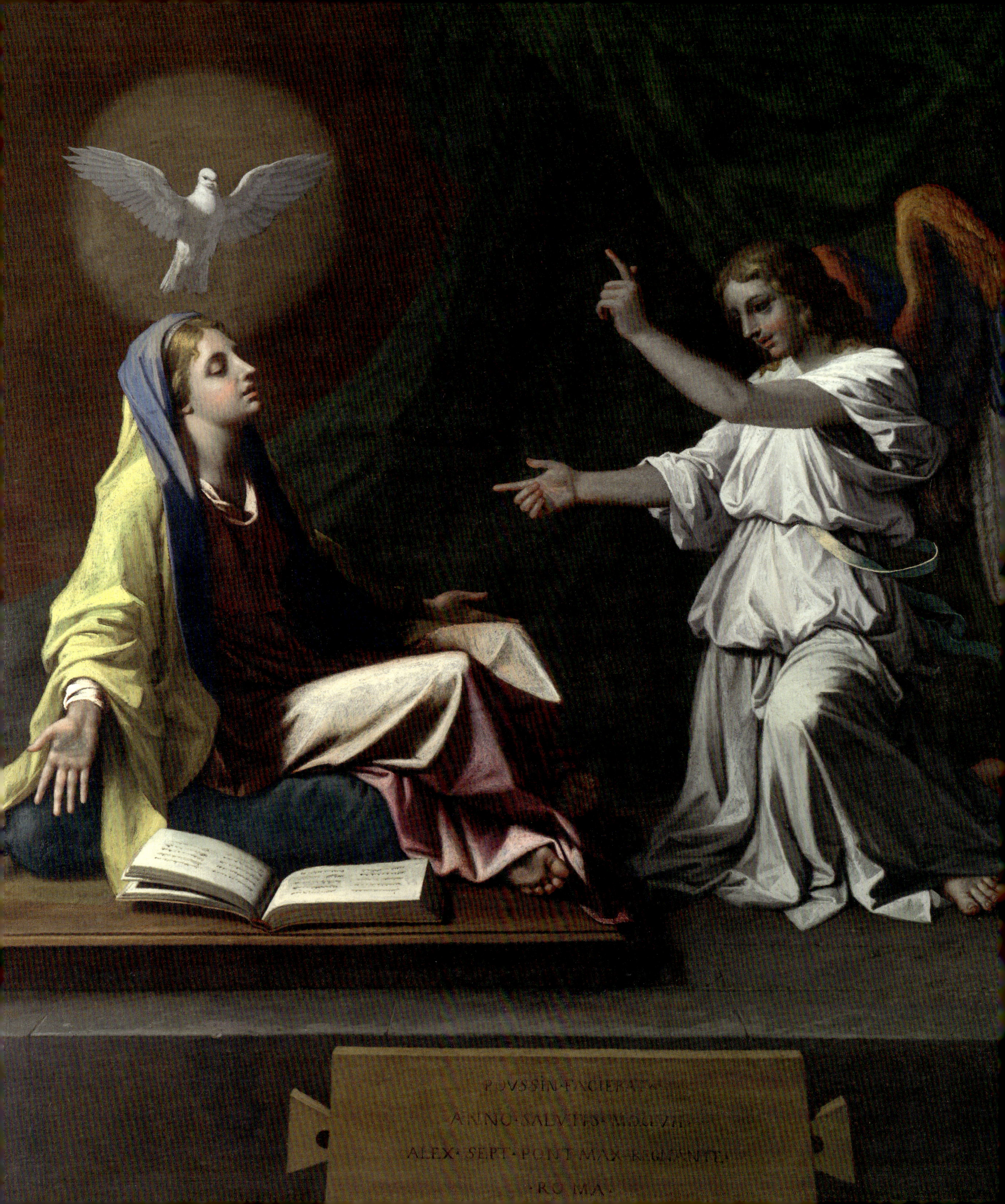
POVSSIN·FACIEBAT
ANNO·SALVTIS
ALEX·SEPT·PONT·MAX
·ROMA·

Annunciations: Three Women Talk Back to Tradition

12.
Nicolas Poussin
The Annunciation (detail)
1657, oil on canvas
138.4 × 135.6 × 12.9 cm (framed)
The National Gallery, London
Bought, 1878
NG5472

Rebecca Birrell

The Annunciation, a scene depicting Mary's momentous visit from the Archangel Gabriel, is relatively consistent across centuries of its representation. In Nicolas Poussin's *The Annunciation* (**12**), a young woman is confronted with an unexpected announcement about her future, the gravity of which even this charged moment cannot quite convey or contain: she has been chosen as the mortal vessel for the son of God. The Angel delivers this as a statement, not as a question requiring her consent, and, without any explanation of how this disembodied conception might occur, Christ's brief life is set in motion. The air is still, and something about the quality of light suggests a deepening silence. We watch as the news settles in, Mary's previous life draining visibly from the room.

The same figures and furniture are arranged almost identically from one picture of the Annunciation to the next. Mary is seated, encased in folds of voluminous fabric, no longer looking at an open book. Always there is a sense of interruption: the passage of Scripture abandoned mid-sentence, her head turned towards the surge of light and flutter of wings. This disturbance is the first of many in the transformation of Mary's life, the domestic routine dutifully rehearsed since childhood relinquished for her holy duties. On the other side of the room stands an androgynous angelic intruder, his arms raised, foot arched in suggestion of flight. A small open window imagines the Angel as entering the room in the manner of a breeze, disturbing the hairs on the back of Mary's neck, becoming as substantial as a bird of prey only once his target is in sight. He is accompanied by a dove, in which resides the Holy Spirit. Clearly this is a significant meeting: expectation ripples in the atmosphere. They are completely alone, enclosed by the privacy of Mary's bedchamber, but they never touch. They face one another, but only rarely do their gazes meet. Their separation is emphatic, crucial to the significance of their encounter. In some renditions, the pair are stranded on their own panels, made to converse beyond the bounds of their frames, across a column of blank space, the walls of another world. Architectural thresholds allude to the boundaries of the body, its integrity and impenetrability: attention is drawn to windows, doors, curtains, corridors, pillars, raised platforms; bolts, locks and keys. Even in compositions that place them close together, a proximity evocative of whispered conversation, a sliver of space – anxiously, insistently – remains between the hems of their garments. Imagine a flame flaring up like a struck match if these lengths of sumptuous fabric were ever to meet. In an arrangement that might otherwise bristle with desire, their isolation states that this shared experience, profound in its spiritual and physical repercussions, refuses intimacy and sensuality as conventionally understood. An intricate network of symbols explains what is unfolding between them, but not without some hints at transgressively fleshly alternatives. For a contemporary viewer, Mary's bed is hard to disentangle from the sexual connotations of the Angel's message, seemingly alluding to more familiar forms of reproduction. When tucked into the background and dressed in a sumptuous red fabric, her bed resembles a metaphor for desire, redolent of privacy, passion and heat. However, theological readings state that this is God's bridal bed, there is nothing erotic about it, and the rest of the room's furniture stands in agreement. White-throated arum lilies are either presented by the angel, or stand erect in a vase on the floor, an assurance of Mary's innocence and purity. Sunlight beams in from an open window, and does more than simply mark the hour or give tangible form to Mary's righteousness, her clarity of spirit. Light carries holy presence, and when it crystallises into a fleet of iridescent rods which move towards Mary's stomach it visualises the divine communication which produces her pregnancy. Other props differ from tradition to tradition, but all convey Mary's virtue, and its rewarding grace from God. A laundry basket overbrimming with clothes refers to her role as a seamstress in the Temple of Jerusalem, proof of a broader domestic usefulness and readiness for spiritual work. A locked door glimpsed through a passageway out of the bedchamber and towards an enclosed garden is a metaphor for Mary's virginity. These objects' metaphorical context is intermingled with intimations of their everyday use: haphazard folds of linen deposited in a basket reveal a hurried hand, an absent mind; pages in an open book curl as though responsive to moisture and repeated touch. Although Mary is there solely as an archetype, an embodiment of humility and submission, emotion flickers beneath her surface. Her hands are eloquent, whether pressed against her chest or lifted in appeal. Her face is often impassive, but rather than indicating blank acceptance, there is a depth to her expression which telegraphs not just listening but thinking. Her thoughts vary. There are paintings in which Mary is more placid, the faintest of smiles lifting the corners of her mouth, but the most powerful are those in which her acquiescence to God's will appears rent with reluctance and confusion. She turns towards the intruder with a cautious look. She trembles; she grimaces. The incline of her head evidences compliance, and angled lower, a resignation indistinguishable from unhappiness. These glimpses of resistance are the only reckonings with the story's seed of coercion, even violence, and they are mild and inconclusive. As a receptacle with roughly the same autonomy as the vase frequently placed at her feet, Mary is not permitted any real defiance or grief. She is shown to shrink from the intensity of

God's demands, but never to act otherwise. However appealing it is to see Mary's scowl as a sign of suppressed wilfulness, it is much more likely to be a reference to her puzzling over the story's central mystery, as she does in Scripture: reproduction without sex. Our response to Mary's plight might contemplate the same problem. These paintings respond to Mary's anxiety and a viewer's speculation through an established set of motifs that imagine conception as a matter of hope and intent alone. Through the Angel's pointed fingers, through particles of light as substantial as marbles, through the announcement itself, which is sometimes written out on to the surface of the canvas to underscore the ability of speech to reshape the given world, Mary becomes pregnant.

Religious paintings served to make the faith's foundational stories more real, transforming the sparsely detailed moral precepts of Scripture into visually arresting models of ethical behaviour. Mary's life, and in particular her submission to God's plan, state the value of women as procreators, cogs in the vast machine of patrilineal power. More broadly they communicate the rightness of women's obedience to men, their duty to self-sacrificial behaviour within the family unit and society at large, and the irrelevance of their own dreams and desires. The fact of Christ being conceived without sex, the status of Mary as both a mother and a virgin, asserts the moral dangerousness of female sexuality, and establishes an impossible ideal in which women must be both chaste and eager to fulfil their obligation to reproduce. As Marina Warner notes, the Virgin Mary was 'built on an equivalence between goodness, motherhood, purity, gentleness and submission'. For all her exceptional goodness, Mary is not even the main focus of these scenes, despite her centrality to the events depicted: by focusing on the purity of Christ's conception, the Annunciation is largely designed to demonstrate God's power. Yet many of these paintings invite readings against their grain. Even if these pictures do not attempt explicitly to imagine Mary's inner life, even if its erasure and irrelevance are implied, even if our attention is relentlessly drawn elsewhere, intimations of her thoughts and feelings remain. Something of the emotional magnitude of Mary's spiritual and physical becoming resonates out of these works, and cannot be extinguished by the source material's lack of interest in her subjectivity. Mary pauses, and recalls the last lines she read to calm herself, heart thrumming within her chest, her hesitation shifting into resolve. What if Mary were not simply giving herself up to the cause, meek and choiceless, but agreeing with some foresight into how this responsibility would enlarge her horizons, take her from her family and all she has known? Speculative entries into Mary's mind in this moment, her intentions and emotions, became a focus for several twentieth-century women artists interested in reworking and expanding works from this tradition.

Gwen John (1876–1939) was fascinated by religion as an artistic tradition and as a spiritual practice: her personal papers are filled with prayers alongside quotes and translations from theological texts, a focus which only intensified after her conversion to Catholicism in 1913. John's series of portraits of nuns in her town spoke to this commitment, as too did her production and sale of small works on behalf of the convent, and the numerous watercolour sketches she would complete over subsequent years of churchgoers bowed in prayer. Yet her paintings of her own domestic life are permeated by more subtle allusions to religious art, and a number are addressed to the Annunciation. In *A Lady Reading* (1911, Tate) a woman with the face of Albrecht Dürer's Madonna, as John wrote of her intentions to the artist Ursula Tyrwhitt, stands by an open window reading a book, a pose reminiscent of the Annunciation which is washed in its characteristic radiant light. The Angel, however, is nowhere to be seen: perhaps he has come and gone, his command ignored, his blessing withdrawn; another receptacle must now be chosen. This Mary is left to read uninterrupted, suggesting an identity and destiny that is all her own choosing. For John, this reinterpretation of the story is not a rejection of God but a proposal of other modes of devotion for women, those rooted in study and solitude rather than reproduction or family. Nevertheless, John's spiritual thesis was no doubt at least in part influenced by the ambivalence she felt about bearing children. Haunting these works is the experience of motherhood as a patriarchal institution that stymied the lives and careers of John's artist friends: Ida Nettleship (1877–1907) died in childbirth at thirty; Edna Waugh (1879–1979) had a serious mental breakdown while raising her children. John's modern Madonna insists upon the sacredness of choice and independence in a culture which valorised women's willing renunciation of those freedoms, even integrating it into its founding myths.

Rather than reckon with the Annunciation, a scene as much about fear and obligation as possibility and youth, Winifred Nicholson (1893–1981) chose to reimagine a scene later in Mary's life. Nicholson situates the viewer inside a familiar scene of maternal devotion, the Madonna and Child, only, daringly, to remove Mary altogether from the composition. *Father and Son* (**13**) shows Nicholson's husband Ben with their child Jake in a tender embrace which resembles the traditional arrangement of the Madonna and Child. The textured blue backdrop recalls the expanse of sky that enfolds Mary and the infant Christ in Renaissance examples, a reminder of their direct link to the heavens, which in Nicholson's rendition become the walls of a cosy kitchen interior. The home, not the abstracted space of the divine, this substitution implies, is where childcare and mothering actually occurs, despite the claims made by centuries of religious art. Ben and Jake's position at the breakfast table surrounded by food playfully echoes the nursing and nurturance of Christ often depicted in these same scenes.

13.
Winifred Nicholson
Father and Son

1927, oil on canvas
102 × 81.7 cm (framed)
The Fitzwilliam Museum, Cambridge
Bought with the assistance of The Art Fund and V&A/ACE Purchase Grant Fund, 2022
PD.72-2022

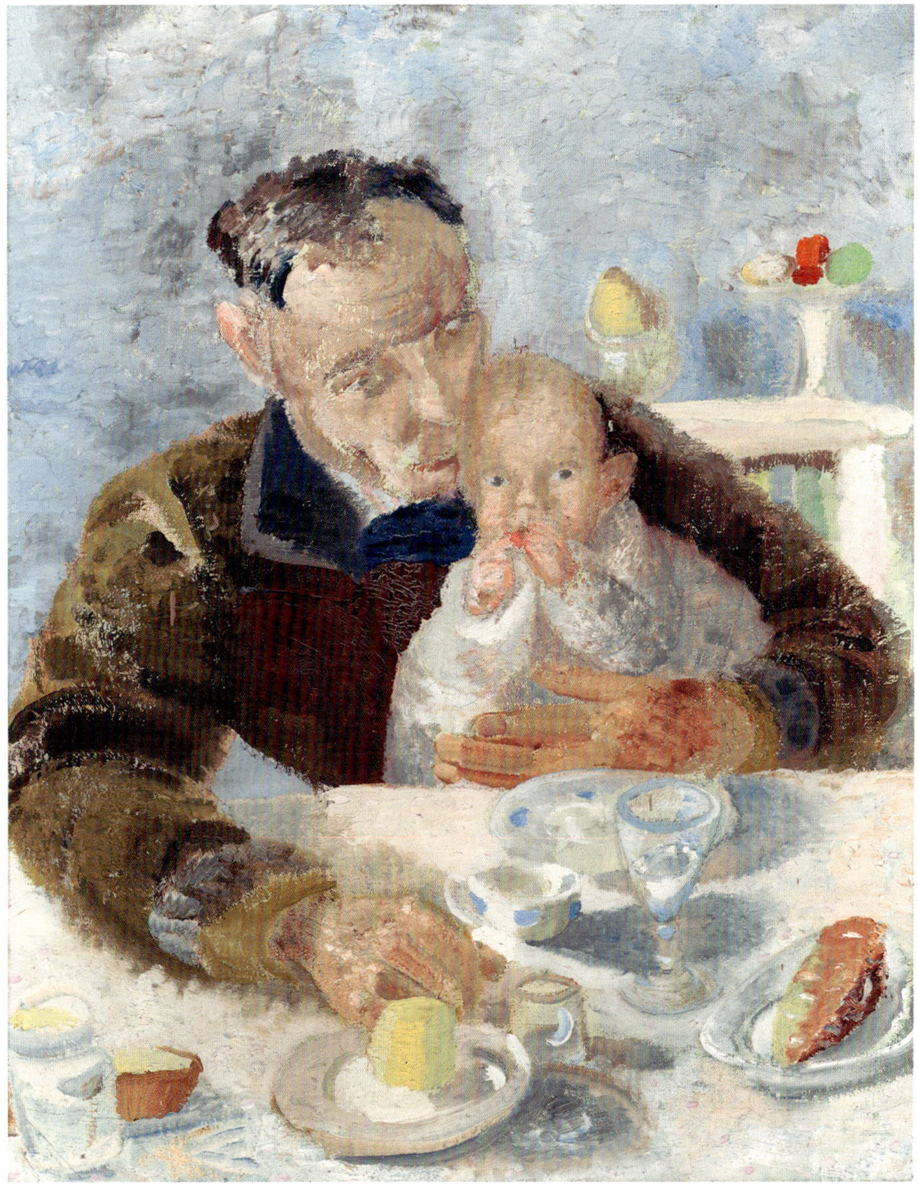

These adjustments are part of a larger act of disobedience: the very fact of portraying a fathering bond went against the ideas at the heart of the Madonna and Child. These paintings imagine Mary's attention and being as entirely oriented around the child in her arms. She holds; she caresses; she watches; she feeds; occasionally she reads to Christ from a devotional book. The glitter of a young woman's thinking and feeling that makes Annunciation scenes so arresting has been stamped out: Mary is a mother now and a mother alone. Explicit within these paintings is the belief that motherhood is an all-encompassing role. In these scenes mothering a child is accomplished via constant vigilance, physical effort, resourcefulness, creativity and a commitment akin to a spiritual vocation, but as the role is natural, allocated by God, it should ask for no reward or renumeration. The father has no part in this intense dyad; Mary's childrearing is solitary, all the more enraptured for being so.

These representations contributed to a broader societal obsession with a maternal archetype centred around self-sacrifice and self-effacement, and a bind – very much alive in Nicholson's time – in which motherhood was at once devalued as work and regarded as women's sole calling. Nicholson's subversion of this imagery was an attempt, even on a small scale, to confront this deeply entrenched problem and its consequences for women, and through a strategy as simple yet transformative as putting the father into the frame. Nicholson's husband feeds and holds the child, indicating that neither of these acts need arise directly from a woman's body. A baby might be passed to its father or to friends, allowing the mother a freedom in which she might set up her easel and begin to paint. By moving herself – the modern Mary – behind the frame, Nicholson also challenges a binary which pit motherhood and procreation against creativity and artistic personhood. Patriarchal ideology has long understood male superiority as arising from their sole claim over intellect and culture, making them natural artists and thinkers, whereas women are stuck in the mire of their physical bodies. The poisonous basis of this binary did not stop it from spreading as an unfortunate, frustrating truth amongst women artists themselves. Towards the end of 1920, the artist Dora Carrington (1893–1932) wrote to her lover (the writer Gerard Brenan) a definitive statement on women, art and motherhood. 'One cannot be a female creator of works of art & have children,' she insisted, going on to list all the women who inspired her who were childless: 'the Bronte sisters, Jane Austen, Sappho, Katy Hester Stanhope, Queen Elizabeth, Le Brun, Julie de Lespernaisse'. Yet the pattern Carrington details – and perhaps she knew this as well as Nicholson – is not about capability, biology or intellect, or a loss of will or desire on the part of artist-mother, but about practicalities surrounding childcare. Mothers could be artists if fathers (or any individual or community of people) took on some of the burden of care, a shift which would only be strengthened if a new set of images were produced to normalise the full participation of both parents. Nicholson proposes a solution in the reconciliation of art and motherhood: a male Madonna might usher in a fairer and more fulfilling existence for women. Nicholson's domestic scene might appear inward, but it had a subtly political intent. Nicholson points to new ways for a mother to see and relate to her child: as an artist unburdened of the urgencies of care, capable of dispassionate observation, attending to colour, form and texture. Nicholson's commitment to representing a personal rather than archetypal motherhood brings to mind the work of Adrienne Rich, who distinguished between motherhood as an institution which enforced patriarchal norms upon women and mothering as it was actually experienced. A painting born out of the rich web of attachments, emotions and interests of mothering rather than the punishing fantasies of motherhood might be a testament not only to love, Nicholson's work proposes, but also to freedom and to pleasure.

The work of photographer Elina Brotherus represents an extension of the visionary thinking of John and Nicholson. *Annunciations* (2009–13) declares its investment in and divergence from divine models in the title itself: Brotherus pluralises an event honoured for its singularity and impossibility. Yet for Brotherus, Mary's experience is not so unique, neither for its distillation of hope, anticipation, frustration and fear into a single moment of revelation nor for its defiance of ordinary reproductive processes, which twentieth-century assisted reproductive technologies have made more commonplace. The hand of God has been supplanted by that of science, which is more generous in distributing benefits from its power, but less precise or predictable in its results. Brotherus's paralleling of biblical storytelling and modern science implies that women have little agency in either scenario, even if the latter, more equitable and humane, is chosen. Undergoing infertility treatment involves submitting the body to figures of authority and hoping – praying – the prescribed rituals and interventions work. In a series of photographs chronicling her unsuccessful attempts to conceive through IVF, Brotherus imagines herself into the classic Annunciation set-up. In *Annonciation 7, Jour de L'Annonciation* (**30**), she is alone in a lustrously lit room, oriented as Mary is at the right side of the composition facing the left. Brotherus draws on and departs from the scene's traditional symbols to detail the humdrum domestic realities in which many women's thinking about fertility unfolds. Although enclosed within a private space, this is not a bedchamber evocative of youth, as in Brotherus's artistic precedents, but a dining room centred around a table set to accommodate a nuclear family. Mary's open book confirms her surprise at being called, but the opposite affect might be gleaned from Brotherus's table, which illustrates a long period of preparation, a readiness which despite her best efforts cannot summon her desired state into being. Light is not beaming in from the heavens, but radiates from an electric bulb, reflecting Brotherus's reliance on artificial interventions rather than the divine. In one photograph, an arum lily recognisable from traditional scenes is set alongside a vase full of flowers wilting under the glare of the overhead light, the ideal of purity and innocence overshadowed by ephemeral, messy earthly life. In all the photographs in the series, Brotherus's solitude appears keen and anguished. Brotherus mimics only one of Mary's repertoire of physical responses, and that is the arms held close to the chest: Mary's gesture embodies cautiousness, Brotherus's a need to be consoled, touched. This aloneness is at once accentuated and explained by the ambiguous presence of the Angel, who is expected on the other side of the room, ready to communicate the news of a future family and God's attention to her plight. However, an arch reminiscent of ecclesiastical architecture blocks the view. Even if the angel were there, he could not be seen or represented, as befits the mysteriousness of the spiritual world, but, from Brotherus's desolate expression, it seems nobody is there. Brotherus shows herself in a state of expectation across a sequence of images of the same room, changes in decor and furnishing tracing the passage of time, waiting for a moment which it is implied might never arrive. The appropriation of religious imagery mourns a world without divine forces capable of circumventing the body's capabilities, but in which a longing for the miraculous persists. There is no doubt that women's bodies are used and brutalised in biblical stories, but Brotherus sees in them too an enviable simplicity. If only the process of conceiving a child were as simple as being informed one morning of its inevitability then waiting it out, safe in the knowledge that the pregnancy was protected by God, destined to succeed. For Brotherus, the realities are not only wildly different from this model, dependent on human contingencies rather than the certainties of the divine, but are painfully isolating. In Brotherus's series, struggling to conceive when most appear to do so without obstacle or complication feels like being repeatedly passed over by some higher benevolent force, denied the grace which others freely receive, left to fend for yourself without any special assistance or care. Brotherus's reworking of the Annunciation ultimately reveals the emotional toll of the story's demands on women. These scenes and their source material express to women that the most valuable and meaningful life possible is one rooted in motherhood. But what if such an experience is unavailable to you, Brotherus asks. What if you want something and, in spite of the centuries of conservative imagery and misogynistic storytelling urging its importance, and even after all the effort of redefining it for yourself, imbuing it with new values, still you cannot have it? The answer, in Brotherus's photographs, is that those images haunt your existence, forever illuminating your perceived failings. A different model of intimacy, belonging and purpose must be pursued, one for which society has few available scripts, and Brotherus is unflinching in her account of the fatigue and grief involved in seeking out this alternative. It might involve testing out certain culturally ubiquitous stories to see if with enough courage or ingenuity they might accommodate other experiences, and it might mean repeatedly finding these attempts futile.

In the 2013 exhibition which displayed this series of photographs, Brotherus also showed two films made around the same time, while she was living in New York. In these works, Brotherus is motivated by an alternative set of references and practices, all at a remove from motherhood and its legacy in art. In *Wrong Face* (2013), Brotherus and another woman maraud around a sparsely furnished Manhattan loft. The film observes them as they cast their reflections on to a series of mirrors, sometimes alone but often together, producing a proliferation of faces and bodies, a multiplication of themselves. Their relationship to one another is unclear, but there is a sense of tenderness and camaraderie. They are bearing witness to one another, signalling this profound emotional bond visually through the play of mirrors. They are building an eccentric form of domesticity – impractical, self-reflexive, stripped of all its conventional constituent parts – and committing it to memory via film. Using a hand mirror, Brotherus layers her own face on to her companion, and vice versa, insinuating an intermingling of selves. One of the joys of motherhood might be, for some, the experience of seeing aspects of yourself reflected back in your child. This part of yourself lives on in another body and mind, and places you in a distant future which you might not personally see. In *Wrong Face*, Brotherus proposes an approach to living outside yourself, in understanding yourself through others, and in building a legacy which does not involve bearing children or settling into a conventional family unit. Brotherus seeks out fresh forms of togetherness, untried avenues of play and pleasure, unexpected means of feeling seen and understood, and records them so others may make use of her discoveries. Art is her chosen mode of intimacy, and it connects her with those she comes into contact with, friends and allies such as the woman in *Wrong Face*, and multitude of others she never will, her audience. In *Annunciations*, Brotherus presents herself as waiting endlessly for the call, but *Wrong Face* illustrates how another vocation had long ago transformed her life. Holding a mirror to the world, what Brotherus does literally throughout this film – doggedly and experimentally, stacking mirrors in new arrangements all over the apartment – is one metaphor for the deep-rooted and abiding ambition of the artist.

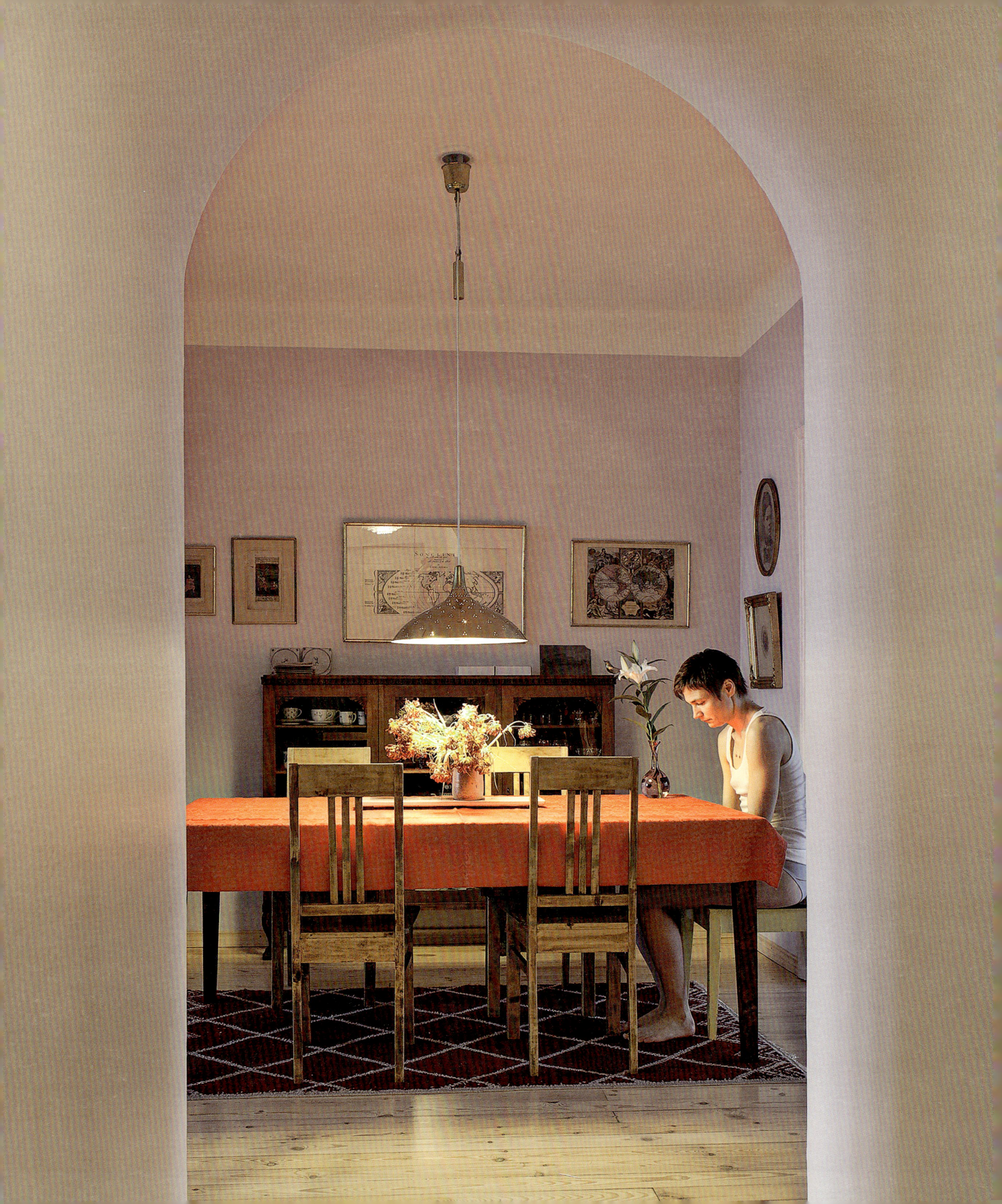

Everyday Madonnas

Detail of **30**, Elina Brotherus, *Annonciation 7, Jour de l' Annonciation*, 2011

Rosie Millard

Throughout the historic art collections of the USA and Europe, the fertility of the Virgin Mary is a pretty popular topic. Whether this be in terms of a dramatic Annunciation, a humble Nativity, a grand *sacra conversazione* (typically a bethroned Madonna and Child surrounded by saints and patrons), or perhaps a sinous Gothic alabaster sculpture, a Victorian stained-glass window or either of the Madonna of the Rocks masterpieces by Leonardo da Vinci (one in London, the other in Paris), artists and their patrons have seemingly never tired of this maternal template.

In his recent book *All the Beauty in the World*, which documents his ten years working as a security guard in New York's Metropolitan Museum of Art, Patrick Bringley is at pains to describe the effect of seemingly interminable rooms filled with serene Madonnas, chubby babies and any number of Gabriels, tourists stumbling from one to the next, almost blinded by repetition.

Such is the legacy of this model that any exhibition of human families today needs to acknowledge it, not least because it has informed and directed nearly every image of a mother and child for the last 700 years, right up to photographs of Princess Diana with an infant Prince William (1982) or Dorothea Lange's famous image of a migrant woman and her children in the American dustbowl (1936). Hence the presence in this show both of the Fitzwilliam's *Virgin and Child* by Flemish painter Joos van Cleve (*c.* 1525–30) (**14**) and the Finnish photographer Elina Brotherus's *Annonciation 7, Jour de l'Annonciation* (2011) (**30**).

The Annunciation is a key – perhaps the key – moment in Christian faith, for it details the moment that God's word became human. Also, what a great subject! The angel Gabriel arrives and tells the Virgin Mary that God has chosen her to deliver the Saviour of the world. If you are going to depict a biblical event, this is possibly the best – fresh, dynamic and starring a young woman and an angel, no less. As the art historian Michael Baxendall explains in his masterly *Painting and Experience in Fifteenth-century Italy*, the role of the painter was 'a professional visualiser of the holy stories'.

Artists commissioned to paint an Annunciation were therefore relieved from the burden of the rest of the canon, and the problems inherent in depicting crowds, miracles, flagellations, crucifixions, empty tombs, devils or people going to Hell. As holy stories go, this one is straightforward. There's the arrival of the Angel Gabriel; virile, winged, thrillingly dynamic, almost always on the left-hand side of the painting. Then, on the right, there is the reaction of the Virgin.

As Baxendall explains, the strict demands of medieval iconography meant this was conveyed through one of five Laudable Conditions, or states attributable to the Virgin. To a modern mind this rigidity of choice seems absurd, but this was the format. The five Conditions in which the Madonna could be seen were as follows: Disquiet, Reflection, Inquiry, Submission or Meditation (when the Virgin would be depicted on her own).

Most Renaissance artists plumped for one of the first four options, therefore at the arrival of Gabriel (usually depicted as having just crash-landed in the vicinity of the Virgin, with his wings open and his robes in disarray). Mary is either shown with her arms flung wide in surprise or folded in prayer, or looking up from a book. As the Renaissance progressed, so did the habitat and behaviour of the Virgin; one can even accurately date the work via an analysis of how the Annunciation was depicted.

Hence Simone Martini's flat, golden Gothic beauty (*c.* 1330), which reveals both a gesturing Gabriel and a startled, reading Virgin firmly in their own pointed, gilded frames, leads to Fra Angelico's serene, tidy Virgin (1420) timidly nodding at Gabriel in an architectural loggia beside a flowery garden, to Botticelli's writhing, urgent couple in a believable room with haloes in perfect perspective (1489). It is a progress revealing the development and changing concerns of Western art at a remarkable moment of cultural transition.

In his 'Treatise on Painting', written around 1499, Leonardo da Vinci describes a particularly dramatic depiction of the scene: '… some days ago, I saw the picture of an angel, who in making the Annunciation, seemed to be trying to chase Mary out of the room, with movements showing the sort of attack one might make on some hated enemy; and Mary, as if desperate, seemed to be trying to throw herself out of the window. Do not fall into errors like these.'

Somewhere in the picture one will usually find Gabriel's totemic emblem, the white lily, either in a vase between angel and woman or lurking on the mantelpiece, windowsill or nearby table. Occasionally he is carrying them. Sometimes there is also an actual representation of the incarnating Holy Spirit, often seen as a tiny little angel, or a bird, with little golden rays speeding towards Mary, as if impregnating her on the spot. Very often she is near a garden, with flowers and nature outside. Typically, Leonardo's own *Annunciation* (1472) has an array of botanically identifiable flora beside his Gabriel.

In contemporary society, however, the focus is not on saints. We don't 'do' God, as a former British Prime Minister once memorably said. We do, however, 'do' ourselves, all the time, both in our psychological concerns and in creativity. Hence it is perfectly apt that Elina Brotherus's *Annonciation 7, Jour de l'Annonciation* (**30**) is not only a photograph of the Virgin, but also a selfie.

Brotherus is sitting, as is customary, on the right-hand side of the picture, with the light coming in from the left, which is the side one might expect the Angel Gabriel to have exited from. To heighten the religious attributes of the picture Brotherus has utilised an arched framing device, much as Simone Martini did 800 years earlier, and the vaguely yellow painted walls act as a contemporary gold-leaf background. The rounded arch resonates with holy significance, heightens the dramatic sensibility of the scene and also plays with the notion that we are looking into a historical moment.

Rather than having a tiny dove shooting rays of light, Brotherus gives us a contemporary pendant light illuminating the table. There is, as one might expect, a vase of lilies between the light and the woman. There is even a floral display on the table, echoing the typical abundance of flowers in historical Annunciate paintings.

In strict medieval terminology, Brotherus is enacting the last of the Virgin's Laudable Conditions, Meditation. She is contemplating what has just happened. Although, a modern twist. Unlike Mary, who is contemplating 'being with child' after miraculous divine intervention, Brotherus is contemplating being child-free after unsuccessful scientific intervention. She has photographed herself sitting at her table after another round of unsuccessful IVF treatment, which, as she has described it, seems akin to 'waiting for an angel who never shows up'.

The miracle of the Annunciation has not been translated into the 'miracle' of modern-day science. The room does not give on to the outdoors, and a vista of flowers and nature. She is surrounded by windowless, plastered walls. There is no existence outside her little room. There is no vision of a future. There is no baby. The chairs are drawn up to the table, and the table is bare. Brotherus is not expecting any guests, let alone one with wings.

The atmosphere is heavy, charged. Brotherus is pensive, restrained and focused, with her hands beneath the table and her bare feet flat on the floor, under the chair. She is not looking at the flowers, or the artworks on the walls. She is looking down, into herself. The photograph acknowledges the miracle, perhaps the sanctity of childbearing, with more than a nod to the past. It is simultaneously ancient and modern.

Joos van Cleve's oil of the *Virgin and Child* (**14**) is as much of its time as the Brotherus self-portrait photograph. Gabriel's lilies are still in evidence on the balcony, but now the Virgin is attempting to suckle a rather sleepy baby Jesus.

As was customary with his Netherlandish predecessors, who were drawn to paradigms from everyday life rather than imaginary scenes from the Bible, Van Cleve has painted a contemporary Flemish woman, not a saint. She is not wearing a halo, but an everyday muslin headscarf, although her fur-lined brocaded cape indicates that this is a classy mother. As one might expect from a North European painter, Van Cleve is using oil, which has an influence

14.
Joos van Cleve
Virgin and Child

About 1525–30, oil on panel
80.1 × 65 cm (framed)
The Fitzwilliam Museum, Cambridge
Bequeathed by the Rev. R.E. Kerrich 1872 (received 1873)
No. 104

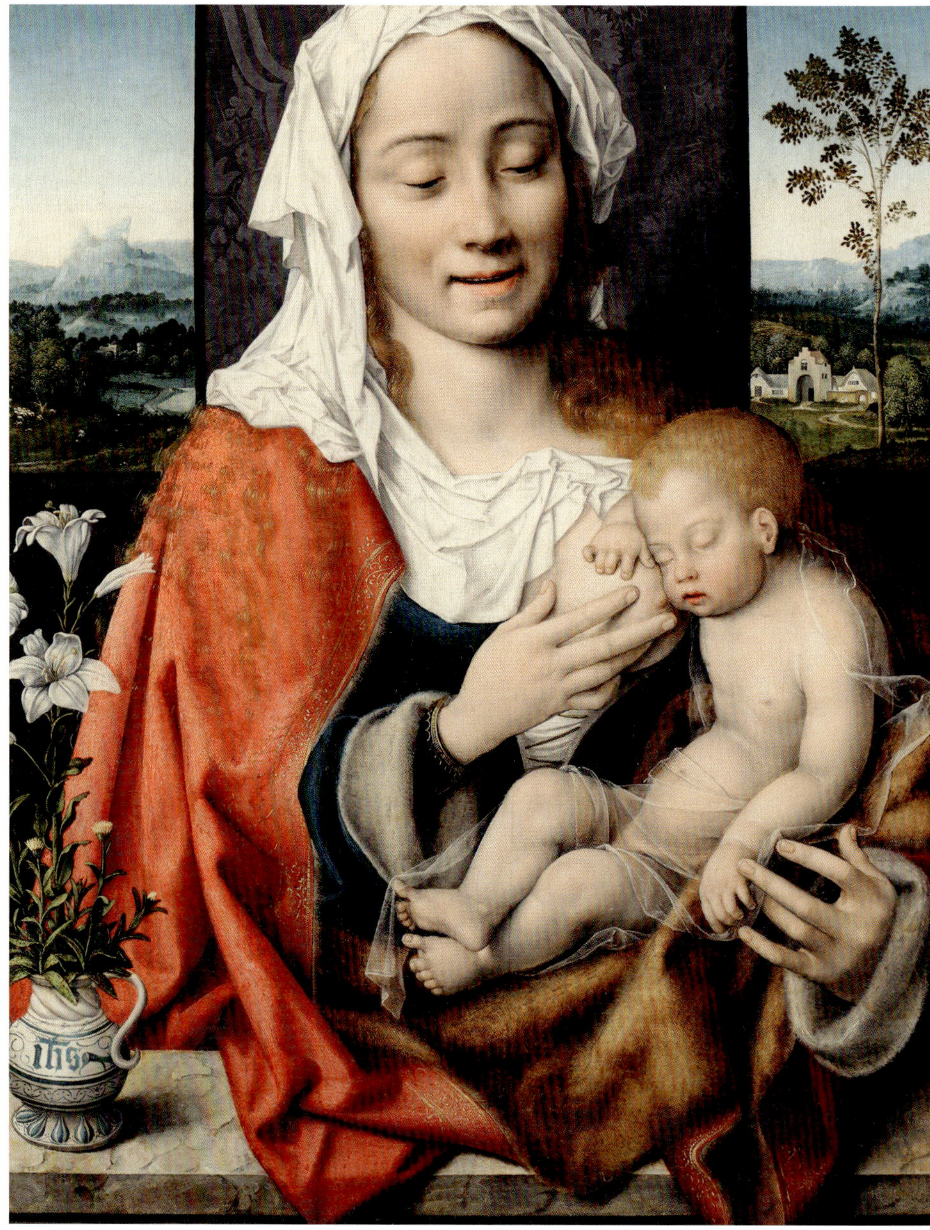

on texture and pattern, alongside the jewel-like colours typical of a Northern Renaissance master.

Meanwhile, the treatment of Jesus is similarly drawn from real life. Van Cleve has clearly observed a new-born baby, sleepy and full from a satisfying and lengthy feed. One hand is still resting on his mother's breast; the other was possibly clutching her finger, but has relaxed as he has nodded off. His mouth is still right beside her nipple, but he has had so much milk that sleep is now the only option. His mother looks down at him, smiling.

In this, Van Cleve is referring to more recent Italian painting; indeed, his happy Madonna is very similar to the joyous *Benois Madonna* (1478) by Leonardo, now in the Hermitage, St Petersburg, which Van Cleve may well have seen. Indeed, the treatment of colour and light, particularly the 'sfumato' (smoky) depiction of the far-off fantasy landscape and the soft emotion around the Virgin's mouth and eyes indicates that Van Cleve was well aware of Leonardo's techniques. He would probably have come across the work of the Italian master at the court of Francis I, where Da Vinci was working as 'the King's first painter, engineer and architect' from 1516 until his death in 1519, and where, a decade later, Van Cleve was sent for to paint the French king.

Indeed, the Flemish painter might have even seen the *Mona Lisa* (1503), which Leonardo brought with him to the court, and which has since always remained in France. Not only with her hesitant smile, but also with the balcony by which the Van Cleve Madonna is sitting and the receding imagined landscape, there are distinct echoes of the *Mona Lisa*, although the details of the view, with its tiny gabled farmhouse and Dutch shepherd tending his flocks, is very much in the Flemish vernacular.

The painting also nods to work by Van Cleve's Venetian counterpart Giovanni Bellini, namely *The Madonna of the Meadow* (1505), now in the National Gallery, London. Here Jesus is also asleep in his mother's lap, but something about the baby, who is stretched out motionless, with Mary's hands folded in prayer above him, looks chillingly as if he has died, prefiguring the posture of his crucified body being cradled by his mother in a formal arrangement known as a *Pietà*.

Surely, for all his Virgin's smiles, Van Cleve is also hinting at a *Pietà*, and the Passion. This is underlined by the presence of dandelions beneath the white lilies in the vase; a contemporary audience will have known that the bitter flower was associated with suffering and sacrifice. Furthermore, if you look very closely at the picture in the landscape you will see, just visible, a wooden cross on the hillside above the flock of sheep.

Here, then, we have a rather thrilling conjunction not only of life and death as experienced by Jesus, but also an immediate snapshot of the artistic influences on painters in the late 1520s. In this single picture, Van Cleve is dealing with both Northern and Italian Renaissance tropes and styles. The determinedly everyday treatment of his ungarlanded, unheralded Madonna, who is expertly expressing milk with her two fingers just as mothers have done for millennia, is typical of Van Cleve's Netherlandish forebears. However, the tonal treatment of light and space, and the modelling of the face of the Madonna herself, acknowledge a keen eye for what was currently going on in artistic circles across Europe, particularly at the French court and Venice.

There is also an intriguing circularity of influence within the picture. As we have already acknowledged, this Virgin is not in some heavenly gilded vista, but sits in an angel-free, everyday Flemish setting, with recognisable trees and buildings visible through the balcony behind her. Indeed, this style of oil portraiture, where a half-length subject is depicted within an actual landscape, was pioneered by Van Cleve's forebears from Bruges, Hans Memling and Hugo van der Goes, artists Van Cleve would have known very well as he lived in Bruges around 1507–11. It was a style which, thanks to Italian patrons buying work and taking it back to Italy, also became hugely influential within Italian Renaissance circles. It's thought that Leonardo must have seen these works before envisaging portraits such as the *Mona Lisa*.

So, while we are keen to assign influences on Van Cleve from Leonardo, we must also acknowledge that Leonardo himself was more than probably influenced by his Netherlandish counterparts, counterparts with whom Van Cleve was also familiar.

The story of the European Renaissance is much more than one geographical location influencing another, or even two separate schools, one in the North, one in the South. Rather, one must envisage circles of influence, aided by burgeoning trade routes, increased literacy and a growing mercantile class feeding and being fed by a fiercely competitive ruling class, royal, ducal and religious, who wanted the best artists, regardless of where they were from. Court artists were the elite footballers of their day, hired across Europe for vast prices, their allegiances only as strong as the latest contract.

Brotherus and Van Cleve are working 500 years apart; one is a religious oil painting, one a self-portrait photograph, but their contemporaneousness connects one to the other. They both depict everyday women; one with a baby, one contemplating a future without one. One has light, and life, and a long-distance view going on around her. The other has flat plaster walls. But both pictures have flowers, and beauty within their worlds, and both show their main protagonist as a cognate individual coping with the immediate demands of her world.

15.

Joshua Reynolds

The Braddyll Family

1789, oil on canvas
238.1 × 147.3 cm
The Fitzwilliam Museum, Cambridge
Given by the National Art-Collections Fund from the Ernest Edward Cook Collection, 1955
PD.10-1955

This portrait represents the traditional notion of family and lineage. Inheritance of land and personal characteristics are illustrated by the backdrop of the family estate and the similarities in pose between father and son. Mrs Braddyll and the dog reflect loyalty and obedience. The family's three daughters do not appear in the portrait. As women, unable to inherit or pass on their father's name, they had no place in this kind of image of family.

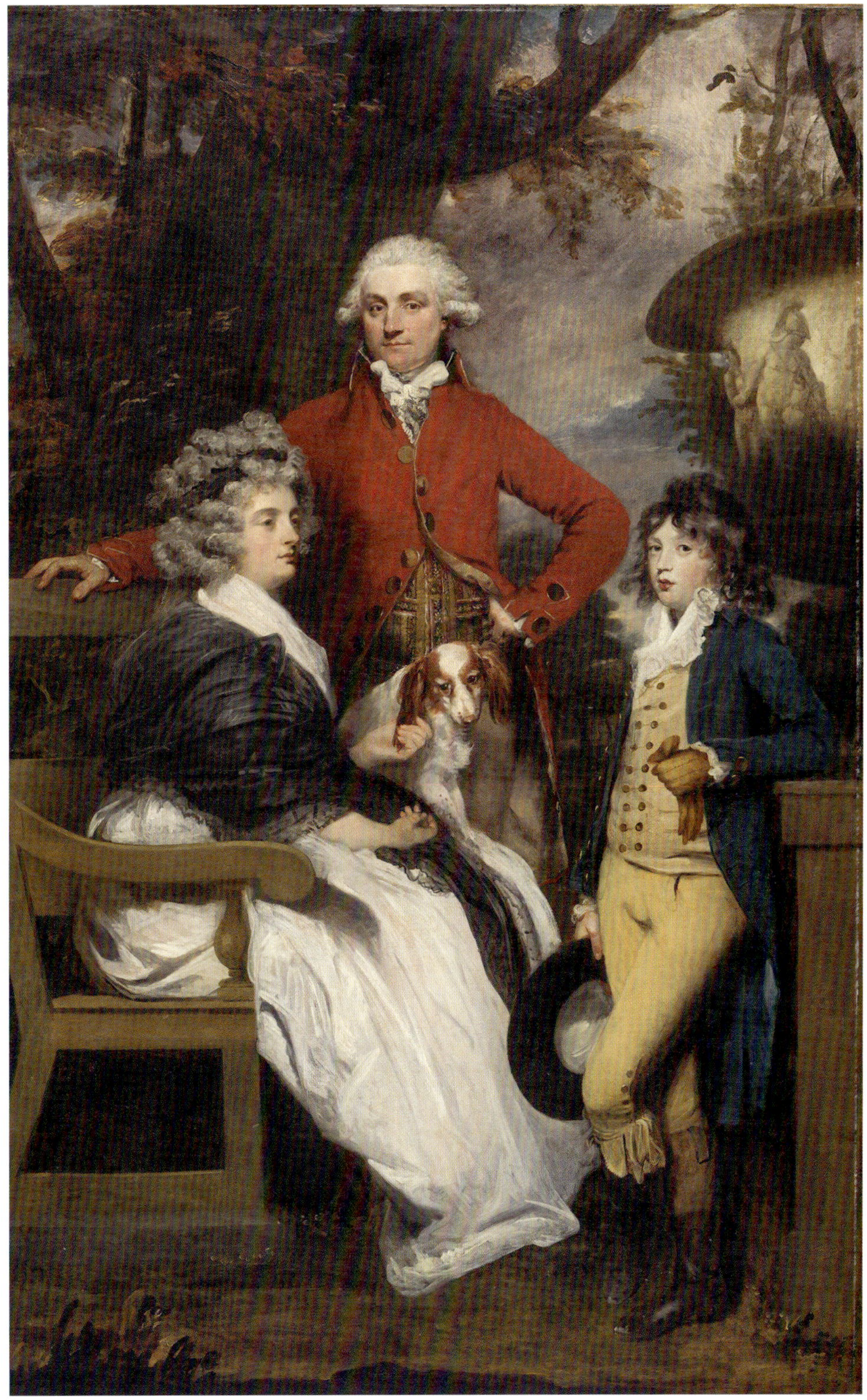

16.
JJ Levine
Alone Time 19

2021, C-print , edition 2/3, 1AP
107 × 132 × 6 cm (framed)
Courtesy JJ Levine / ELLEPHANT

This portrait appears to show a traditional family of a mother, father, son and daughter. Look more closely, and you will see that the mother and father are the same person, and the son and daughter are the same child. The artist, who identifies as queer and trans, questions the idea that gender identity, gender roles and sexuality are unchangeable.

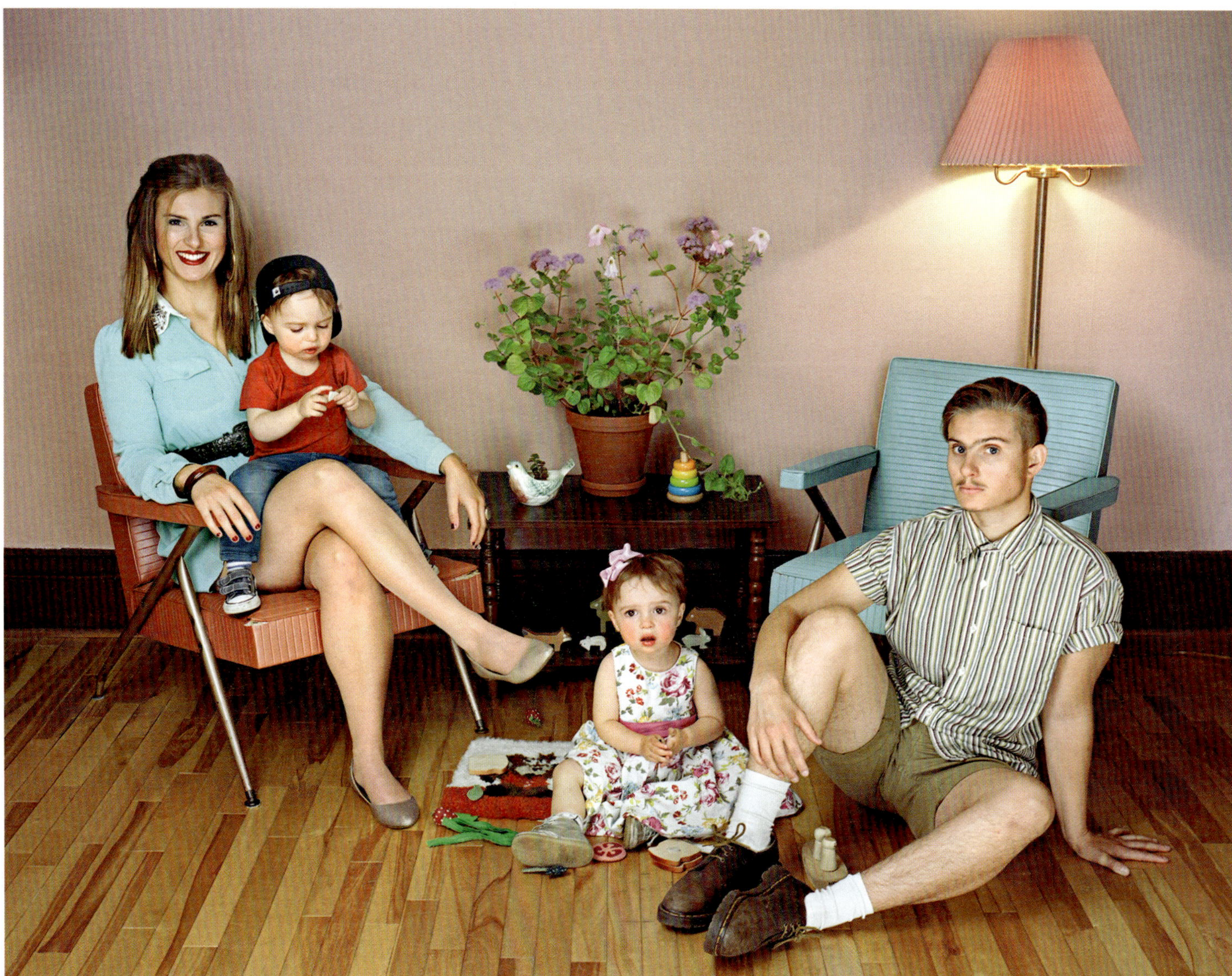

17.
Joseph-Marie Vien
Sarah Presents Hagar to Abraham

1749, oil on canvas
98 × 134.5 cm
Musée Fabre, Montpellier
2015.21.1

Abraham needs an heir, and because his wife Sarah is unable to conceive, he impregnates Hagar, their Egyptian slave. Some scholars read this story as an early example of surrogacy. Others see Hagar as a victim of exploitation. Biblical stories illustrate anxieties felt by ancient societies around the importance of a male heir, which put enormous pressure on women's ability to bear sons.

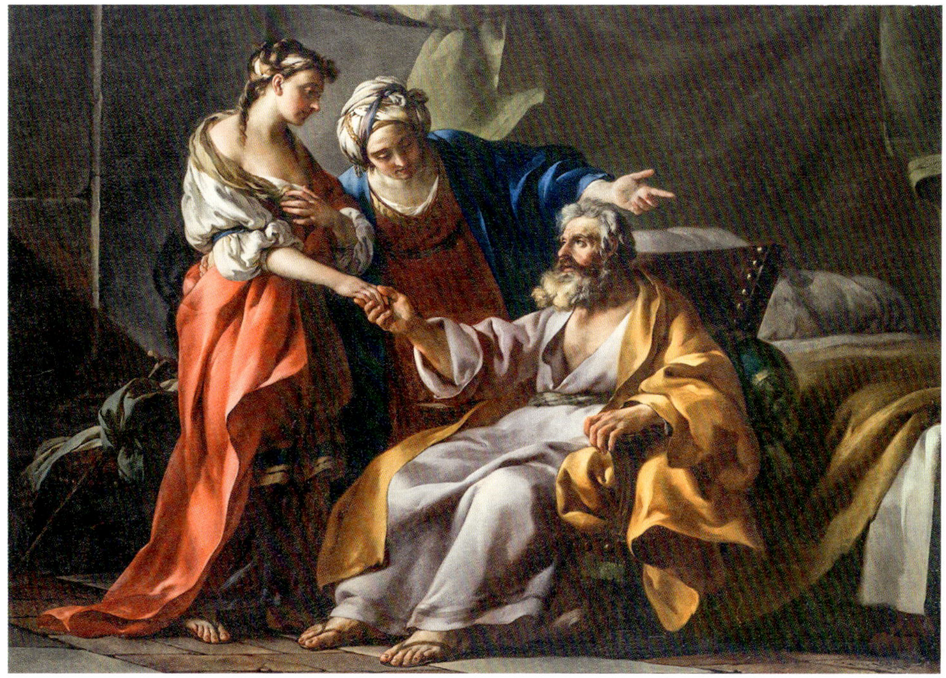

18.
Bart Heynen
Milo with her fathers and sister. New York City

From the photographic project *Dads*
2021, inkjet print on photo rag paper
60 × 45 cm
Courtesy Bart Heynen

Bart Heynen is a gay father. 'We all come from straight parents and have very few role models. So I wanted to see what other families with gay dads were like. Also, for my kids, it was important to meet other dads and kids. They were the only ones with two gay dads in their school.'

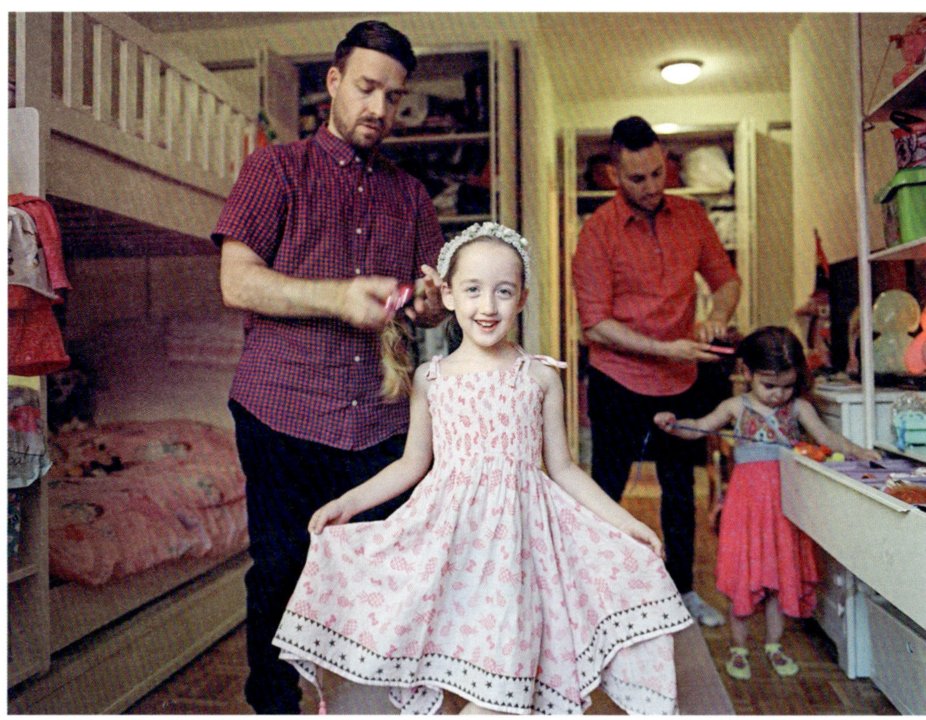

19–21.

JJ Levine

Harry Pregnant, 2015

2015, C-print, edition 2/3, 1AP
107 × 132 × 6 cm (framed)
Courtesy JJ Levine / ELLEPHANT

Harry and Joah, 2016

2016, C-print, edition 2/3, 1AP
107 × 132 × 6 cm (framed)
Courtesy JJ Levine / ELLEPHANT

Harry, Joah and JJ, 2018

2018, C-print, edition 1/3, 1AP
107 × 132 × 6 cm (framed)
Courtesy JJ Levine / ELLEPHANT

The first portrait shows Harry, a transgender man, pregnant with Joah. The second is of Harry with Joah as an infant. The third shows Joah aged two, with her two parents, Harry and JJ, the artist. In the Centre's research on families with transgender parents, the children said that it's not having a transgender parent, but other people's reactions to it, that they find upsetting.

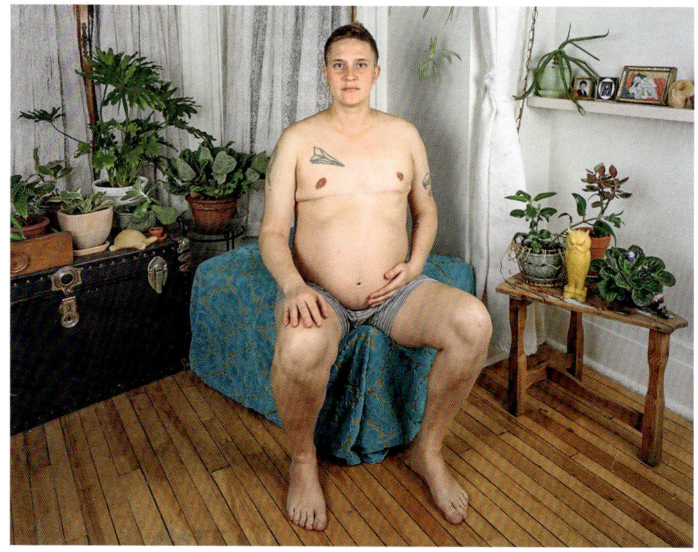

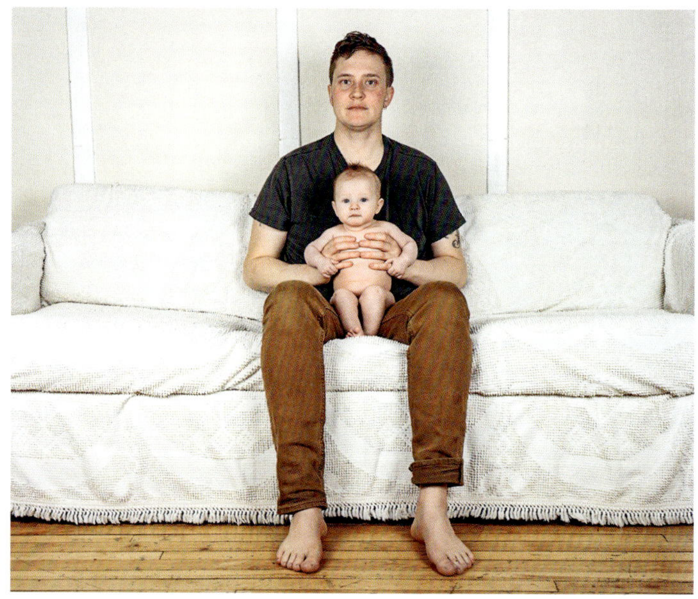

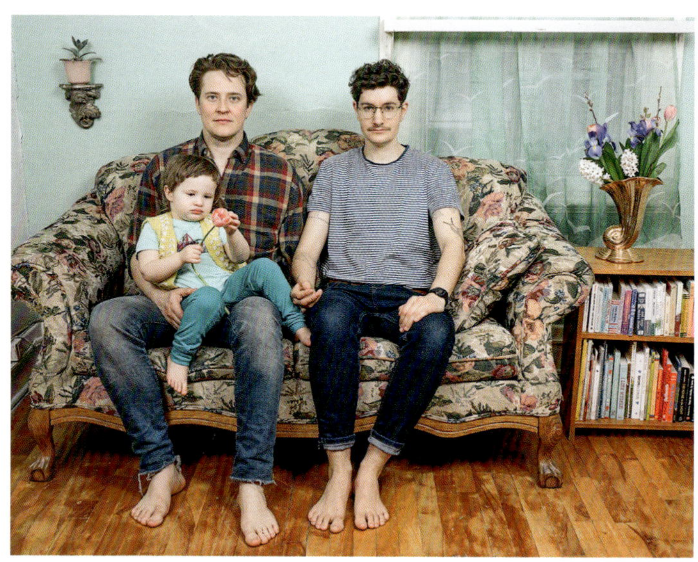

22.
Loulou d'Aki
Sandra and Lilje

A portrait from the series *Mother of Choice*
2019, giclée print on Hahnemühle paper
50 × 60 cm
Courtesy Loulou d'Aki

In 2016, the law changed in Sweden to give single women access to assisted reproduction. Lilje was born after insemination treatment with eggs donated from Sandra's sister. 'When the doctor came in and told me I probably shouldn't wait too long to have a child, I thought I'll just do it – straightaway! One year later, I was pregnant.'

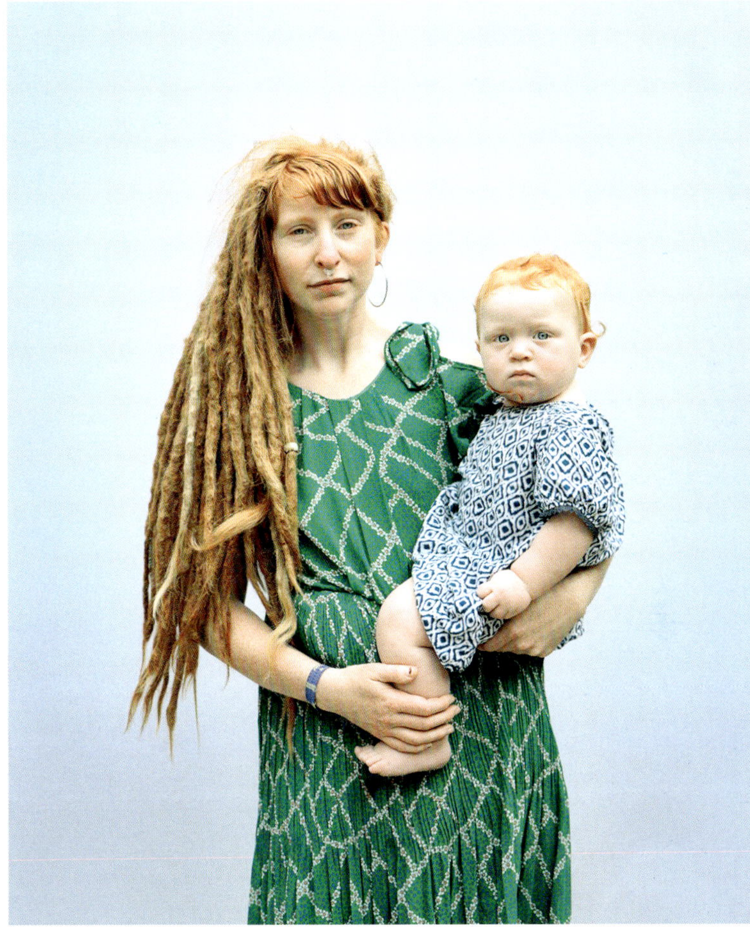

23.
Harry Borden
Jonathan with Xavier

From the photographic project
Single Dad
2021, C-type print
45.7 × 45.7 cm
Courtesy Harry Borden

A small but increasing number of men, like Jonathan, are becoming single fathers by choice. 'I'd always felt that one day I'd be a dad, but I'd never imagined that becoming one would be so daunting. With the help of fertility specialists, lawyers, an egg donor and an awesome gestational surrogate, Xavier was born in Southern California, September 2013.'

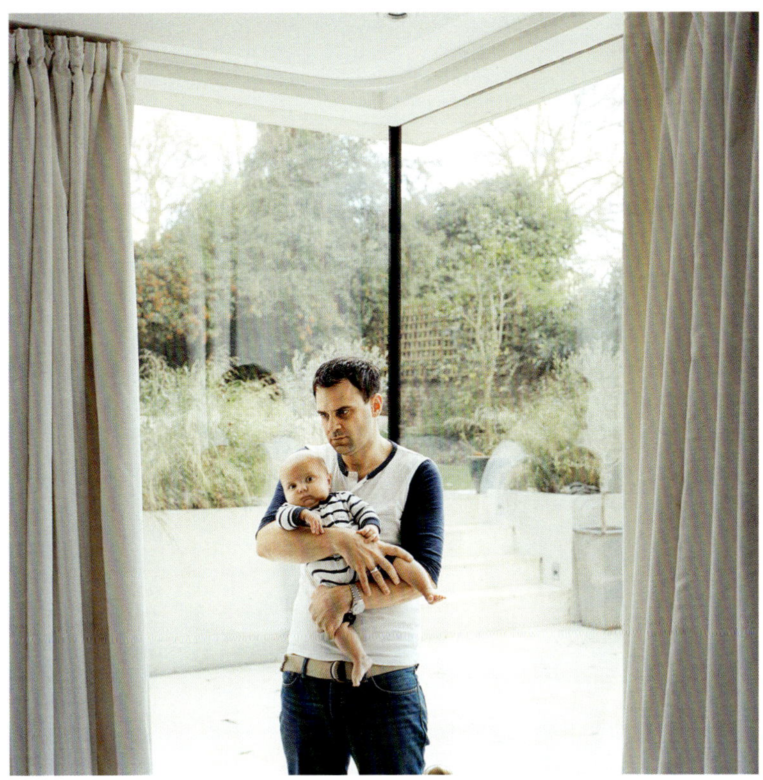

24.
Harry Borden
Tony, Emma and Louise

From the photographic project
Single Dad
2021, C-type print
45.7 × 45.7 cm
Courtesy Harry Borden

There has been a rise in divorced or separated fathers raising their children alone. 'The girls' mum and I shared care for several years after we split up. But then she decided to move away, for love and for work. I knew their childhoods would pass quickly so I decided to slow my life down, to enjoy every moment of fatherhood.'

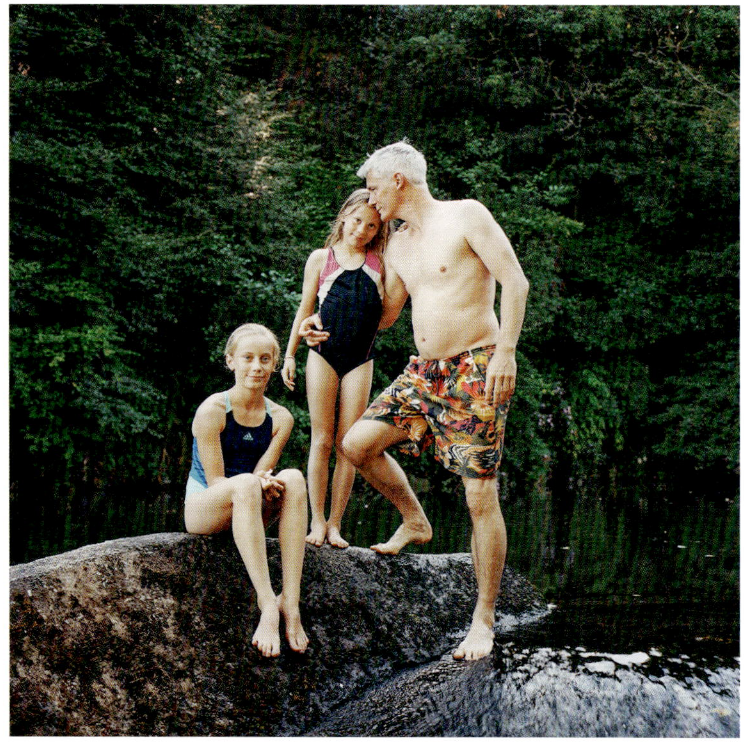

25.
Harry Borden
Florian (the Photographer's Son)

From the photographic project
On Divorce
2023, C-type print
61 × 50.8 cm
Courtesy Harry Borden

The artist's son reflects on his parents' divorce. 'I was so surprised when you told me. I still remember it all exactly. I now certainly wish it hadn't been so quick .... I'd say probably when I was little, all my friends' parents were together. Now 70% must be divorced. Nothing is certain.'

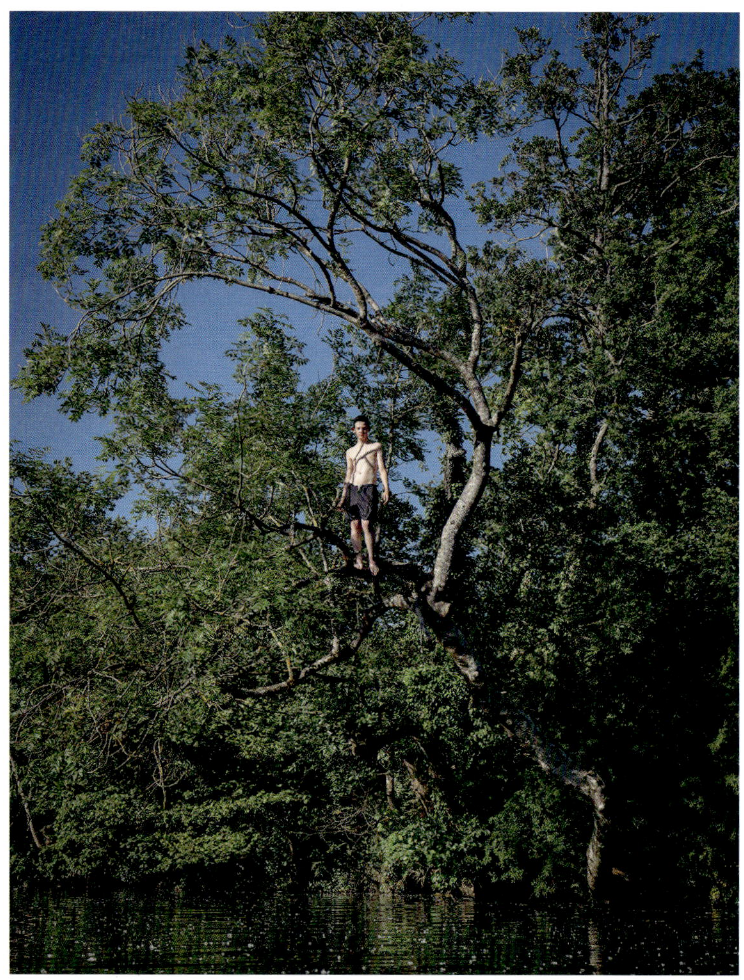

26.
Diana Markosian
Not too long ago, my father had another child. I should be happy for him, but watching him play with her, feels like a bruise someone keeps pressing

From the photographic project
My Father, The Stranger
2013–14, archival inkjet print
40 × 60 cm
Courtesy Galerie Les filles
du calvaire, Paris

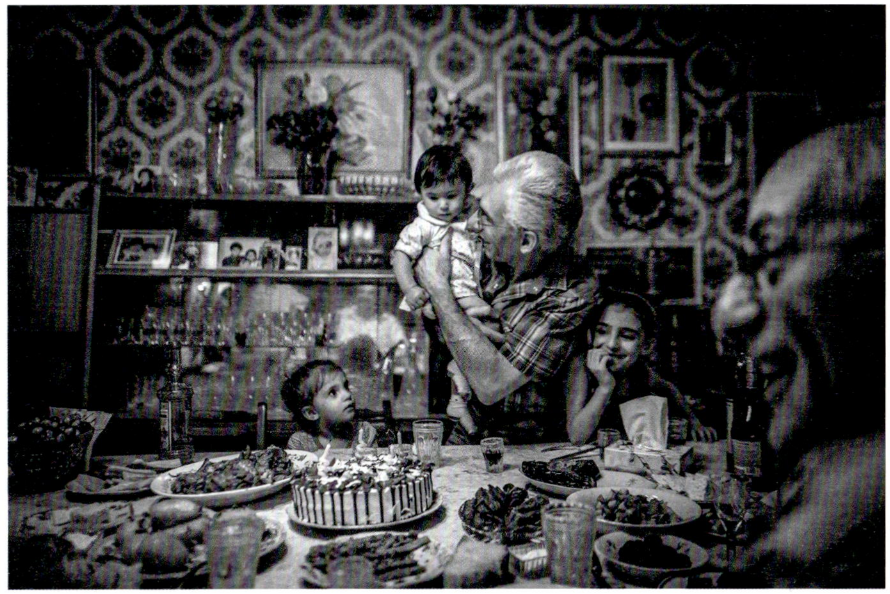

27.
Sassoferrato
The Holy Family

1660–85, oil on canvas
134 × 104.8 cm
The Fitzwilliam Museum, Cambridge
Bequeathed by
Charles Brinsley Marlay, 1912
M.74

Mary carries God's baby and Christ is always known as 'the son of God', yet Joseph is shown raising Christ as his own son. He kisses his child's hand, a sign of reverence for his divine status, and a reflection of their loving bond. Their relationship is striking because so much of the Bible is concerned with the status of sons and male ancestral lines.

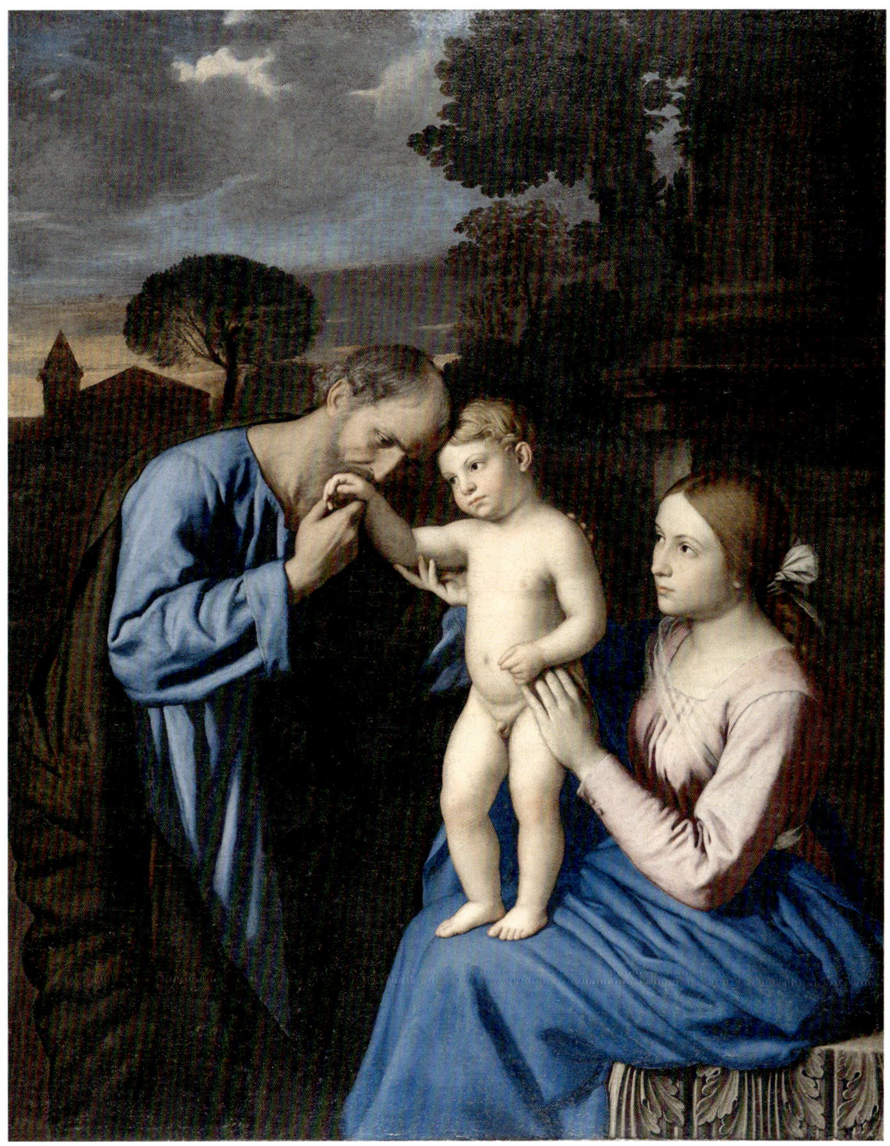

28.
Marcantonio Bellavia
Romulus and Remus Discovered by Faustulus and his Wife, Louva

1688–70, etching on paper,
bound into an album, state II/II
12.3 × 17 cm (image)
26.5 × 19.5 cm (sheet)
The Fitzwilliam Museum, Cambridge
Bequeathed by Richard, 7th Viscount Fitzwilliam, 1816
31.H.6-8

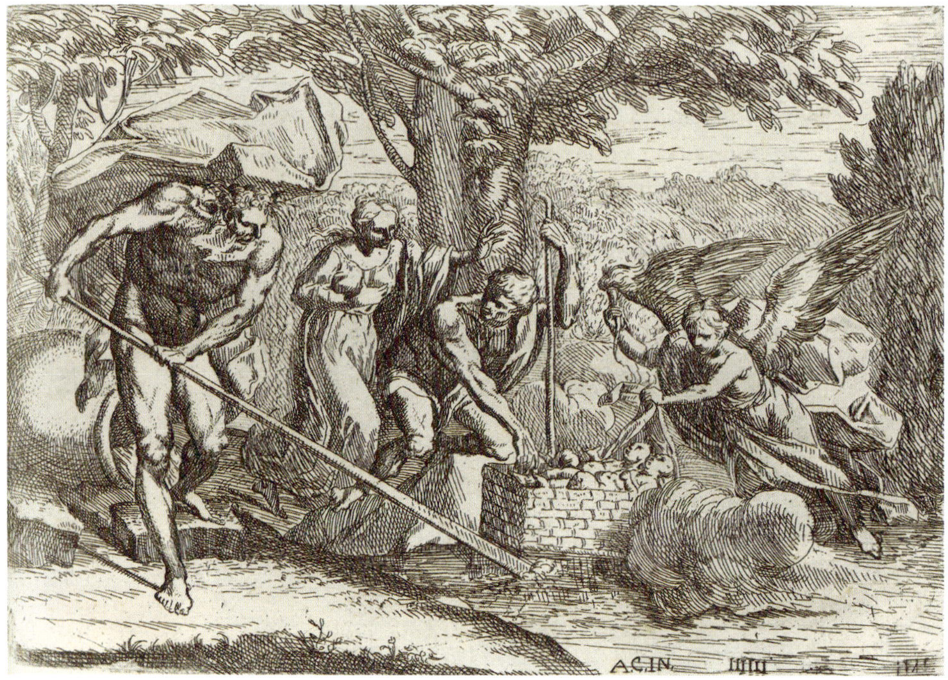

In a story from Roman mythology, twin brothers Romulus and Remus are deserted and left to die on the banks of a river by their jealous father, the king. The pair are kept alive by being suckled by a female wolf, then raised by a shepherd unaware of their royal lineage. The abandoned and rescued child was a common theme in stories from the ancient world, which suggests an interest in adoption as a practice.

29.
Unknown maker
Vacuum desiccator bell jar

About 1968–77, glass,
rubber stopper
40 × 30 × 30 cm
Bourn Hall Clinic

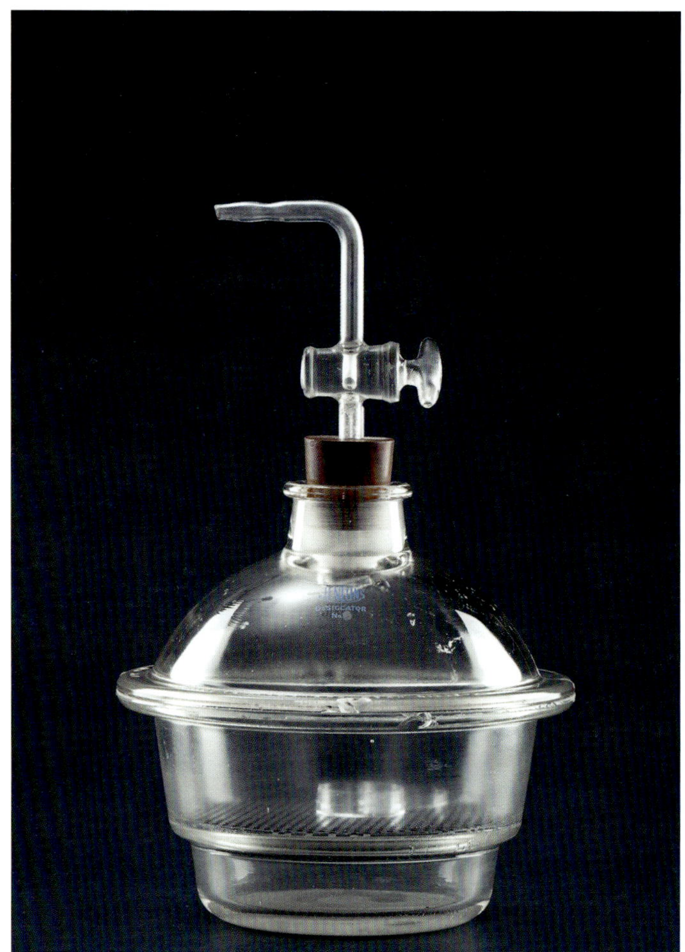

Louise Brown was the first baby in the world conceived outside the human body. She was born in 1978 through *in vitro* fertilisation (IVF) in Oldham, Lancashire. This became possible through the scientific work of Robert Edwards at the University of Cambridge and the obstetrician Patrick Steptoe. The first IVF babies, and possibly Louise Brown, were conceived in this glass jar.

30.
Elina Brotherus
Annonciation 7, Jour de l' Annonciation

2011, pigment ink print on barytha paper from digital original mounted on aluminium
50 × 61 cm
Courtesy of the artist

This work relates to the artist's five years of unsuccessful IVF treatment, and reflects the experiences of women undergoing IVF, anxiously waiting to discover whether they are pregnant. Brotherus references the Christian Annunciation, in which the Angel Gabriel informs Mary that she will conceive a child. The artist described her own experience as 'waiting for an angel who never shows up'.

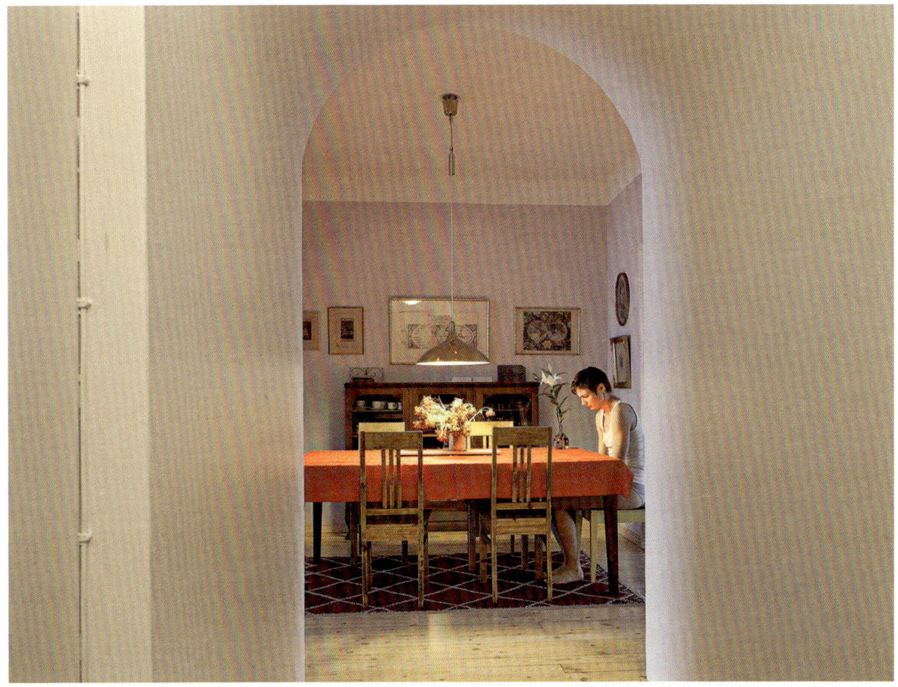

31–32.
Tabitha Moses
Investment: Emma's Gown

2014, hand-embroidered threads, mirrors, beads, linen, cotton binding
105 × 55 × 2 cm
On loan from the artist

Jon Barraclough and Tabitha Moses
Investment: Tabitha

2014, giclée print on Hahnemühle photo rag paper
92 × 67 × 2 cm (framed)
On loan from the artist

Tabitha Moses's hand-embroidered hospital gowns depict the experiences and objects that were meaningful to her and Emma, a patient at the same fertility clinic, while trying to conceive. These include syringes, a thermometer, fertility figurines, embryos, blood and tears. The emotional roller-coaster of fertility treatment, the hopes and fears of the women who experience it, the magical thinking that can accompany it, and the deep sense of loss of a failed treatment cycle, are embedded in these embroidered images.

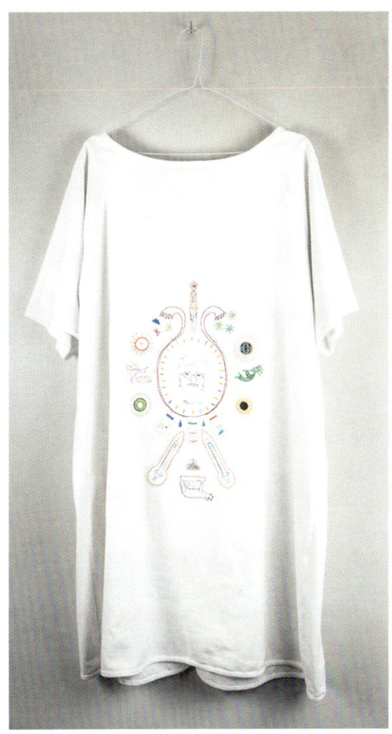

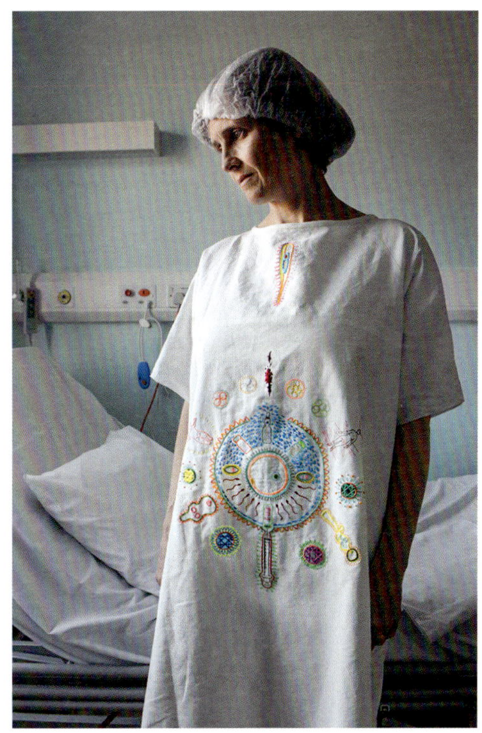

33.
Britt Thomas
No Heartbeat
and
Little Rainbow

From *Lullabies for Loss*
2018, rocking chairs and binaural lullaby recordings performed by Ashlynn Ivy-Tamez, dimensions variable
Courtesy of the artist

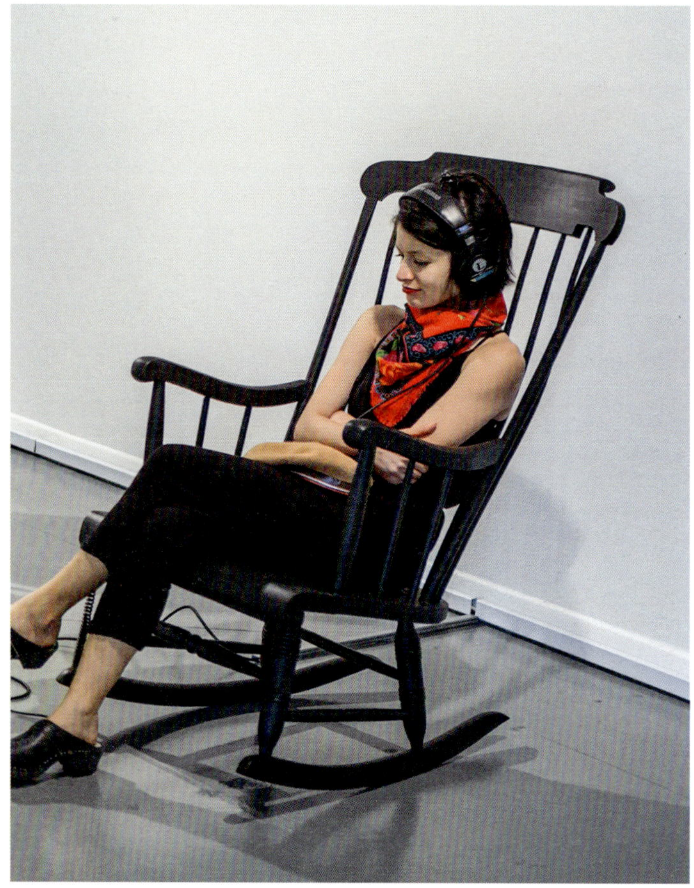

No Heartbeat, set to the melody of Brahm's *Lullaby*, evokes the trauma of discovering through a routine ultrasound scan that a longed-for baby has died in the womb. *Little Rainbow* refers to rainbow babies, the name given to babies born following miscarriage – the rainbow after the storm. These works, based on the artist's own experiences, draw attention to the grief of losing a baby.

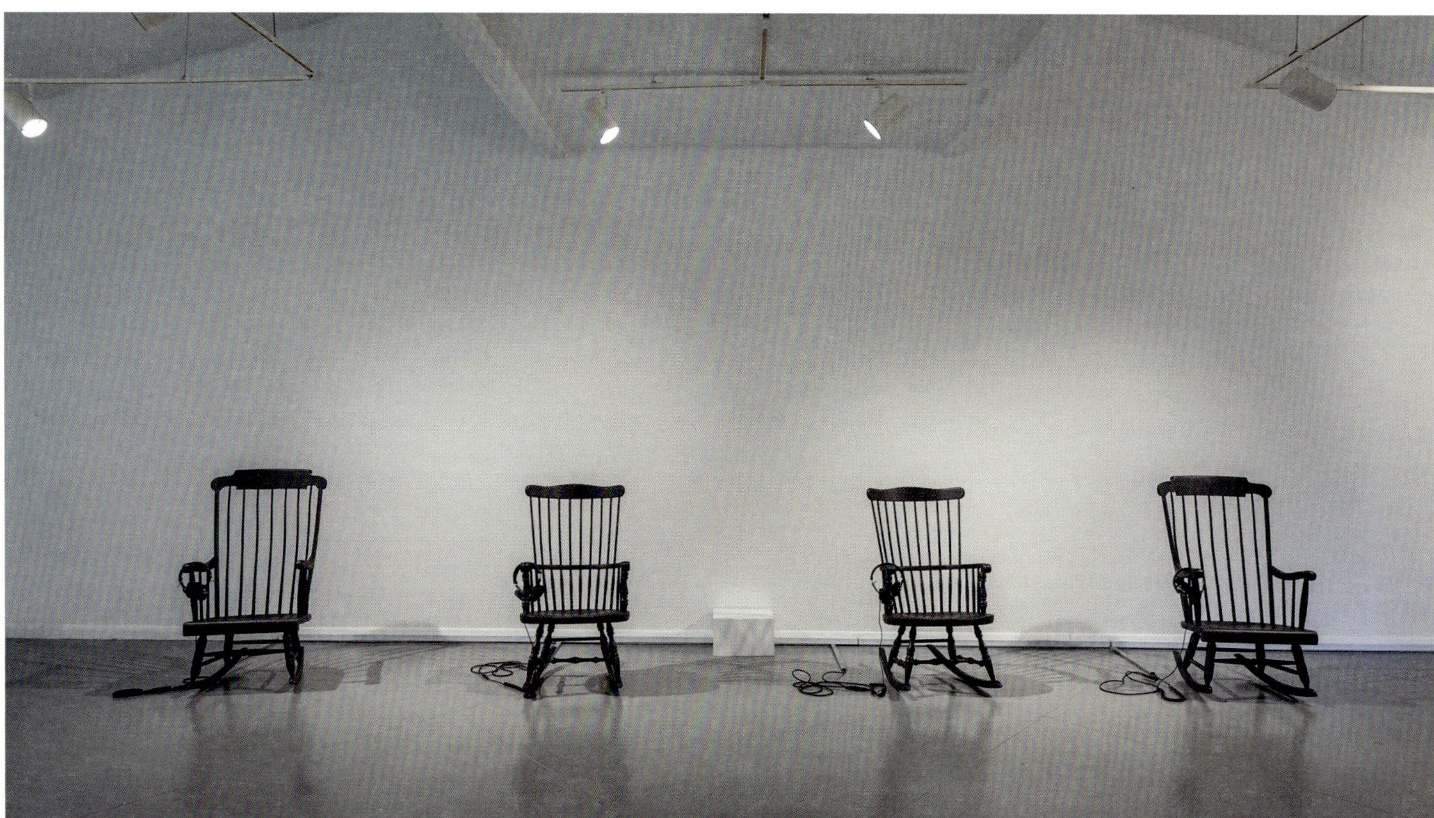

34–37.
Miriam Schaer

Untitled #1 ('Your not having children was the biggest disappointment of our life')

From the series *Babies Not On Board: The Last Prejudice?*
About 2012, hand embroidery on baby cotton rompers / dresses
38.1 × 48.2 cm
On loan from the artist

Untitled #11 ('Children are what makes a real family')

From the series *Babies Not On Board: The Last Prejudice?*
About 2012, hand embroidery on baby cotton rompers / dresses
38.1 × 30.5 cm
On loan from the artist

Untitled #15 ('Yes, you're married …')

From the series *Babies Not On Board: The Last Prejudice?*
About 2012, hand embroidery on baby cotton rompers / dresses
35.6 × 45.7 cm
On loan from the artist

Untitled #13 ('You are not a real parent if you have only one child')

From the series *Babies Not On Board: The Last Prejudice?*
About 2012, hand embroidery on baby cotton rompers / dresses
48.3 × 40.6 cm
On loan from the artist

Miriam Schaer, who was unable to have children, embroidered baby clothes with insensitive comments made to women without children to express her anger about the way they are made to feel.

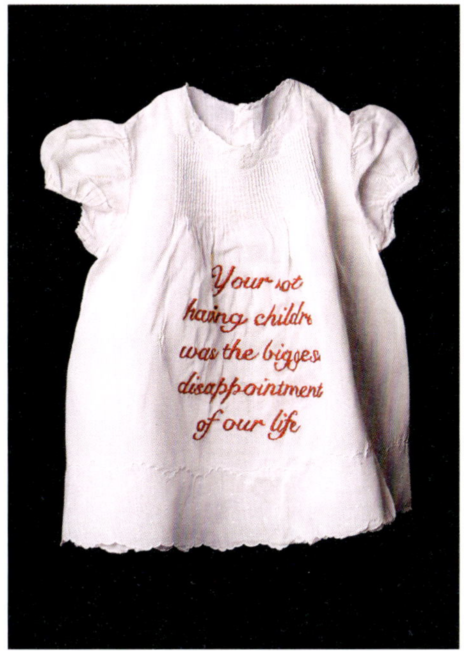

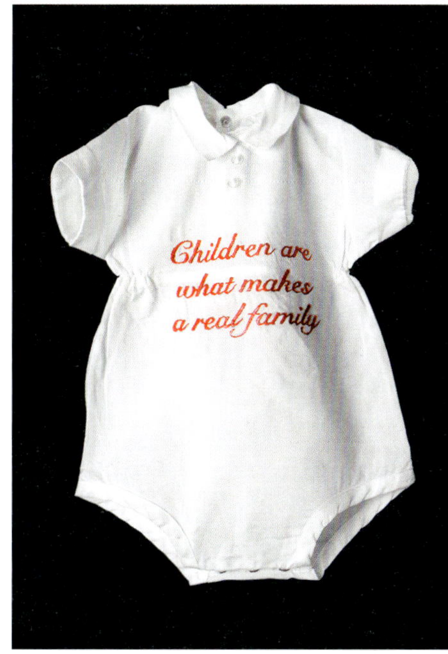

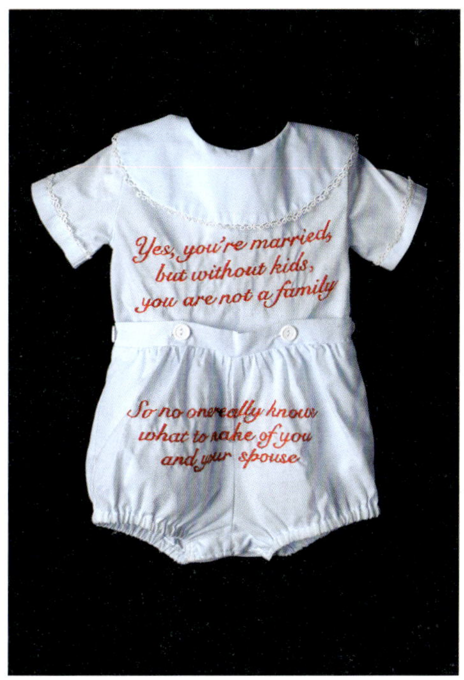

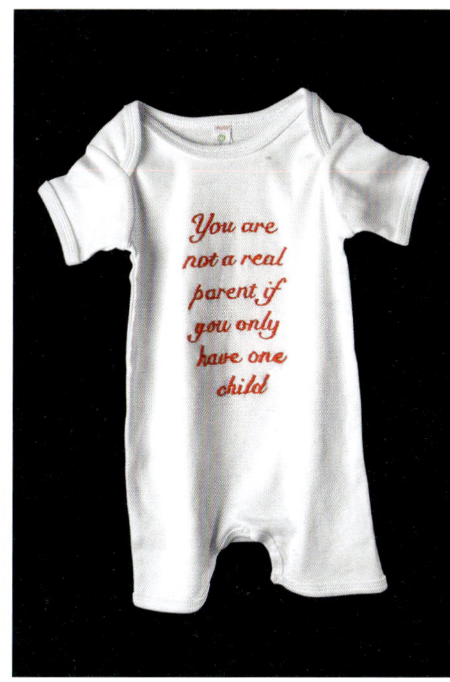

38.
Elina Brotherus
My Dog is Cuter than Your Ugly Baby

2013, pigment ink print on paper
82.2 × 56 × 3.2 cm (framed)
Louisiana Museum of Modern Art, Humlebaek
Acquired with funding from The Augusting Foundation
50-15-4019

Elina Brotherus described this work from her *Carpe Fucking Diem* series as an attempt to find meaning in a life without children, a future that she had not expected. 'I don't have children so I don't need to adopt any preconceived role of an adult. I can give normality the finger.'

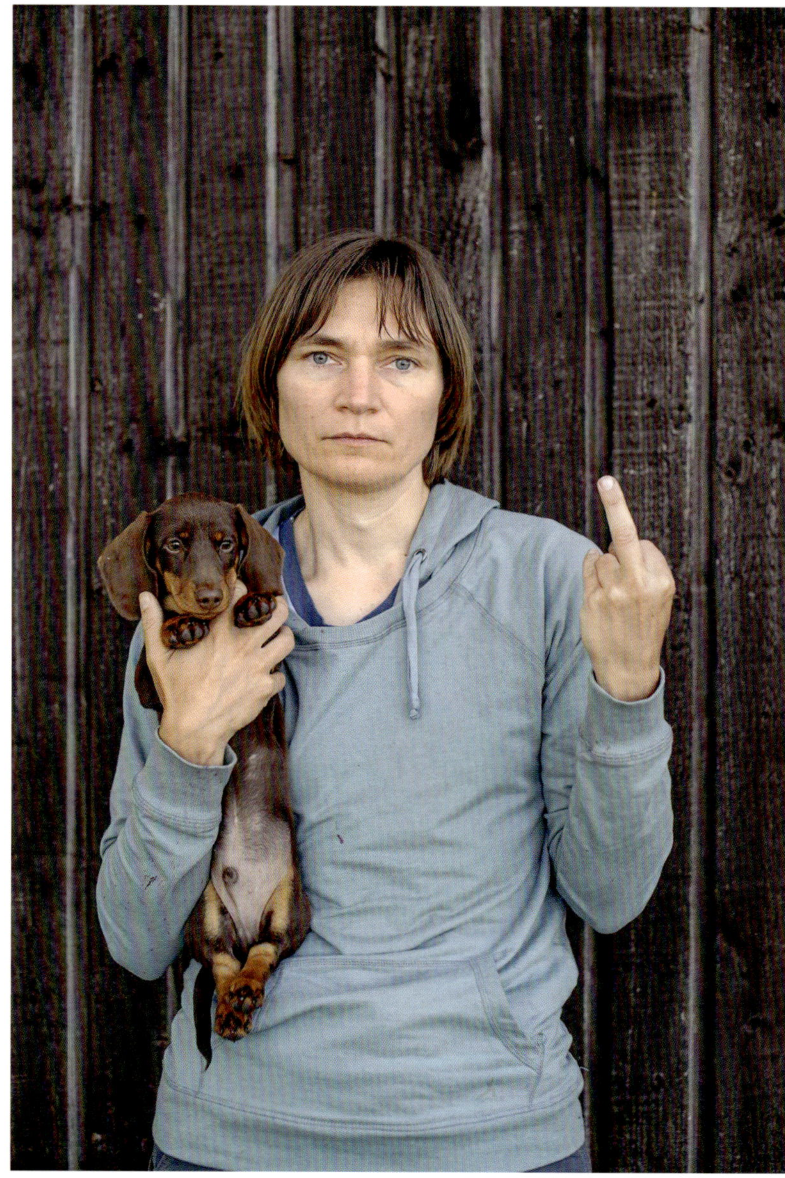

39.
Sunil Gupta
Shalini, Rudi, Sunil, Léo, 3425 Stanley

About 1974, pigment print on archival paper
30.6 × 42.9 × 0.5 cm
On loan from the Harris Museum & Art Gallery, Preston. Presented by the Contemporary Art Society to the Harris through the Collections Fund at Frieze, 2021/22
PRSMG: 2022.3.1

In the 1970s, when there were barriers to forming families outside the context of a heterosexual relationship, some LGBTQ+ people began to form chosen families based on mutual support rather than blood ties, and not necessarily including children. Gupta's photograph of his chosen family of friends and lovers was taken in his flat in Montreal's Gay Village, Canada.

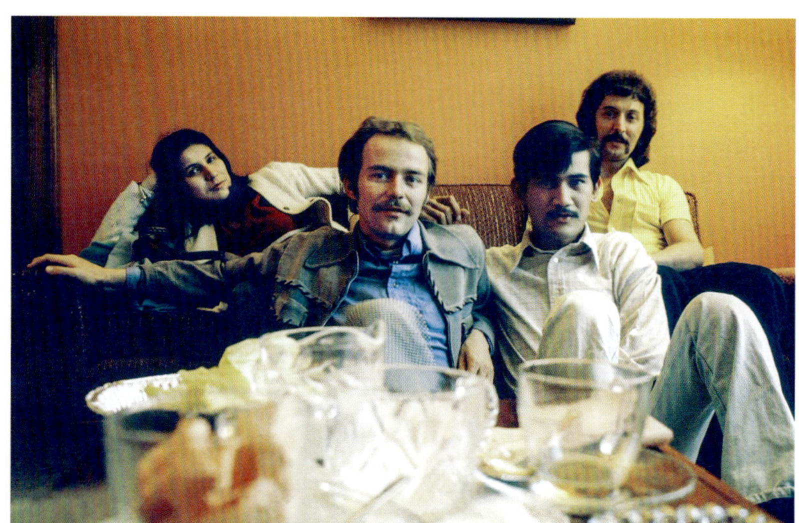

40.
Tejal Shah
You too can touch the moon – Yashoda with Krishna

From the *Hijra Fantasy Series*,
2006, digital photograph on archival photo paper, dry-mounted on aluminium
147 × 96.5 cm
Richard Heaton, Warden of Robinson College

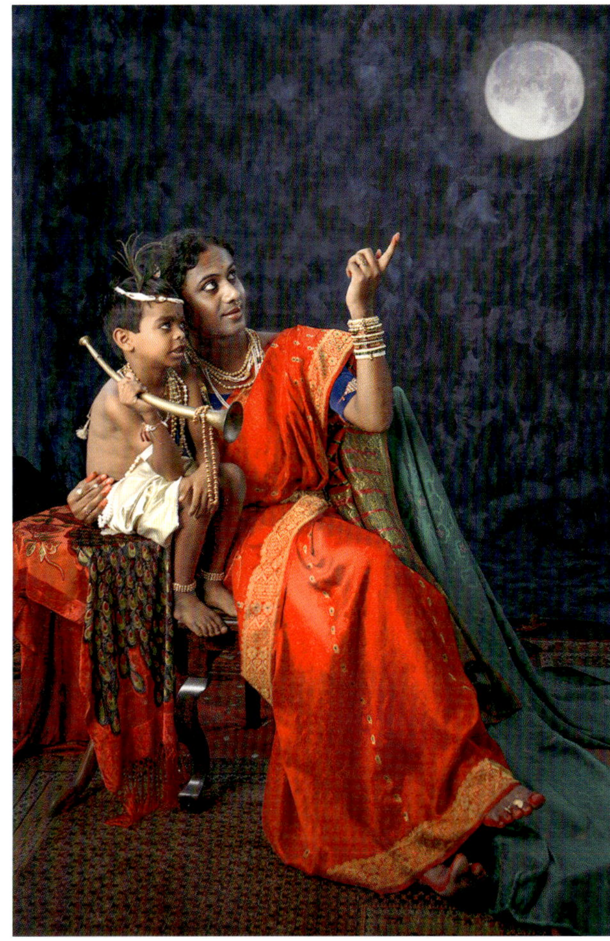

The mother-son story of Yashoda and Krishna is shown here with a person from the Hijra community of eunuchs, intersex and transgender people in India as Krishna's devoted foster mother. It speaks to loving relationships between parents and children in families with non-biological and queer parents.

41.
Sophie Calle
Today My Mother Died (Aujourd'hui ma mère est morte)

From the series *Autobiographies*, 2/5 EN
2013, colour photography, text, wooden frame
130 × 50.5 cm (framed)
Courtesy of the artist and Perrotin / © Sophie Calle / ADAGP Paris, 2023, Photographer: Claire Dorn

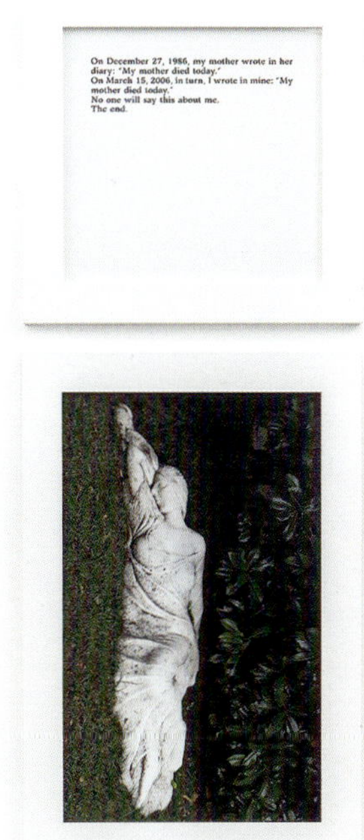

On 27 December 1966, my mother wrote
in her diary,
'My mother died today.'
On 15 March 2006, in turn,
I wrote in mine, 'My mother
died today.'
No one will say this about me.
The end.

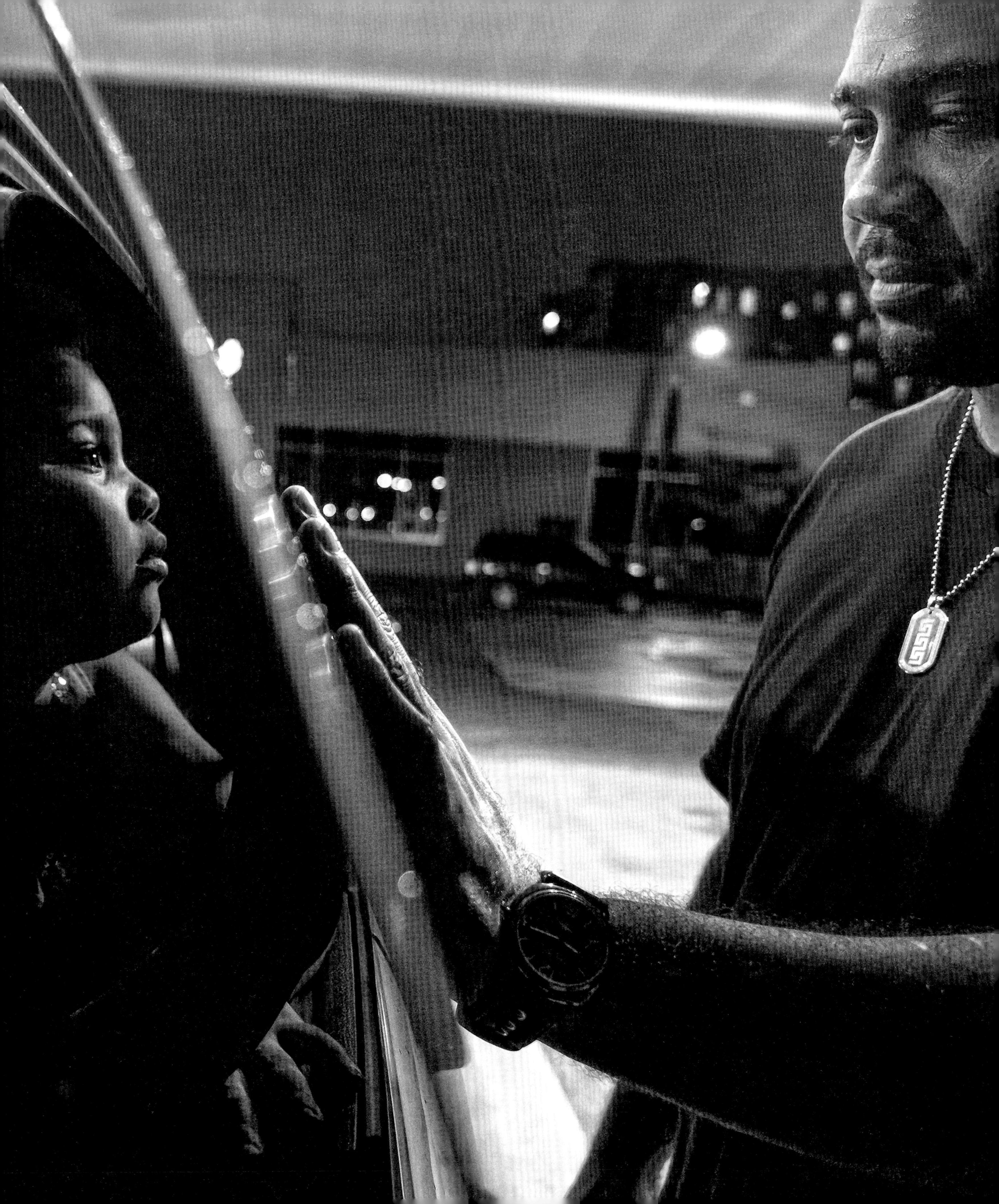

Relationships between different family members change over time. The impact of these relationships on psychological well-being is the focus of the work of the Centre and of artists. The emotional bond between mothers and their children from infancy through to adolescence, and a father's role in the development of their children, are explored. The artworks on siblings speak to the dynamic and intense relationships that exist between them from early childhood onwards, and those on grandparents and grandchildren highlight the benefit of having each other in their lives. Adults are often faced with the expectation that they will care for their parents, something that can produce mixed emotions, including feelings of obligation and resentment as well as closeness. Artists convey these complex thoughts and feelings through portraits of their ageing parents.

Family Transitions

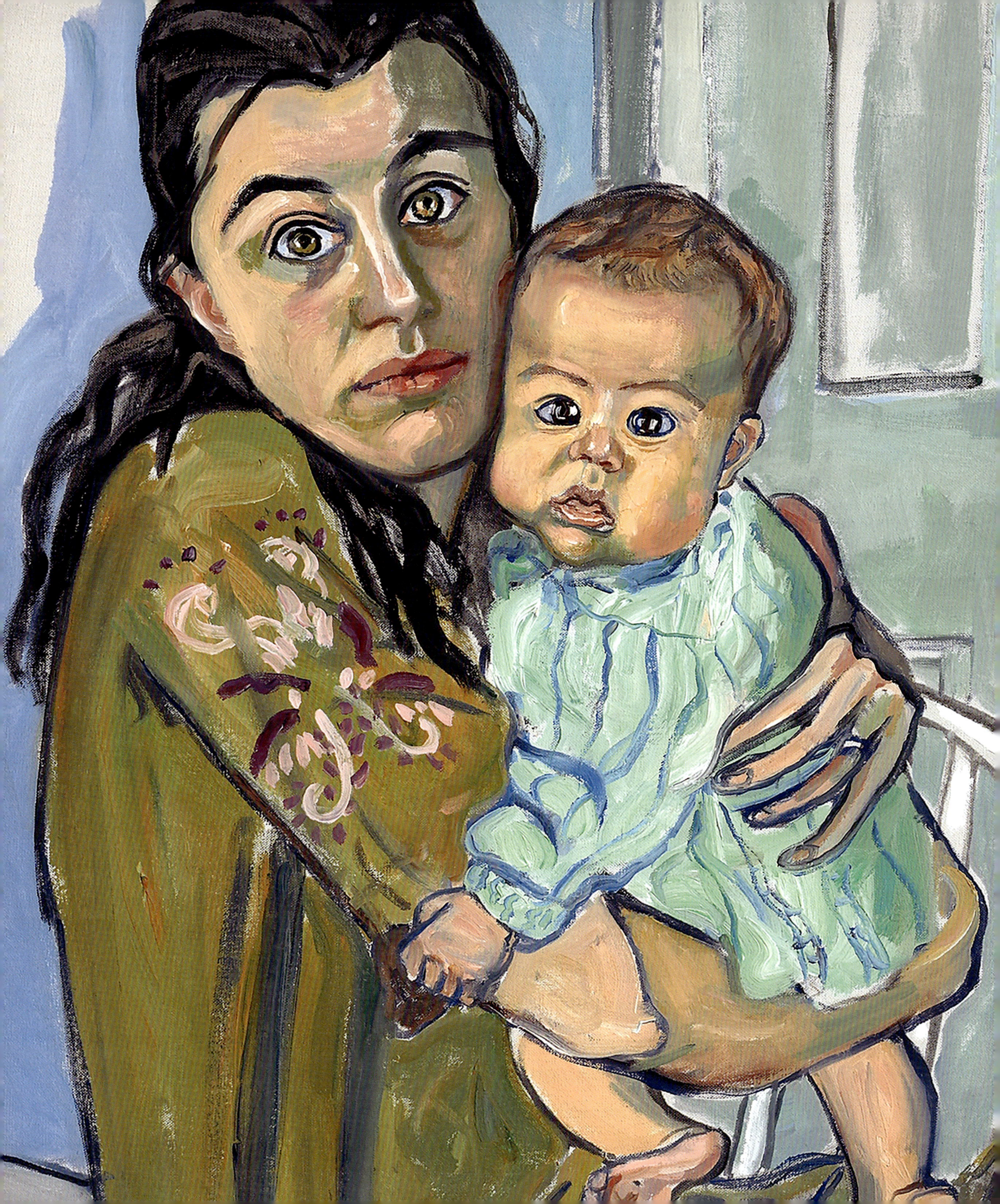

Legitimising Motherhood

Detail of **52**, Alice Neel, *Nancy and Olivia*, 1967

'Alice Neel showed me that it's possible to paint and be a mother. Not only that, she makes the subject of motherhood seem legitimate,' the artist Chantal Joffe told me when I asked about the effect Neel has had on her practice.

For centuries, the subject of motherhood has been contentious. When we think about images of the subject from Western art history, so often it has been dictated by the male gaze. From the Renaissance and the birth of 'humanism' – which sought to show man's lived experience – to the late nineteenth century, artworks have commonly presented the mother-child relationship as idealised – as an immaculate, virginal Madonna doting on her cherub-like son. But has this skewed our understanding of the realities of motherhood, and presented to us a false narrative? Rarely have we been witness to the messy realities of parenthood in painting, the complex emotions that come with it, and the body's physical transformations. Historical European Painting has almost exclusively fed us one perspective. But Alice Neel has helped drive the change away from this. Through her art, she showed us pregnancy, grief, love, complicatedness – one might say, truth. As Joffe continues, 'Seeing [Neel's] painting of *Margaret Evans Pregnant* (1978) makes it seem incredibly exciting to paint a pregnant woman from the inside'. It is the notion of painting from the inside that says it all.

Neel, born on the stroke of a new century, on 28 January 1900, was one of America's greatest painters. Her chosen subject was people – she described herself as a 'collector of souls' – and she worked from the early 1920s right up until her death in 1984. Neel captured people from all walks of life who she knew and admired from her various neighbourhoods – Havana in Cuba, and Greenwich Village, Spanish Harlem and the Upper West Side in New York. Her sitters ranged from artist Andy Warhol and playwright Alice Walker to her landlord's son Benjamin and her cleaner, Carmen. But for me, it's her images of motherhood and families – and the dynamics that come with these roles – that are the most profound.

Always working from life, Neel captured her encounters with mothers in all different capacities – new mothers, old mothers, grandmothers, mothers-in-law; mothers in love, mothers tending to their unwell child, and mothers experiencing grief. The nature of the slow, time-based act of sitting for a painter means that an artist can really see their subject. Stroke by stroke, they are able to capture the conversation that played out, how the sitter might have felt at that moment, the energy of the room. Painting involves this longer duration – it's different from a photograph where a subject can

Katy Hessel

switch moods from one minute to the next, but it's also as much of a self-portrait of the artist themself as it is of their subject. When we look at her images of motherhood, we must consider Neel's own role and experiences.

Neel was a mother to four children. In 1926, she gave birth to her first child, Santillana, but, just days before her first birthday, Santillana tragically died of diptheria. As quoted in Julie Phillips's *The Baby on the Fire Escape*, Neel recalled, 'After Santillana's death I was just frantic. Then I was already in a trap. All I could do was get pregnant again.' The following November she gave birth to Isabetta, but eighteen months after that Isabetta would be taken from Neel back to Havana by her husband's family. She would only meet her a handful of times. (One of Neel's most challenging images, for me, is a reproduction of a portrait of *Isabetta* from 1934–35. It indicates the stark distance and the lack of intimacy between mother and child.) Neel went on to give birth to Richard (1939) and Hartley (1940), with two different fathers, children who she raised as both a single mother and a full-time artist. It must have been the opposite of easy, but knowing this background I find allows us a greater understanding of her work.

Empathy and a mutual trust are ubiquitous in Neel's paintings – especially when it comes to mothers, loss, or the onset of loss. One of Neel's most emotional paintings is *Carmen and Judy*, a later work from 1972, which depicts her Haitian cleaner, Carmen, who is attempting to breastfeed her unwell and disabled baby, Judy. In this work we see tenderness – between mother and daughter, and through Carmen's gaze that determinedly meets Neel's. Although Carmen is smiling, Neel reveals a helplessness in her eyes, perhaps a knowingness that she is unable to feed her child. As Hilton Als writes in a recent letter addressed to Neel, cited in *Hot off the Griddle*, 'There is not one of us who has not been Judy – life has harmed us, injured the brain and heart, and yet there is the softness of the woman who holds us'. The scene is also full of tension. Whereas Carmen's right hand is protecting her child, her left hand is in a different mood entirely: it is tense, out of place, eerily spider-like as it grips on to the blanket underneath her child.

This is not a warm, happy image, but rather a painful and brutal depiction of motherhood. One might even question why Neel would want to immortalise such a scene. Although it is unsettling, it conveys the sad reality that some mothers have to go through. When we consider Neel's biography, it may also speak to her own suffering in the last few months of Santillana's life. Because, unbeknownst to them, baby Judy would die shortly after this painting was made. Like Neel, who no doubt wanted to cling on to her children forever, the fact that she has immortalised Judy through paint allows her memory never to fade.

Thinking about this, I was reminded of the artist Nan Goldin's approach to photography, and her series *The Ballad of Sexual Dependency*. Goldin took up photography after her sister, Barbara, committed suicide, when Nan was just eleven years old. She has since dedicated much of her work to her late sister, writing: 'I don't ever want to lose the real memory of anyone again'. The power of art is that it can immortalise people.

The act of painting can serve as a form of therapy – perhaps Neel working through her own experiences of grief and loss, something not ubiquitous in the history of art when it comes to motherhood. In her essay for the Barbican exhibition, Eleanor Nairne wrote: 'Creating art became crucial for Neel's recovery. The studio was a space in which she felt free from social pressure, and where her acute sensitivity could be repurposed as strength. As she [Neel] explained in an interview with [Cindy] Nemser, "When I painted I was completely and utterly myself. For that reason it was extremely important to me. It was more than just a profession. It was even therapy, for there I just told it as it was."' No matter how painful the subject, Neel painted with honesty. And that honesty allows people – and mothers – to feel seen.

Throughout her career, Neel painted the many stages of motherhood, and, in her images of pregnancy, presented it not as perfect, but as the life-affirming yet terrifying experience that it can be. One of her most powerful images is *Margaret Evans Pregnant*, where we see a woman both in physical discomfort (from her bulbous belly and protruding breasts that almost squash her fragile and dangly legs) and also emotionally anxious (from her piercing wide-eyed gaze). Sitting uncomfortably upright with her hands firmly gripped to the yellow chair below (that appears to be almost shrinking from view), it is as though Evans is bracing herself for what is to come.

I discussed this image with the artist Christina Kimeze, who responded: 'I think the way she paints these women alone, naked, pregnant sitting or reclining takes it to the psychological'. On a pregnant woman's specific mindset she writes: 'I think that's deeply moving as you try to consider how your life is going to change – but it's also a complete unknown for a first-time mother and Neel, and all of us, bring to the painting our own experience of that.'

As if to disrupt the scene by combining both her own experiences as a mother and Evans's future, Neel paints a second portrait to the left of her subject – Evans reflected in the mirror, as a slightly slimmed down and less youthful version of herself. Ambiguous and warped as she is, the picture could be signalling Evans's future, enhanced by the wrinkle that appears to stretch down the side of her face. In this one image, Neel presents the many aspects of pregnancy. Here, we see a bodily transformation, a universal anxiety about change, and a nod to the ever-lasting commitment of parenthood – something Neel was well aware of by the time she painted the image, being then herself a grandmother at seventy-eight years old.

When we consider how artists have also documented the complications of this subject, the Impressionist Berthe Morisot is someone who formed

42.
Alice Neel
The De Vegh Twins

1975, oil on canvas
121.9 × 101.6 cm
Private collection.
Courtesy Tracy Williams
Art Advisory, NY

new representations of the subject. Working slightly before Neel's birth, at the end of the nineteenth century, Morisot grappled with the subject's complexities. This is exemplified in her painting *The Cradle*, 1872, of the artist's sister, Edma, and her new-born baby, Jeanne. Edma, who was once a promising artist, at first glance might appear to be gazing lovingly at her child. But her thoughtful stance, and the diagonal line that separates the two figures, might hint at the complicatedness of her role. (After all, she was forced to renounce all artistic pursuits in favour of marriage.) Additionally, in contrast to stereotypical images of mothers, Edma's choice of fashionable dress (a white ruffled shirt, striped blazer and black choker) might suggest that she was still striving to live life as an independent and modern woman.

In *Nancy and Olivia* (**52**) Neel portrays a mother and her new-born child. Like Morisot's *The Cradle*, both works are of family members – Nancy was

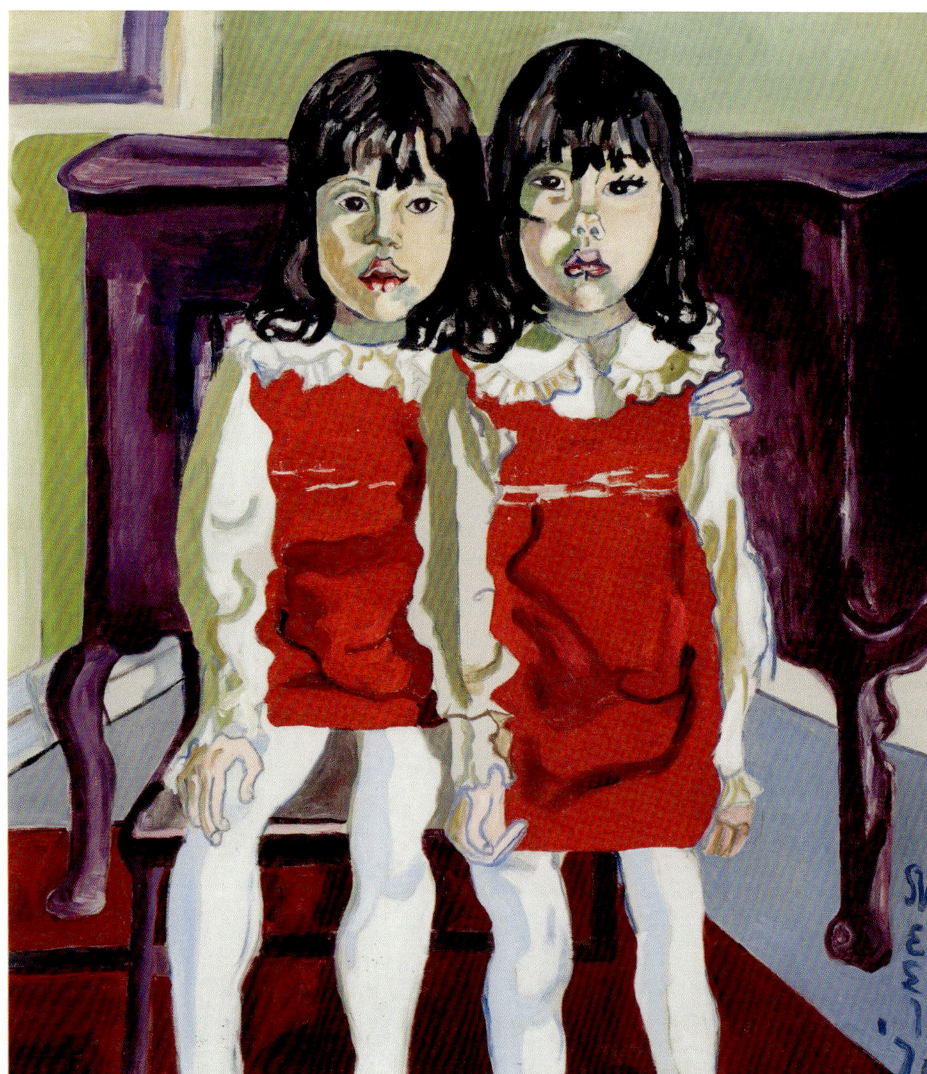

Neel's daughter-in-law – and show an acute sensitivity to and understanding of the reality of being a mother. Although Nancy is physically clenched to Olivia, Edma isn't touching Jeanne; and while Nancy and Olivia stare intensely at us, Edma's gaze is focused on Jeanne. Both paintings illustrate the reality of having a new-born child and the simple differences that might be only minutes, or even seconds, apart – when a mother has returned to her baby after a long day, or before she is about to leave the house.

These nuances are what Neel captures so poignantly. She documents the complicatedness, the tensions, the grief and the love that motherhood entails. But what one also has to keep in mind is that Neel was 'mothering' on the job. Her studio was set up in her apartment, and in the 1940s and 1950s she was tasked with raising two young boys. It's an issue, like much discussed in this essay, that has rarely been spotlighted in history. But, as is the case with so many professions, when you are parenting it is difficult to find the freedom to make art. As quoted by Phillips, Neel once recalled: 'I always had this awful dichotomy . . . I loved Isabetta, of course I did. But I wanted to paint.' Isabetta was told that her mother had once left her on a fire escape because she was painting. Does that make Neel a bad mother?

Neel also painted other people's children – as is the case with the portrait of the De Vegh twins (**42**), sisters who appear worlds apart from the settings Neel's children grew up in. Almost comically matching in scallop-collared silk shirts and red dresses, the twins feel significantly more distant from the painter than her own children. The twins were the daughters of Geza de Vegh – a close friend of Neel's, who restored her paintings – and while she knew them well, through her painting she demonstrates the uncomplicatedness of painting another's child.

What Neel accomplished was extraordinary. Although she was barely recognised until her 70s, and died in an apartment on the Upper West Side stocked full of unsold paintings, she showed that it was possible to do both – mother and paint. The artist Antonia Showering told me: 'Knowing her life story has always made me feel less alone. She overcame and endured so much but this only made her more determined as a painter. Alice makes you understand you can be both a mother and an artist, and, although it might not always be easy, it's certainly doable – she did it.' Neel showed us the emotional, physical and psychological truth of being a mother – and, as Joffe says, 'makes the subject of motherhood seem legitimate' – and in turn gave a generation of artists permission to do the same.

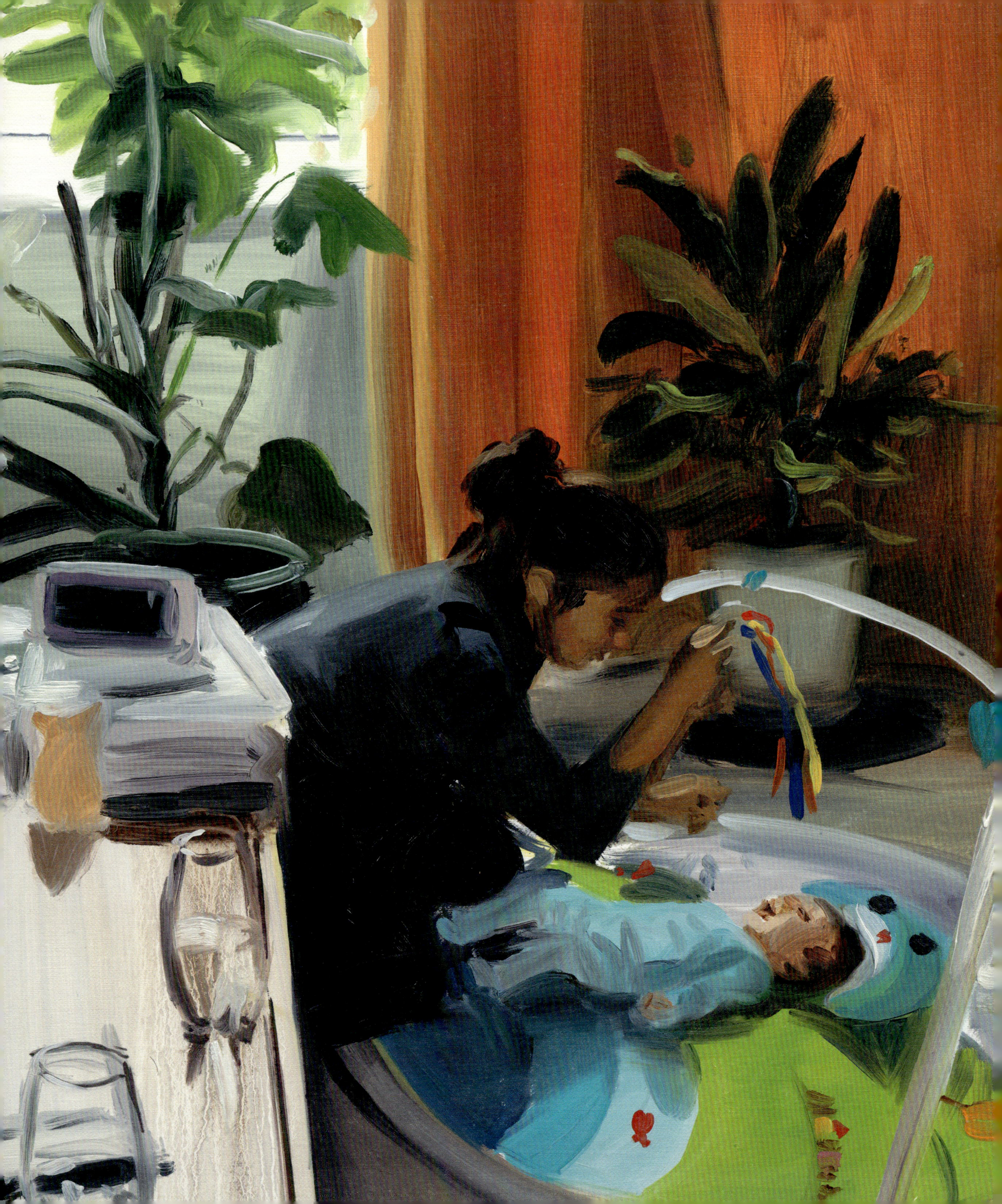

Attachment and Human Experience

Detail of **54**, Caroline Walker, *Study for* Refreshments, 2022

When you think about it, being a psychologist is a weird thing to be. You observe people, compare them against each other, codify their behaviour, write down theories about them – how you think their thoughts and feelings work – and try to make it all systematic and predictable. For outsiders it must seem like a bizarre and probably impossible job. I rarely even stop to reflect on it. But it's a fair question: how do you study the profoundly personal and hidden things that go on in people's minds, like the experience of connection, intimacy, joy, self-doubt and grief? How can you systematise people's relationships and feelings about each other? So much of this is deeply human and subtle – like how the present is imbued by our early experiences or how barely conscious fears shape our sense of the here and now. Or how a look, or a tone of voice, can put you at ease or throw you off guard. Can you really make a science out of people's lives or make families and children measurable objects of research?

I've been in this business long enough now to have a humble respect for the enormity of that task and I don't know if I have a good answer to those questions. I certainly began my academic career full of confidence we could find scientific answers to these sorts of questions, but, as time goes on, I'm much less clear about that. I am cautious about our attempts to measure people or build grand theories, and try to respect the complexity of human experience and development. So, when I am grappling with a problem in psychology – a question about human behaviour or human relationships – I always try to bring it back to what real life is like. Put down the textbook, forget the theory and just look around you. You need to be able to shift back and forth flexibly between analysing and observing, letting them sit in some sort of creative tension with each other. The art is to allow your analytical mind to see patterns in the thicket of moments – so to look beyond them – while at the same time allowing one's emerging conceptual understanding to be drawn back to and tested against the immediacy, the detail and the messiness of human experience. You'd be surprised how disconnected some psychological theory and writing is from real life, and indeed how little training the average psychologist gets in pure observation. I think this basic interest in observation is part of what drew me to Lisa Sorgini's work. Unlike some more symbolic or rhetorical artworks, her photography comes as close as it feels possible to do to the momentary experience of being a person and, most importantly for me, of being a person embedded in a network of human relationships – in families, communities, cultures. Sorgini observes,

Pasco Fearon

non-analytically, the everyday moments of family life, with a tender and compassionate eye, keeping us close to the real stuff that we psychologists can get carried away theorising about.

My own research has focused on what is called attachment theory, which sets out to explain the nature and dynamics of the bonds between children and their parents. It's a beautiful attempt – arguably one of the best attempts so far – to systematise something so seemingly human and intimate. The theory was developed by the British psychiatrist and psychoanalyst John Bowlby in the 1950s and 1960s and it has had a huge impact on the field of developmental psychology, as well as on wider society. His insight – which at the time was genuinely ground-breaking – was to think of this bond as something rooted in our biology. Bowlby argued that evolution and the process of natural selection created a complex protective behavioural system, designed – as it were – to ensure that babies and young children survived and flourished despite being highly immature and vulnerable for a long period of their development. According to Bowlby, infants instinctively form selective bonds with familiar and reliable caregivers and use them as a source of comfort and protection when under threat. Over time, a whole range of different behaviours and emotions become organised around these key individuals and are activated when the child feels anxious or vulnerable. They reach out or cling, cry or protest, crawl towards their parent and ask to be picked up; they snuggle in, and mould themselves to them, as if absorbing comfort through the skin. These are what we call attachment behaviours, and they all have the predictable consequence of bringing about contact with, and support from, a trusted attachment figure. When you think about the exceptional vulnerability of a young baby, this pattern of behaviour makes so much sense, both psychologically and evolutionarily. So, according to Bowlby, the tie between a young child and their carers is instinctive and serves vital survival functions; it is a product of our evolutionary history.

So, when I look at Lisa Sorgini's piece (**43**), I am reminded of the timelessness of this scene. This is contemporary Australia (I think), but rearrange the physical surroundings and we could be looking at a mother and child anywhere in the world, at more or less any time in our history. A mother and child, passing the time together, some invisible thread keeping the child in the mother's proximity, as she plays and explores. There is a sense of peaceful normalness; of toddlers doing what toddlers do, under the watchful eye of an older and wiser parent. There are reasons these scenes recreate themselves every generation: our societies and communities are patterned in fundamental ways because of the way we raise children, and these patterns are shaped, no doubt in complex and conditional ways, by biological forces. When you look at this picture, you are seeing the simplicity and beauty of some of the fundamentals of what make us human – we raise children and we form attachments. I think this is part of the reason the image captures your attention. Like seeing a sunset or a verdant landscape, there is something here that resonates deeply with our basic humanity.

In the early days of his writing, Bowlby's work on attachment was largely a theoretical enterprise. He gathered a wide array of information to support his ideas from existing research and clinical observations, but he didn't conduct much research on the subject himself. The study of attachment really took off as an empirical subject through the work of an American-Canadian psychologist called Mary Ainsworth, who came to work with Bowlby in the early 1950s. Mary Ainsworth was surely an exceptional observer of the minutiae of the everyday. Inspired by Bowlby's thinking, Ainsworth began her observational work in Uganda, where she spent many hours quietly watching and recording mother-baby interactions in rural villages near Kampala. She was particularly interested in how infants used their caregivers as a source of comfort and safety – a so-called 'secure base' – and how the caregiver's responses supported that or not. She continued this observational work when she returned to the United States, similarly observing, in acute detail, the care-giving and -receiving interactions of mothers and babies.

Two absolutely critical innovations were to emerge from this work. Firstly, Ainsworth came to realise that a crucial variable, from the infant's point of view, but also in the more statistical sense, that distinguished some mother-baby pairs from others, was the extent to which the mother was closely aware of the infant's subtle signals, how accurate her interpretation of them seemed to be, and how helpful and timely her responses were (**54**), as depicted in Caroline Walker's painting. Some dyads were harmonious and in-tune, and the child appeared easily able to explore and to return for comfort when needed. Others were more distant, inharmonious or conflicted, and the mothers tended to ignore or frustrate the infant's bids for contact. These differences in caregiving that Ainsworth identified came to be known as 'caregiver sensitivity', and the evidence gathered since that time is quite overwhelming in pointing to its importance for children's development. It's worth underlining one critical and sometimes misunderstood aspect of this concept: this is not a picture of perfect parenting Ainsworth is painting, or indeed one that is highly demonstrative or full of parenting tricks, 'good jobs!' and high-fives. It's often low-key and ordinary, and yet responsive to the baby's subtle or not-so-subtle communications; it's present, and responsive; available.

In introducing Mary Ainsworth's work, we have shifted from a focus on the baby and its selective attachment to her parent to a focus on the parent and how they respond to the baby. Although Bowlby's writings were almost entirely dedicated to understanding the evolution and development of the baby's attachment to their caregivers, it stood to reason that this evolutionary trick to ensure infant survival and optimal development would only work if there were a caregiver to be attached to, and who was invested in

43.
Lisa Sorgini
Lise (36 weeks) and Lulu

From the series *Mother*
2019, giclée print on
Hahnemühle paper
76 × 102 cm
Courtesy of the artist

and responsive to the child's bids for contact and comfort. These things must have evolved together. So, throughout our history, there were young children playing and pottering around their caregivers, now and then needing support, contact or care and signalling their need for it, and caregivers keeping a watchful eye, knowing their needs and dispositions, anticipating the next mishap, and responding with comfort and protection. You get a little hint of that in Sorgini's photograph – her hand held up, slightly extended, as if in a warning to be careful, or in readiness to catch Lulu if her roly-poly doesn't quite go to plan.

The second key innovation that came out of Ainsworth's work at this time was the development of a now famous observational procedure for studying a child's attachment behaviour, which she named the 'strange situation'. Her impression from her observations in the home was that sensitive and responsive caregiving facilitated the child's use of the parent as a haven of safety and secure base from which to explore the world, but, to test that idea more scientifically, she needed a separate measurement of the child's attachment, distinct from the observational context from which she had

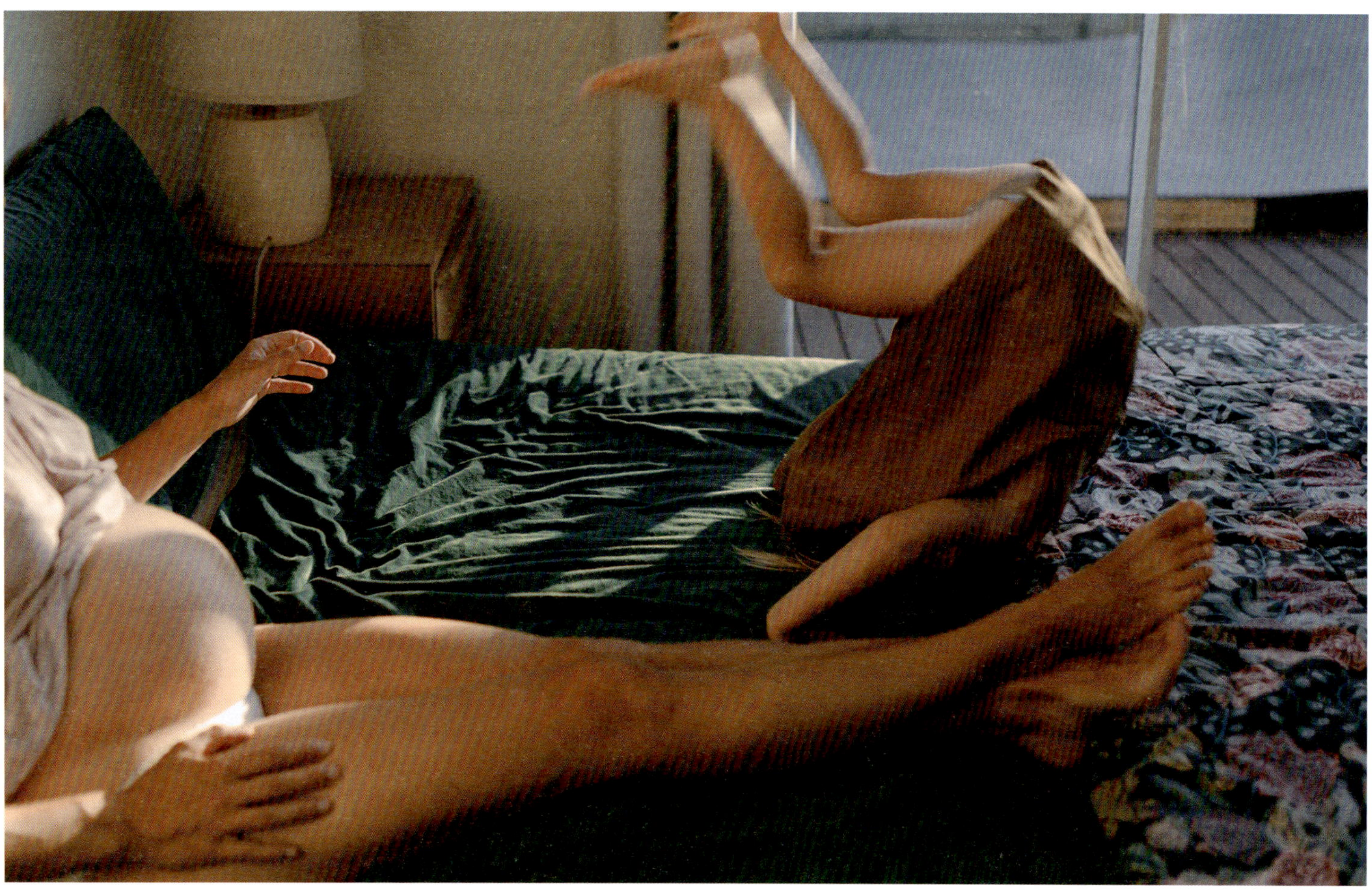

derived an assessment of the caregiver's sensitive behaviour. The 'strange situation' procedure created a set of conditions outside the home to reliably elicit the child's attachment behaviour, and it did this by introducing the child to a series of mild 'cues to danger' – first meeting a stranger, and then on two occasions being briefly separated from her parent, in an unfamiliar setting. This procedure was much less naturalistic than Ainsworth's home observations, deliberately so. It was designed to limit too much variation in what the parent did, so that the child's attachment behaviour could be observed more clearly in its own right.

When young children are introduced to the Strange Situation, you see a rich variety of behaviour and interaction. The parent and child may be close to each other at the start, but slowly the baby gets curious in the room and starts exploring, checking back now and then, maybe returning to 'touch base', smiling, chatting, pointing out what's interesting. A stranger enters the room and sits down nearby. The baby tucks herself, perhaps, between her mother's knees for a moment, staring watchfully, now and then looking up at her mum for reassurance, or just clarification, twiddling her hair with mild anxiety. A friendly conversation between the adults breaks the ice and the baby relaxes, playing on the floor, or even cautiously offering the stranger a toy. The stranger sits next to her and invites her to play with the toys with them. Glad of the playmate, the baby joins in and now they are getting on famously. After a little while, the child's mother stands up and casually says, 'I'll be back in a minute', resting her hand briefly on the child's shoulder. The sight of her mum leaving the room in this unfamiliar place immediately unsettles her and she stops playing, and heads towards the door, calling out. Despite some valiant efforts to distract her with toys and friendly invitations, the stranger isn't able to persuade her to come back to play, and indeed the longer the delay, the more upset she becomes, and she starts to cry. The door promptly opens, and mum returns, calling to her and extending her arms, waiting for the baby to make the first move. Sure enough, she dashes forwards, raising up her arms just before reaching her mum. Mum, in kind, reaches forwards, tucking her hands under the child's arms, lifting her up. After a brief snuggle in the space between her mum's neck and shoulder she sits upright, and points to the stranger, as if to say, 'Let me introduce you to my friend'. And before you know it, she's off again, trotting around the room, rearranging the toys and chatting to herself, the little drama apparently over.

It was in this situation that Ainsworth made a key discovery. The majority of babies behaved more or less like this little girl, and, while every observation was different, there was a patterning that could be seen from one child to the next – one that makes sense in the light of Bowlby's theory of attachment. In the scenario I just described above, when faced with cues to danger, the baby's behaviour and emotions all became organised towards one goal – regaining contact with her parent. And when that contact was achieved a sense of security and safety was restored, and she skipped right back to play. The attachment behavioural system – as Bowlby referred to it – was doing exactly what it was designed to do. However, a striking minority of babies in Ainsworth's studies did not do this. Rather than use their parent as a secure base in this way, they either avoided contact – for example by averting their gaze and gently pushing the parent away when they approached – or seemed unable to derive comfort from contact, demanding it, but remaining angry or listlessly tearful. Ainsworth was able to relate these different ways of responding to what she had seen in the home, and came to the conclusion that the differences could be explained by the sensitivity of the interactions they had experienced with their caregiver. This connection Ainsworth made between caregiving and the organisation of a child's attachment behaviour launched a great wave of research, corroborating and extending her findings, which continues to this day.

Ainsworth had made a vital discovery. And she did it by paying close attention to the everyday interactions between babies and mothers, while at the same time being alert to patterns and how they might fit into a broader conceptual framework. She balanced these different ways of apprehending with extraordinary dexterity, and the result was a whole new paradigm for thinking about and studying children and families. The idea that our feelings of security are derived in large part from our perception that the people we care about are there for us, are available and ready to respond if needed, is such a familiar and mainstream one it's easy to overlook how critical Bowlby and Ainsworth's work was in planting it so firmly in our consciousness.

I've got this far without mentioning the rather obvious fact that Lisa Sorgini is 36 weeks pregnant in this picture (just four weeks to go ...). So, we are observing a moment in a family that is on the brink of a transition to something new. Lisa will be a mum to (at least) two soon, and Lulu will have a new baby brother or sister. Everything will be different. A sense that these two are approaching a fork in the road is palpable – a kind of calm before the storm. Lisa must be thinking about it a lot. Lulu surely is too. Surprisingly, attachment theory has remarkably little to say about how having a new sibling affects children's attachments. So much of the research that has been done has stuck closely to Ainsworth's paradigm, which looked exclusively at one parent and one infant, focusing on the dyad to the relative neglect of more complex constellations of family members, but that's changing and there are clear indications from research that the arrival of a sibling has an impact on a child's attachments. Research shows for example that even quite young children are quite sensitive to their mother's attention being absorbed by another baby – for example, giving the parent a realistic toy doll to hold can clearly elicit some attachment behaviour in the child, as if the sight of it is itself a cue to danger. The arrival of a sibling brings with it plenty of excitement, but also uncertainty and anxiety. I remember when our son was born; our daughter had just turned two. I look back on photos of that time and I'm struck how, in every one, she is beaming, almost manically, as if warding away anxiety through sheer relentless positivity. Or perhaps she was shining as brightly as she could to make sure we didn't lose sight of her. After a few weeks of this, almost as an aside, she turned to us and asked, matter of factly, 'when's he going back?' It sounds apocryphal, but those were her exact words, and we were stunned. A sudden insight into a child's-eye view of this situation, so startlingly different to our own or to what we had imagined. 'This is your brother, he'll be living with us now, we'll all be together.' 'Oh, OK' (as if to say 'Well, you might have mentioned this'.) And of course, this challenge to her sense of security, combined with our hopefully supportive reassurance that we were still there for her, no doubt expanded her sense of what can be tolerated and navigated, widening the circle of experience within which she could feel secure. Change and growth. I guess that's something else you can see rather unmistakeably in Sorgini's picture.

Mary Ainsworth herself was aware of her own remarkable ability not just to observe interactions but to take a *child's-eye view* when doing so – to notice the child's ever-so-subtle communications, the rapid exchange of signals, the inner states of feeling motivating them, the child's perceptions of the social world around them. Reading Ainsworth's writings leaves you with no doubt just how steeped in the momentary dramas of everyday caregiving she was, and how in tune she was with the child's experiences of them. So, when viewing this piece, take a moment to try to imagine all the things this child might be aware of, or might be feeling or thinking. Try to immerse yourself in what this child's experience might be in the here and now. Imagine you are looking through the child's eyes and play that scene forwards.

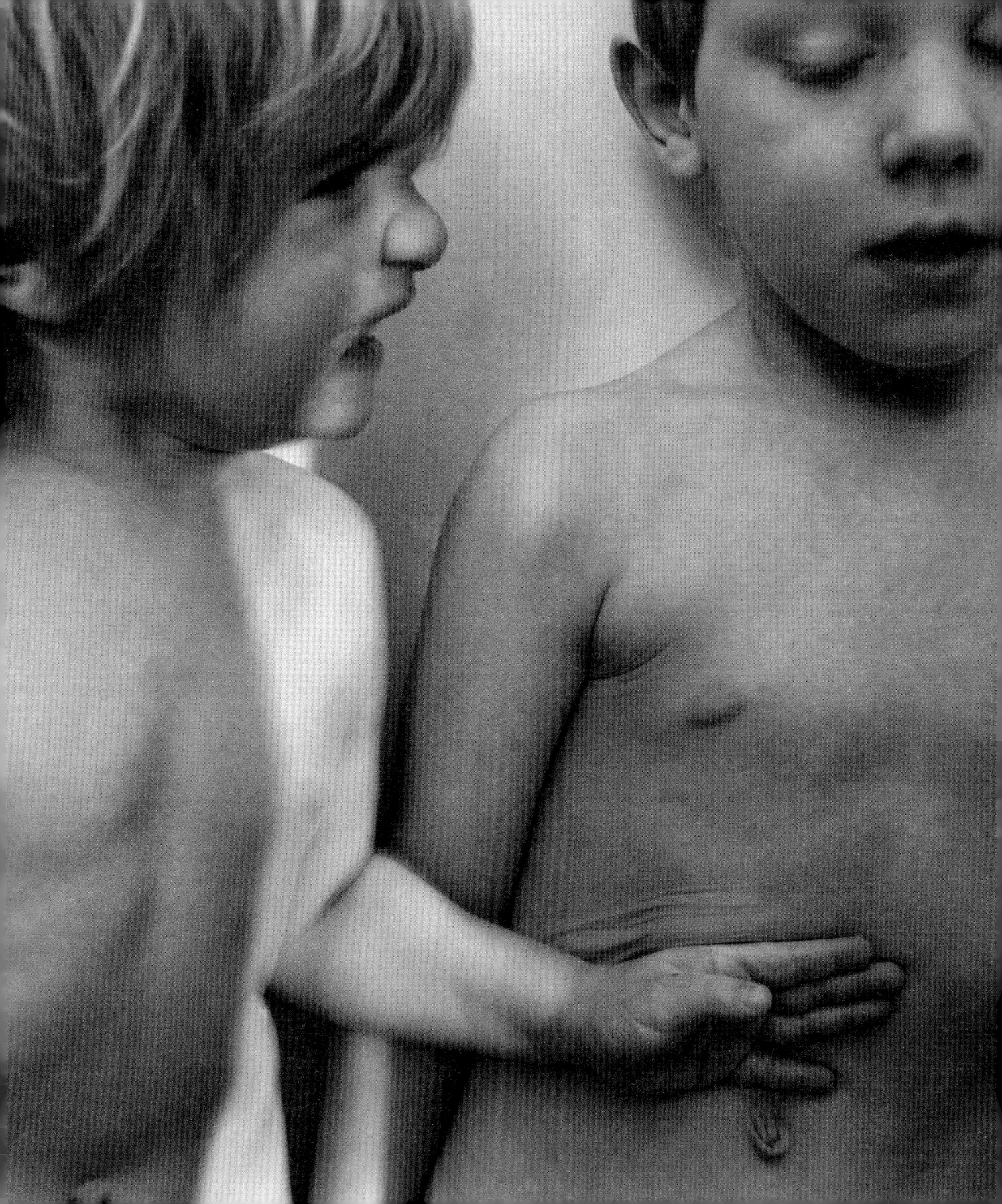

Siblings: A Love–Hate Relationship

Detail of **65**, Nicholas Nixon, *Clementine and Sam, Cambridge, Massachusetts*, 1989

As most parents who have more than one child will recognise, sibling relationships often involve a complex mix of rivalry and support, loving and loathing. This 'love-hate' quality makes sibling relationships stand apart from other close relationships. From an early age, children understand that maintaining friendships require effort, but that siblings remain siblings no matter what. The involuntary nature of sibling relationships provides a simple explanation for this unique quality of ambivalence. Children can express feelings of anger, disgust and frustration toward their siblings unfettered by any concern as to whether they will lose their sibling. In contrast, children are often motivated to restrain expressions of negative feelings that might jeopardise a friendship. As a result, sibling interactions often have a 'no-holds-barred' quality, which can be seen in Nicholas Nixon's intriguing photographs of his children *Clementine and Sam, Cambridge, Massachusetts* (**65**) and *Sam et Clementine, Cambridge, Massachusetts* (**44**). In the early years at least, siblings spend many hours in proximity – leading to a high level of familiarity. Our siblings know us 'warts and all' and this knowledge means that siblings are ideally placed to comfort and support but can also tease and provoke more effectively than almost anyone. Thus, sibling relationships are both a crucible for the development of care, concern and cooperation and a training ground for aggression and other forms of antisocial behaviour.

This familiarity is evident in the way *Clementine and Sam* stand together unclothed. Her hand is pushing against his belly, yet her attention is elsewhere. In *Sam et Clementine*, this familiarity can be seen in the way Sam grabs his little sister by her clothes, in a way that I imagine he'd be unlikely to act either with his peers or with younger children from outside the family. While parents may find it difficult to watch these uninhibited sibling interactions, research evidence suggests that there are benefits for children's social development and understanding. Studies show that children with fewer siblings are, on average, more advanced in aspects of intellectual development such as vocabulary, but children with siblings are typically ahead of their peers in their use of complex forms of social interaction such as joking, engaging in deception, and understanding mistaken beliefs. The photographs of Clementine and Sam provide a powerful illustration of at least three reasons why this might be so.

Claire Hughes

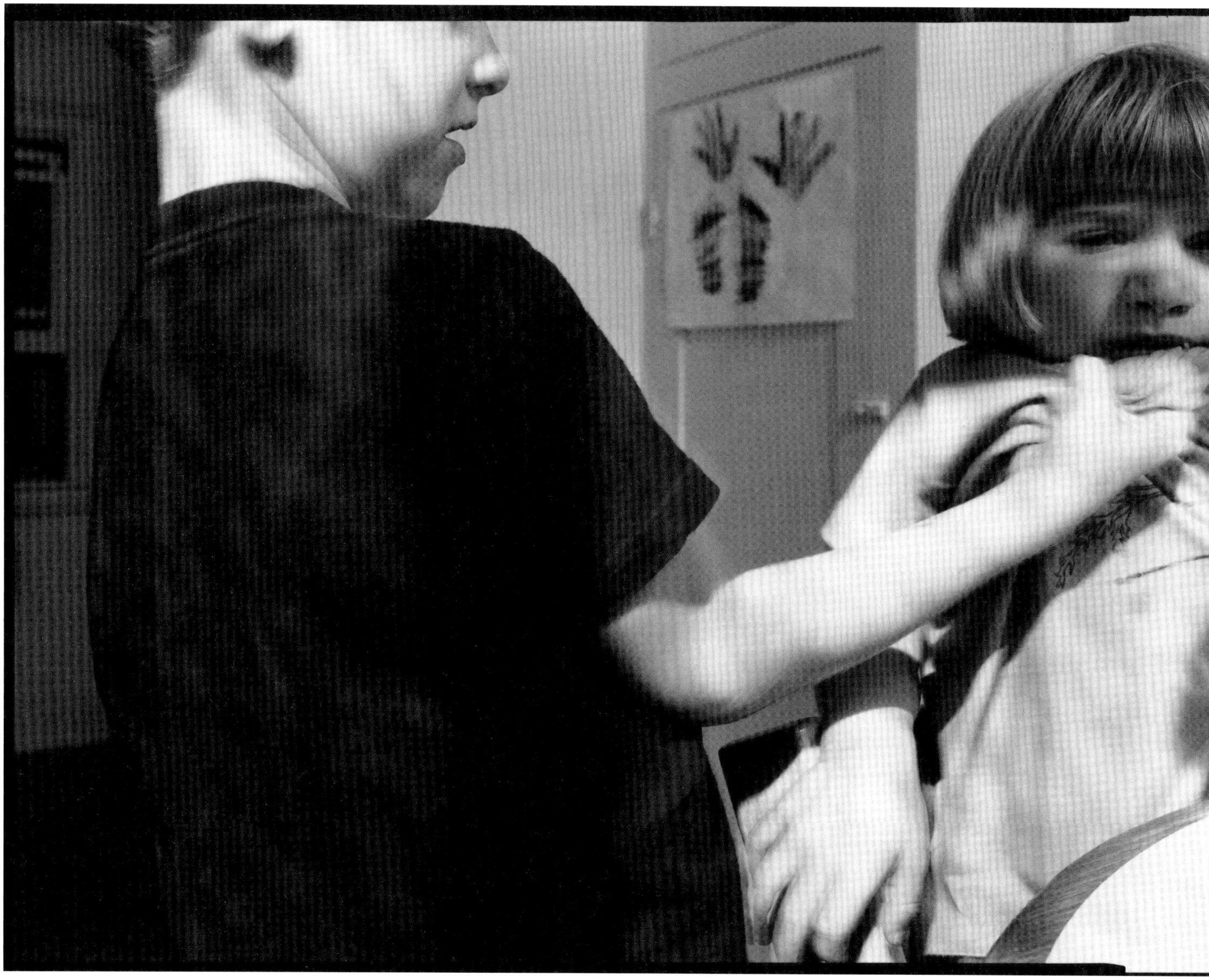

44.
Nicholas Nixon
Sam et Clementine, Cambridge, Massachusetts
1990, gelatin silver print
35.6 × 43.2 cm (framed)
© Nicholas Nixon, courtesy Fraenkel Gallery, San Francisco

First, the high level of familiarity means that Clementine and Sam are likely to understand their sibling's intentions exactly. With friends we may be able to mask how we really think and feel, but it is much harder to do this with a sibling. Secondly, giving full vent to feelings makes differences in points of view obvious – and the pleasure of returning to an enjoyable game or activity is a powerful motivator for children to find ways of resolving these differences. Thirdly, their squabbles may motivate Clementine and Sam to persuade their parents that they are blameless, even if this means trying to pull the wool over their eyes – and so provide an opportunity for children to engage in deception. While sibling alliances made to oppose parental plans can be frustrating, parents can take comfort from the fact that these alliances foster a sense of solidarity that may be much needed in years to come.

The presence of a sibling also affects how parents engage with their children, so that some of the sibling advantage in mindreading may be indirect. That is, having a sibling provides lots of opportunities to eavesdrop on their conversations with a parent – watching a sibling getting into trouble (and out again) can be very instructive! There are, of course, limits to the learning opportunities embedded within sibling squabbles. A review of research on conflict between siblings has shown that greater conflict is linked to increases in both behavioural problems and emotional problems such as anxiety or depression. Relevant to the photographs of Clementine and Sam, these effects were stronger for opposite-sex siblings, for close-in-age siblings, and in early childhood as compared with adolescence.

These photographs of Clementine and Sam also highlight the fact that, although childhood peer relationships are often strongly segregated by gender, sibling relationships offer children the opportunity to form a close bond with a child of the opposite sex. Evidence from a large study of British pre-schoolers shows that gender-stereotyped behaviours are more common in pre-schoolers with a same-sex older sibling and less common in pre-schoolers with an opposite-sex older sibling – relative to children without older siblings. Differences in the kinds of toys available to children who have older brothers versus older sisters may explain some of this effect, but imitative behaviours are also likely to play a role, as young children typically hero-worship their older siblings.

The transition to siblinghood

For many children, the arrival of a baby sibling is their first encounter with a major life event. Early psychoanalysts such as Alfred Adler viewed this transition to siblinghood as akin to a 'dethronement' – a shift from having a monopoly of parental attention and affection to competing with a small but powerful new rival. Adler was developing his ideas in the late nineteenth century, when Europe had extremely high rates of both infant mortality (100–250 per 1000) and maternal death in childbirth (5 per 1000). Given the uncertainties surrounding childbirth outcomes, it is understandable that parental norms did not include preparing children for the transition to siblinghood. Medical advances and societal changes mean that most children today find becoming a sibling a very positive experience that affirms their identity as the big sibling and opens new opportunities for taking on roles of protector/entertainer.

Nevertheless, around a quarter of children will experience difficulties in the early days, weeks and months following a baby's arrival – a period when parents are often sleep-deprived and anxious, so that bids for attention may be missed and minor misdemeanours may attract parental censure. Imagine, then, being a four-year-old boy whose mother has just given birth to triplets

45.
Barbara Hepworth
Group of Three Magic Stones

1973, silver on ebony base
12 × 37 × 31.6 cm
Kettle's Yard, University of Cambridge
BH 5

and is also coping with the loss of her partner (the triplets' father) as he returned to his first family, leaving her alone with a small child and three very small infants. I am, of course, referring to Barbara Hepworth, who spent several years as a single mother, and whose triplets are thought to have inspired the sculpture *Group of Three Magic Stones* (45). When her babies were small, Hepworth was living in Hampstead, and a recent book about the Hampstead Modernists by Caroline Maclean includes letters that show Hepworth torn between her creative needs and the needs of her much-loved children. The views of her four-year-old son Paul are not recorded, but it is not hard to imagine a storm of mixed emotions.

Thinking about numbers helps explain why the arrival of a new baby can be both challenging and a catalyst for growing in social maturity. In a family with two parents and a child there are three relationships (the

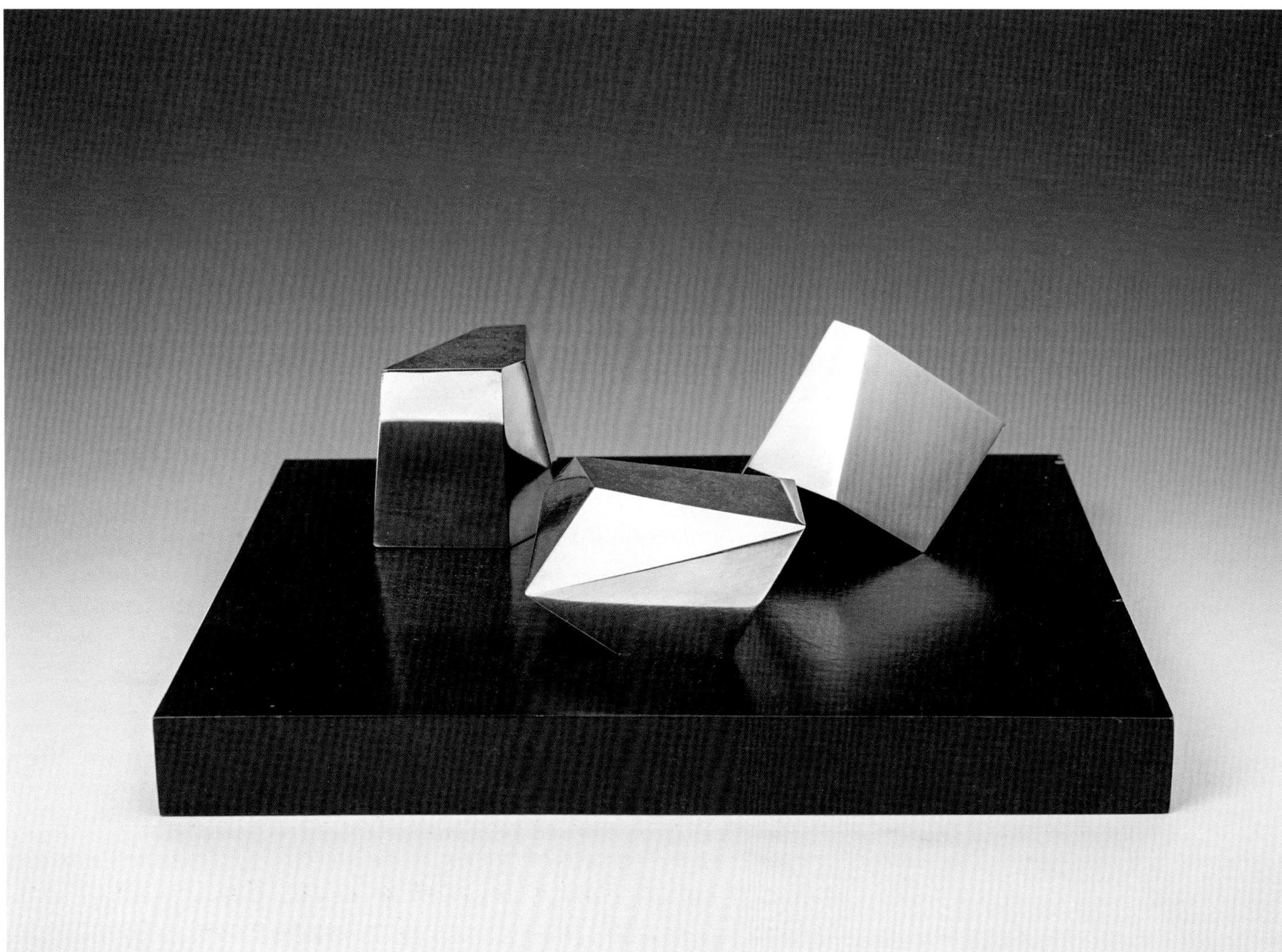

couple relationship and two parent-child relationships). When a new baby arrives, this number doubles to six: the couple relationship, four parent-child relationships, and the sibling relationship. Adding a third child brings the number to ten: the couple relationship, six parent-child relationships, and three sibling relationships. For Barbara Hepworth's son Paul, the social upheaval associated with the arrival of triplets is hard to fathom. At the same time, this new rich palette of family interactions provides fertile territory for the development of empathy and helpfulness – and the processes involved may be both cognitive and affective. For example, parents with a boisterous toddler become much more invested in communicating clear messages about being gentle when there is a new baby on the way. Equally, parents with a new baby are likely to be quick to praise their older child for any small act of kindness to the baby – such that they will feel valued and more likely to share, help, and comfort their younger siblings.

Parental favouritism and sibling rivalry

The unfairness of primogeniture is now largely a thing of the past: today, most parents would like to believe that they treat their children equally. Yet good parenting is tailored to the child, and so differential parenting is appropriate when siblings differ in maturity or needs. Problems emerge, however, when differential parenting is perceived as unfair. One famous example of adolescent resentment of parental differential treatment comes from John Forster's (1892) biography of his friend Charles Dickens, who was highly aggrieved when his older sister Fanny was sent to the Royal Academy of Music in London while his own education appeared forgotten. For both good and ill, sibling influences on children's understanding of fairness are interwoven with parental treatment.

One reason parental favouritism can be damaging is that our self-esteem rests on comparisons with others – the familiarity of siblings makes them prime candidates for comparisons. Two common forms of parental favouritism that persist across the lifespan involve contrasts in siblings' experiences of (a) parental warmth and support (aka differential positivity) and (b) criticism and rejection (aka differential negativity). The prevalence of these differences in parental behaviour is worrying, as exposure to parental favouritism casts a long shadow. For example, in late adulthood sibling relationships are typically warm and low in both conflict and parental favouritism, but siblings who report parental favouritism also report more frequent symptoms of depression, anxiety, hostility and loneliness.

Esau Selling his Birthright to Jacob (**46**) can be seen as a tale of the consequences of parental favouritism. While their father Isaac preferred Esau, the skilled hunter, their mother Rebekah favoured his younger twin brother Jacob, whose talents in the kitchen were evident in his ability to charge

46.
Pieter Rodermondt after Rembrandt Harmensz. van Rijn

Esau Selling his Birthright to Jacob

1639–60, etching and engraving
27 × 19.5 cm (image)
Sheet trimmed within the platemark
The Fitzwilliam Museum, Cambridge
Transferred by Cambridge University Library 1876
AD.12.39-22

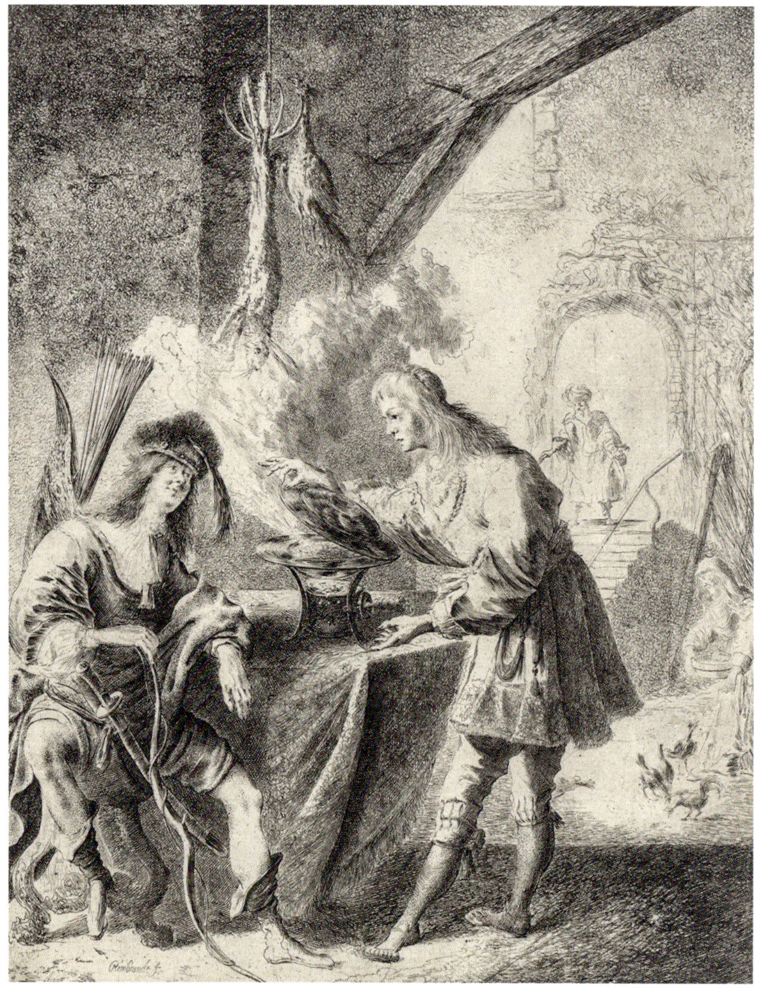

his hungry brother a birthright for his soup. In this story, both brothers appear at fault – Esau clearly held his birthright in low regard, while Jacob not only manipulated his twin brother but later tricked his father (the name Jacob is thought to mean deceiver). To their credit, however, the brothers were eventually reconciled. This is notable: recent findings from a study conducted in partnership with the charity Stand Alone indicate that parental favouritism can lead to long-lived sibling estrangement.

Alongside the story of Jacob and Esau, many other tales of sibling rivalry and violence can be found in the Old Testament. Two famous examples are Cain and Abel (thought to have inspired Robert Louis Stevenson's story of Dr Jekyll and Mr Hyde) and Jacob's son Joseph, whose brothers sold him into slavery after Jacob gave him a coat of many colours. These stories still resonate today; evidence shows that sibling violence is the most common form of family violence. And studies of other species indicate that sibling rivalry is a powerful evolutionary force. For example, research on birds shows that survival in the nest hinges on outdoing one's siblings in competitive begging behaviours. Moreover, those who survive this brutal competition often enjoy greater success as adults than nestlings reared singly, who have no need to compete.

The long-term negative consequences of parental favouritism raise the question of whether any specific characteristics of the child or family make favouritism more likely. A large-scale Canadian study that addressed this question showed that children's age had a strong influence on differences in parents' positivity towards siblings. Intuitively, this makes sense: little children have magic powers in their laughter, eliciting warmth from parents who might be disgruntled with older children. Differential positivity was also more common within larger families and for low-income families, while marital dissatisfaction was related to both positive and negative forms of parental favouritism (especially for mixed gender sibships). Perhaps the simplest explanation for this is that parents are only human, and so have only finite levels of time, attention, patience and support, which are likely to be reduced by marital conflict. As a result, parental behaviours become less intentionally equitable and more reactive, so that child characteristics and parental preferences have more sway. More recent work has also shown that this relationship is two-way, in that parental favouritism can also lead to marital tension. Children from families facing challenges may therefore be doubly disadvantaged, experiencing both an overall reduction in parental warmth and attention and an unfairly small share of parental warmth and attention. The take-home message is clear: it is important that your children understand they are loved equally, even if there are good reasons why they cannot be treated equally.

One context in which parents must treat their children differently is when children have different needs – for example, children with disabilities or chronic illness often need extra help and attention. Long overlooked, siblings in such families are now a focus of concern for clinicians – and the evidence suggests that extra care is indeed needed. A Canadian study – involving 5,000 families with a child being treated for cancer – has shown that both mothers and siblings have a greater need for help for mental health problems when compared with the general population. Likewise, a review of research on siblings of autistic children noted a range of both positive and negative experiences. Although sibling experiences are far from being all 'doom and gloom', it may be helpful to alleviate some difficult sibling experiences via interventions such as learning strategies that support mental health, providing opportunities for peer support, and relaxation therapy. On a more positive note, a recent study involving interviews with adult siblings of autistic individuals has shown that these siblings often report increased empathy and compassion.

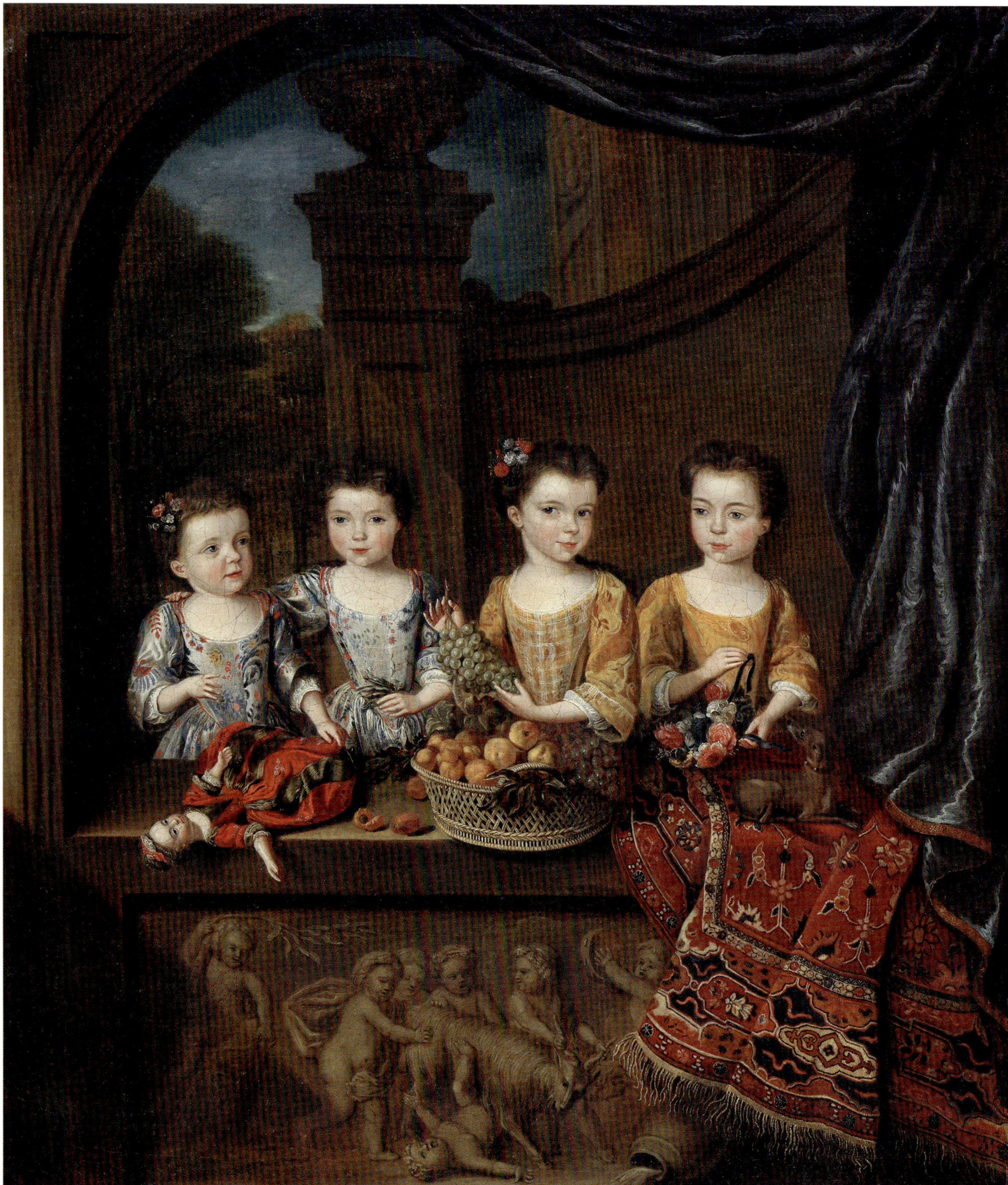

Sibling support

We can see that there are several hazards in having a sibling – from losing a birthright to missing out on parental attention or being made a scapegoat, to getting bashed about or pushed out of the nest. Yet, for most of us who have siblings, this relationship is a long-lasting source of fun and companionship, as well as affection, support and understanding. This is evident in the heart-warming scene shown in Jan van Meyer's late seventeenth-century painting, *The Daughters of Sir Matthew Decker, Bart.* (**47**). These little girls appear happy, at ease with each other, and indulged – each of them is holding a personal treasure. Sir Matthew Decker's only son died in infancy; had he lived, perhaps this picture of four sisters would not have been commissioned. Counterfactuals are, however, unknowable – what is clear is the warmth and security that emanates from this picture. These four sisters appear a close-knit group – their gold and silver dresses indicate pairings between the older two sisters and the younger two sisters, but just one from each pair is wearing a garland in her hair, indicating closeness too between these two different age pairs.

Like parents, siblings can act as a 'secure base', enabling children to explore new situations, safe in the knowledge that there is a place of comfort to which they can return. Being part of a quartet of affectionate sisters is likely to have given each of these girls a strong emotional foundation for their futures. Indirectly, we are the beneficiaries of that. When Sir Matthew Decker died with no male heir, he was able to pass on his fortune to his oldest daughter Catherine, who later had seven children, including Richard Fitzwilliam, 7th Viscount, who founded the Fitzwilliam Museum.

In a landmark study that helped shift the focus within sibling research from rivalry to support, researchers conducted detailed observations of how young children learn to build a model windmill when supported by older peers or by older siblings. They found that young children were much more active learners when paired with an older sibling than with a peer – evidenced by higher rates of watching, imitating and asking questions. Equally, older siblings gave learners more control of the task than did older peers and offered more explanations and positive feedback. Another example of sibling support comes from a large UK study that showed that, following stressful life events, such as parental separation, children with supportive sibling relationships report fewer symptoms of depression than do children with unsupportive sibling relationships.

More recently, my own work on families' experiences in the stressful early months of the Covid-19 pandemic also shows that older siblings act as sources of support. This formed part of a study of more than 2,000 families from six different countries that demonstrated that lockdown restrictions and school closures had widespread negative effects on children's adjustment

47.
Jan van Meyer
The Daughters of Sir Matthew Decker, Bart.
1718, oil on canvas
77.5 × 66.1 cm
The Fitzwilliam Museum, Cambridge. Bequeathed by Richard, 7th Viscount Fitzwilliam, 1816
No. 437

(the only country in the study that did not show elevated child peer problems was Sweden, which was also the only country to refrain from mass school closures). Children with infant siblings displayed marginally higher rates of emotional and behavioural problems than did children without siblings, indicating that caring for infants left parents with less time to support other children in the family. However, the study also revealed that children with older siblings showed fewer emotional and behavioural problems than did children without siblings. In short, at a time of family stress, most children appear willing and able to step in as sources of support for their younger siblings.

Studies of twins

Overall, family researchers have paid much less attention to sibling relationships than to parent-child relationships. However, there is one important exception, as twins are widely included in research as a means of assessing the heritability of given traits, i.e., the extent to which genetic rather than environmental influences underpin variability in people's characteristics and behaviour in the population.

Identical twins – such as *The De Vegh Twins* painted by Alice Neel (**42**) – share 100% of their genes. Despite being dressed identically, the De Vegh twins' individual personalities are clearly distinct in Alice Neel's arresting portrait. One sister's gaze is outwards, and she sits with her dress hitched up; the other sits more demurely, with her thoughts turned inwards. However, the portrait also captures the warmth and closeness of the twins' relationship – the two girls are sharing a seat, their bodies fitting together to create a unit. As with siblings, this companionship is a powerful motivator for twins to resolve differences, and comfort each other when needed.

Do twins have a special relationship? Although this is a fascinating question, research findings are inconclusive. We do know that twins are more likely than singletons to experience both biological and social challenges, at least in the early years. On average, expectant mothers with twins give birth at 36 weeks, four weeks sooner than the average length of pregnancy for mothers carrying singletons. Coupled with the experience of sharing a womb, this early birth can give rise to several medical complications: twins are about twice as likely as singletons to be born with abnormalities of the heart, gut and neural tube. Even when these abnormalities are taken into account, language development often shows a mild delay in twins. Perhaps underpinning this delay, rates of sensitive and stimulating interactions with parents appear lower for infant twins than singletons, a difference that may reflect the increased rate of postnatal depression among mothers with twins. There is also evidence that language delay is more common in twins

48.
Tracey Emin
Me and Paul – The Twins

1963–93, Memorabilia and text (seven parts) all framed
1. 34 × 40 cm
2. 16.5 × 12 cm
3. 29 × 26 cm
4. 29 × 37 cm
5. 16 × 18 cm
6. 26 × 22 cm
7. 15 × 17 cm
Courtesy Vanessa Branson

who share a special language (estimates for this group vary from 15 to 58%). It is also known that – in the preschool years at least – most twins share their friends, and around one in five preschool twins don't have many friends apart from their co-twin. Overall then, young twins may have fewer opportunities to engage in one-on-one conversations with peers, which may also contribute to language delays.

By adolescence, however, the picture for twins looks much more rosy. Findings from a large Finnish study show that twins receive higher peer ratings of social adaptability than singletons. This shift from the more negative picture of twins in early life is both reassuring and intriguing. One possibility is that the experience of being a twin, whilst often challenging, may be a source of social learning that enables twins to develop resilience.

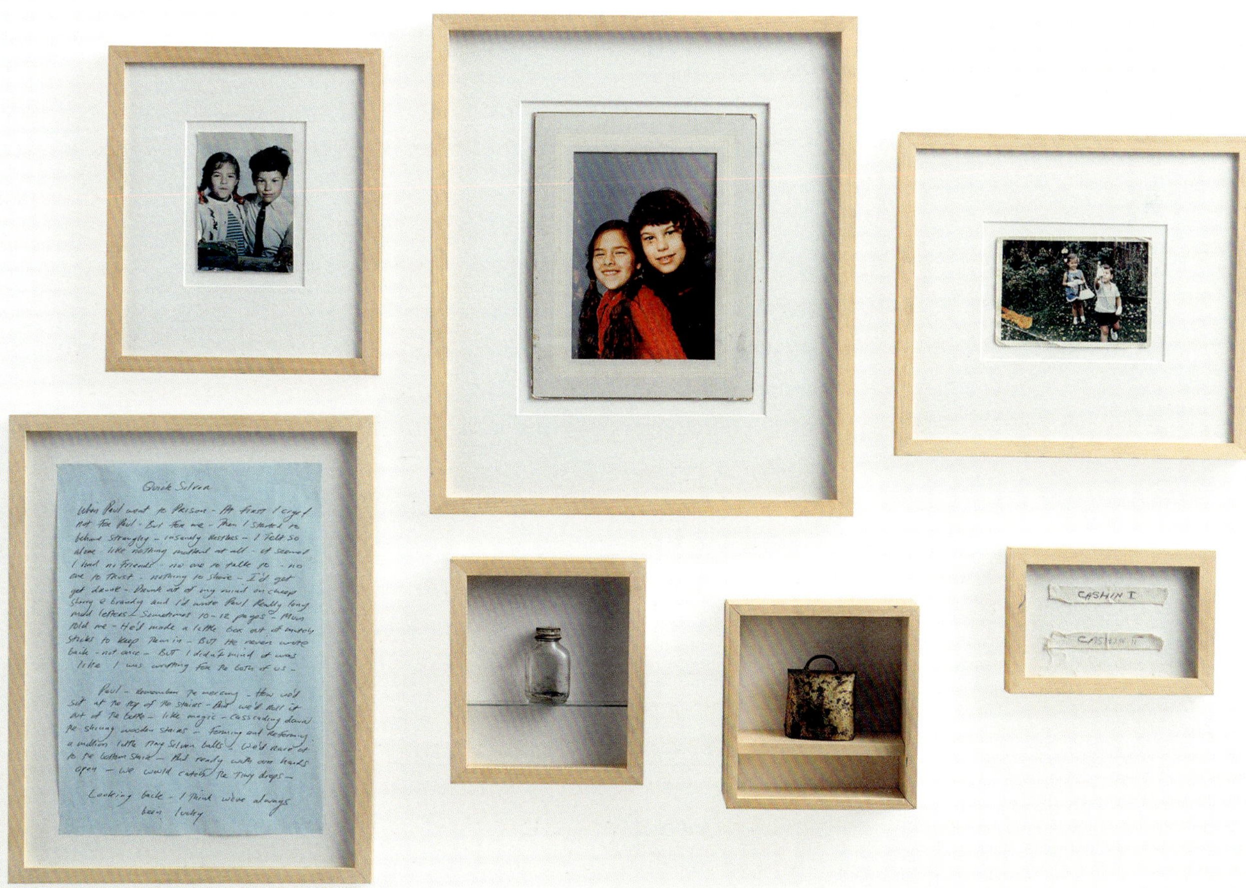

Another possibility is that this shift reflects age-related differences in what matters for children. By adolescence, most children seek emotional support from their age-mates rather than their parents – having the companionship and understanding of a co-twin may therefore come into its own as children grow up.

Non-identical twins, such as Tracey Emin and her brother Paul, who are the focus of her work, *Me and Paul – The Twins* (**48**), on average share only 50% of their genes. In a highly cited review of almost 3,000 twin studies (involving a total of more than fourteen million twin pairs) it was found that overall effects of genes and environment were equal in size, but their relative salience varied widely across different traits or characteristics. Here, three points about heritability deserve note. First, with a few rare exceptions (e.g., Huntington's disease), genetic factors do not have a deterministic impact – instead, they simply predispose individuals to certain traits. Secondly, heritability estimates are higher in more egalitarian societies – when environmental differences are small, it follows that genetic effects will be large. Third, genetically influenced traits can be changed by interventions. For example, improving nutrition leads to population-level increases in height, even if genetic factors underpin within-population variability in height. That is, showing a genetic influence doesn't mean that environmental effects don't matter; indeed, genetic effects are often indirect. For instance, children with sociable temperaments elicit more social input from family and friends, creating a virtuous circle that boosts their social development. Likewise, young people who show creative talent may receive encouragement and time from creative adults in their communities. These are examples of 'evocative' gene-environment interactions and are found alongside equally important effects of 'active' gene-environment interactions, which refer to the way in which children and young people seek out environments that suit them.

This 'active' gene-environment interaction is easy to see in the case of Tracey Emin, who left school at thirteen and moved to London at fifteen, before studying fashion at the Medway College of Design in Rochester at seventeen. These proactive steps led to joining the Royal Academy of Art and a flourishing creative career, and enabled Tracey Emin to evade the snares that drew her twin brother Paul along a very different path. In the poem 'Quicksilver', Tracey Emin describes the impact of Paul going to prison on her own life – an account that illustrates just how important it is for researchers to go beyond a simple partitioning of 'nature' and 'nurture' to include the influence of the sibling relationship itself.

Of course, confidence in the findings from twin studies hinges on the accuracy and reliability of study measures. Traits such as height are easy to measure, but other traits, like creativity, are much more elusive. Twin-study researchers in this field have therefore adopted a belt-and-braces approach.

49.
Li Tianbing
Autoportrait sur neige (Self-Portrait on Snow)
2007, oil on canvas
172 × 177 cm
Collection Mr Eric Fitoussi

For example, two large German longitudinal twin studies have included measures of both perceived and tested creativity. These two creativity measures yielded different results regarding genetic effects, indicating that genes play a role in tested, but not perceived, creativity. Twin studies include the special case of reared-apart twins. For example, the famous Minnesota Twins Reared Apart Study involves more than 100 pairs of twins reared apart; these twins were identified in the 1970s and have been followed over many years. For many different measures of personality, temperament, interests and social attitudes, findings from this study suggest similar levels of similarity for identical twins reared apart and reared together, indicating that, for most psychological traits, individual differences show quite strong genetic influence.

Children without siblings

Just as the sudden arrival of siblings is likely to stir up a deep well of feelings, so too might the loneliness of being an only child. This is reflected in Li Tianbing's *Autoportrait sur neige* (**49**), a moving portrait of himself as a child

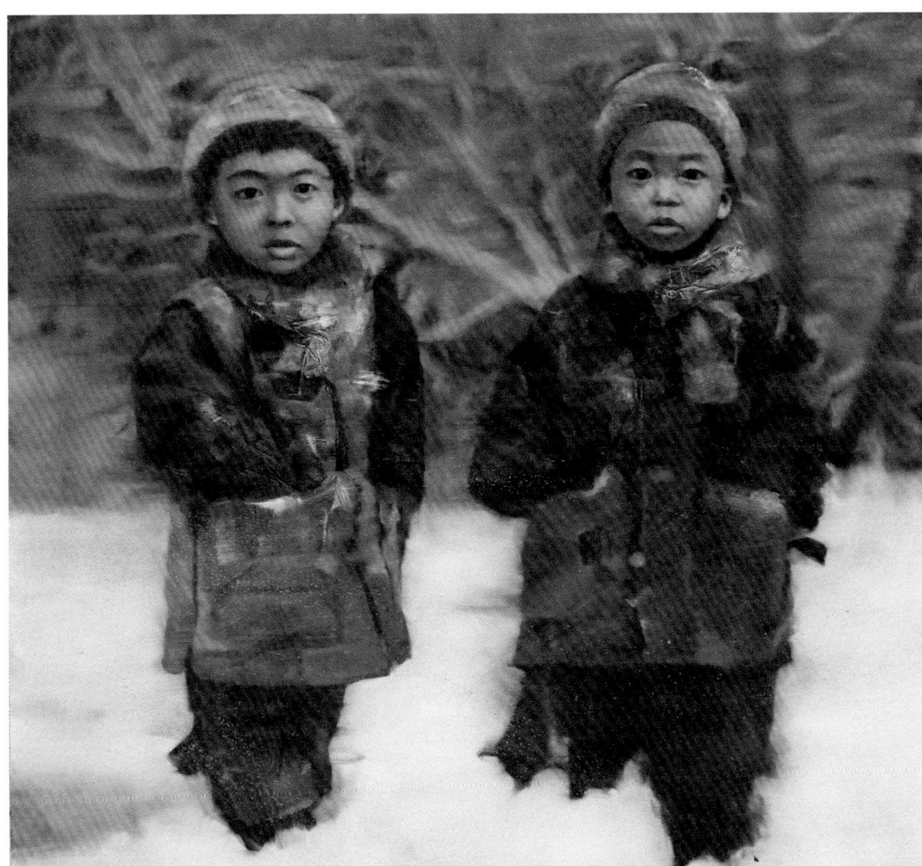

with an imaginary brother. Li Tianbing's work can be seen as a response to China's 'one child' policy, which began in the 1970s in response to rapid population growth in the 1950s and 1960s. This policy is credited with having curbed population growth, aiding economic growth, and improving the health and welfare of women and children, but tragically has also led to female infanticide. The policy ran until 2016, leaving a full generation of Chinese people to grow up without siblings – a generation whom the Chinese government is now trying to encourage to have two or even three children. The impact of this policy may therefore extend across multiple generations.

Negative perceptions of children growing up without siblings are common but mistaken – a popular view is that such children are overly sensitive and spoiled. This misconception harks back to a nineteenth-century survey of 200 American adults, which found that nearly all the respondents described children without siblings as excessively spoiled. From the very beginning, then, the notion of 'only child syndrome' has been based on perceptions rather than reality. Findings from empirical studies from China directly challenge the view that children without siblings are more likely to display social difficulties.

Another historical misconception is that the creation of imaginary companions – depicted in Li Tianbing's moving portrait – is a marker of social maladjustment. Imaginary companions are now thought to play valuable roles – for example in compensating for the lack of a real companion. Consistent with this view, first-born children appear almost three times as likely as other children to have an imaginary companion. However, the creation of imaginary companions can also be inspired by siblings and are described by children as giving comfort and company, boosting motivation and self-control, and enriching their lives. Thus, rather than reflecting social maladjustment, imaginary companions are increasingly seen as a creative solution to loneliness. Indeed, in a recent review, it was concluded that children who create imaginary companions are likely to exhibit a deeper understanding of others' emotions and a greater capacity for creativity, with this advantage persisting through to adulthood.

Conclusions

The sibling-related works of art in this exhibition shine a light on the many ways in which siblings can transform our lives. Of the many features that set sibling relationships apart from other close relationships, two deserve special mention. First, sibling relationships are involuntary in nature, leading to a 'no-holds barred' love/hate quality of interaction. Some (perhaps most) sibling relationships are highly affectionate and supportive, but other sibling relationships can be distant or conflictual. Thus, compared with other close relationships, sibling relationships show striking individual differences that make it hard to draw general conclusions about the influence of siblings on each other. Secondly, siblings are the most enduring of all close relationships; this creates a high level of familiarity, so that siblings often know exactly how to support, but also know just how to provoke. While the closeness of siblings may wax and wane over time, sibling pairs who are close as young children typically remain close. Thus, while it might be tempting for parents with young children to divide their time and arrange one-to-one activities with individual children, it is shared experiences that will foster the sibling alliances that can act as a port in a storm in adult life.

Siblings are our fellow travellers, the people who share our childhood memories, as well as acting as sources of support (and sometimes strife) across the lifespan. Below is a long-forgotten memory that popped into my head when I was first asked to write this piece.

> Scene: a family visit to the National Gallery, in a room full of portraits depicting the Madonna and Child. I am about 9 years old, and my younger sister Elizabeth is 7. She has just become a fluent reader and so is interested in the labels next to the artwork. She is looking at one of these with our mother, when she calls out to me in excitement from the other side of a grand gallery. 'Hey, Claire, guess what? I'm a virgin!'

Memories like these are priceless – a source of mirth in future years, the glue that binds us and provides the foundations for the special intimacy between siblings, who often know what the other one is thinking, long before words are said. Siblings are, in my view, a hugely important and often overlooked element of family life. I hope the research findings outlined in this essay convince you too – and perhaps evoke some fun sibling memories of your own.

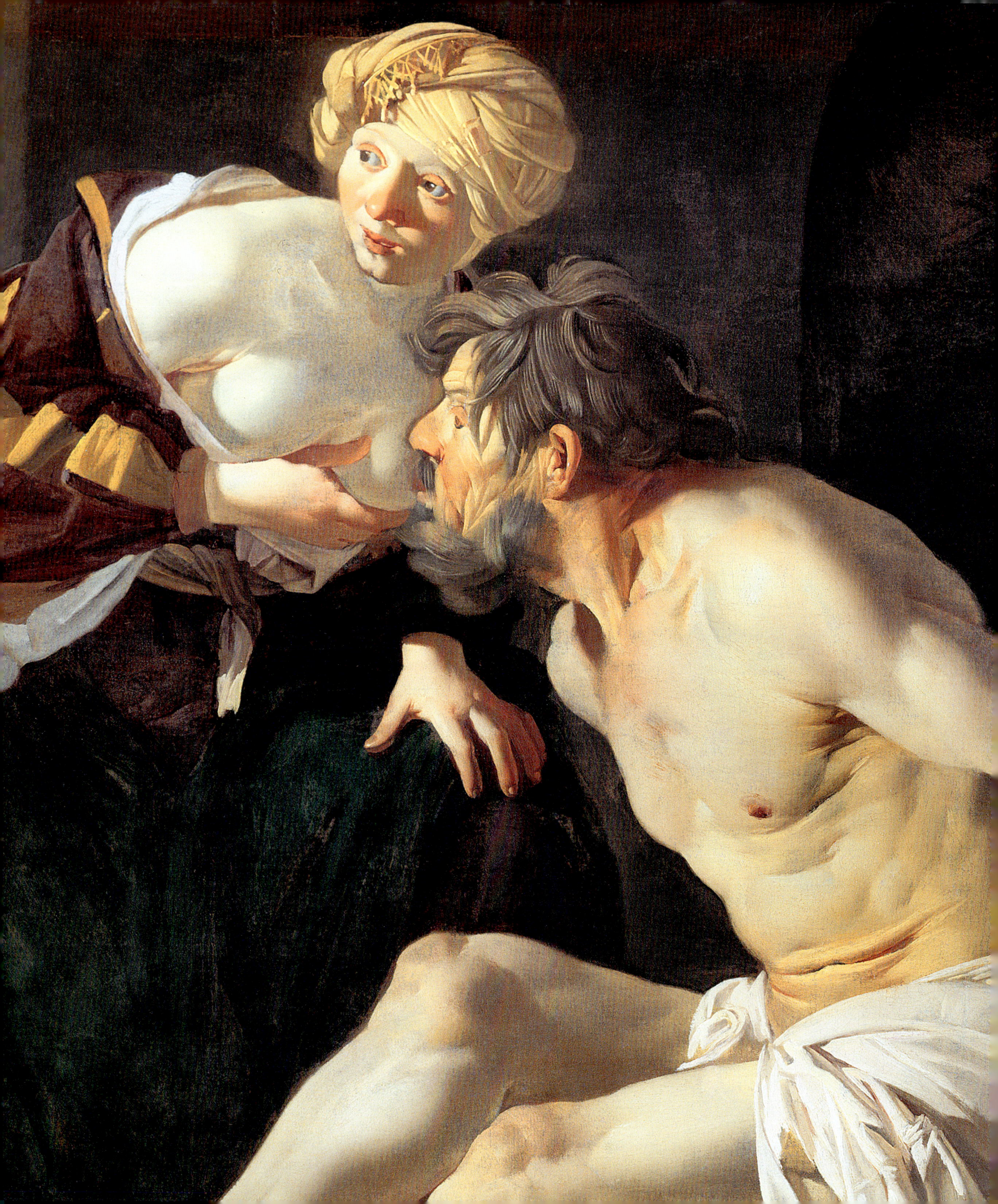

Roman Charity and Modern Families

Detail of **50**, Dirck van Baburen, *Roman Charity, Cimon and Pero*, 1618–24

When I first saw Dirck van Baburen's *Roman Charity, Cimon and Pero* (**50**), it took me a long time to work out (or face up to) what was going on in the painting. An elderly man, obviously a prisoner, with his hands chained behind his back, is sucking on the nipple of a young woman who offers him her breast. She, meanwhile, turns her head away, as if she has been startled or has just realised that she has been discovered – perhaps sensing the presence of the figure, very likely the jailer, who is peering through the tiny barred window.

It should not have taken me so long to get the point. For this is a seventeenth-century version of an ancient Roman story, preserved in a collection of moralising anecdotes and exemplary tales of vice and virtue, compiled in the first century CE by Valerius Maximus, under the title *Memorable Deeds and Sayings* (*Facta et dicta memorabilia*). Though now little known outside the seminar or lecture room, this was once extremely popular. There are hundreds of medieval manuscripts of the collection (more than of any other Latin prose text apart from the Bible), and it was a best-seller across Europe in early printed editions, both in the original Latin and in translation.

Valerius Maximus tells this particular tale in the fifth book (out of nine) of *Memorable Deeds and Sayings*, in a section devoted to stories of *pietas*, the usual Latin term not just for piety towards the gods, but as here for family loyalty, or duty to your parents. He explains that, when an old man by the name of Cimon (he is also sometimes known as Micon) was starving in prison, his daughter Pero visited and saved him, by suckling him with her own milk. It adds to the shock value for most modern viewers when they realise that the painting shows a daughter breastfeeding her own father.

But that is only part of it. In the same section on *pietas*, Valerius Maximus tells a variant of the same basic tale. An elderly woman, unnamed this time, was in prison, condemned to death. The jailer who had decided to kill her by starvation, rather than by strangling, allowed her daughter to continue to visit, provided she brought no food. He had not reckoned on the young woman feeding her mother from her own breasts. When this was discovered, the daughter's *pietas* was deemed so impressive that, instead of further punishment, her mother was freed. Another version of this tale is recounted in an ancient Roman encyclopaedia by Pliny 'the Elder' (as he is called, to distinguish him from his nephew 'the Younger'). Here even greater rewards are specified. Both mother and daughter were granted food for life at public expense and, to commemorate the daughter's devotion, a temple dedicated to

Mary Beard

the goddess *Pietas* was built on the site of the prison. We cannot now recover the historical facts behind any of these stories. Like many of the moral tales collected by Valerius Maximus, they are often now carefully described as 'semi-mythical' or 'highly embellished'. But, almost certainly, most Romans would have assumed they were true – and that 'truth' was paraded in the temple.

The scene of the father and daughter (though not of the mother and daughter) was common in Roman art. We find it on ceramics, and no fewer than six versions – a couple are now lost – have been discovered painted on the walls of houses in Pompeii and Herculaneum. But it was even more popular in later centuries, usually featuring the father, but occasionally the mother too. The story was retold, for example, by Boccaccio and by Christine de Pizan in their compilations of 'famous women' (one fifteenth-century illuminated manuscript of Boccaccio shows a decidedly puzzled jailer, scratching his beard, when he notices what is going on between mother and daughter in his prison). And it was especially prominent in European art from the sixteenth to the eighteenth century, often going under the title 'Roman Charity'. There are hundreds of versions of it in museums and galleries, in paint and engraving, in porcelain, amber, marble and more. You do not now see these as often as you might expect, given the number of them, for the simple reason that very many have ended up, out of view, in storerooms and basements. Curators tend to think that this version of family relations is not one that appeals to modern viewers. They may well be right. When I showed Van Baburen's painting to a focus group, to gauge their reactions, the commonest response, after I had explained the story, was some version of 'Ugggh'. A father suckling at his daughter's breast does not now signal dutiful devotion. It is closer to incest, the right and proper order of the family turned upside down, the erotic and nurturing aspects of the breast uncomfortably confused.

For the most part, this scene remains on public display only when the artist is too famous to be consigned to the storeroom, or when the work of art concerned cannot easily be removed. Caravaggio's version – in which the daughter is not actually inside the prison with her father but offers him her breast, from the outside, through the bars of the window – still survives in a church in Naples. Painted around 1607, it is part of the church's altarpiece, depicting the 'Seven Works of Mercy'. Alongside burying the dead, sheltering the homeless and so on, visiting the imprisoned and feeding the hungry are symbolised by the scene of Cimon and Pero. Not long after Caravaggio, Rubens produced five versions of 'Roman Charity' (the most famous, in the Rijksmuseum Amsterdam – now thought to be largely the work of Rubens's assistants – shows Pero turning away, but with her arm tenderly around her father as he sucks at her breast). Most aggressively public, as well as immovable, is the sculpture of the pair integrated into the façade of an eighteenth-century annexe to the medieval belfry in Ghent, above the doorway. The *Mammelokker* ('Breast-sucker'), as the sculpture is popularly called, has given its name to this whole part of the building, which once formed the entrance to the city prison (it is now the office of the city ombudsman). What on earth the prisoners, their families or their guards made of this rather stern image of the daughter feeding her chained father is hard to know.

That raises the question of what the scene, and the underlying story, is all about. What is it saying about the ancient family, or the modern? One argument is that in the Roman world, as Valerius Maximus and Pliny suggest, the story of Cimon and Pero (and the version with the anonymous mother) represented the highest form of family love and the greatest service a daughter could provide for her parents, even commemorated by a temple to honour the deed in the centre of the city. That is the implication of the modern title, 'Roman Charity', too – charity or *caritas*, in the sense of selfless love.

But, even in the ancient stories and paintings, there are hints that it was more complicated. There is a shadow of incest here and of family relations gone wrong, and a sense that the images of Cimon and Pero could be unsettling to Roman viewers, as they are to us. Even Valerius Maximus points to the perhaps uncomfortable oddity of what is said to have happened. This is 'strange', he writes of the case of daughter and mother, 'unheard of'. And referring explicitly to paintings of the scene, he recognises that people do admire the example of virtue when they look at the father and daughter, but that they are also 'confounded' by them (the Latin word *stupent* has a range of meanings from 'amazed' to 'aghast'). Some of that ambivalence is vividly captured by a painting that still survives in Pompeii.

This is in the 'House of Marcus Lucretius Fronto' (so-called after one of its likely owners), a large property and particularly elegantly decorated. The painting of Pero nursing her father is a panel in the centre of one of the walls of a small room in the more public area of the house, just off the central hall or *atrium*. It is now badly damaged, but enough remains for us to be certain that the old man was shown sitting on the floor at his daughter's feet, suckling from one breast while his hand touched the other through her clothing. Better preserved is the six-line Latin poem, painted in white letters in the upper left-hand corner, which offered a commentary on the scene (here calling the father 'Micon'). The first four lines explain that 'unfair Fortune' has turned food for infants into food for a father and they highlight his veins swelling as he draws on his daughter's milk. But a careful reading of the final two lines gives a different view. For they point out that, with their faces brought together, she is 'caressing' him. Or so some modern translations put it. In fact, that misses (or disguises) the sense of the word *fricat*, which means something much closer to 'rub' – and which is also used in Latin with an explicitly sexual sense ('rub up'). In other words, it exposes the erotic side of the image, one that is confirmed by the last line of the poem: 'there is sad shame (*pudor*) along with the filial devotion (*pietas*) here'. The poem is asking viewers to confront what *kind* of love between father and daughter we are witnessing. Can it ever be as innocent as is sometimes assumed? How shameful is it?

Some of the other paintings in the same small room intensify these issues. In the domestic decoration at Pompeii, there are often meaningful connections between the images on one wall and on those that are adjacent or opposite. Here, on the wall directly facing Micon and Pero, only a couple of metres away, in exactly the same central position, is an image of the mythical Narcissus, almost naked, dreamily gazing into a pool, falling in love with his own reflection. Are we meant to see a strong contrast between these two scenes – Narcissus representing an extreme form of transgressive erotic love (a man falling in love with *himself*) versus Micon and Pero representing proper dutiful affection within the family? Or do *both* scenes depict versions of sexual transgression – from narcissism to incest? That is certainly what the last two lines of the poem suggest, as do the flying cupids that are another element of the decorative design (though quite how the demure faces of two children, painted on either side of the main door, fit into this, I am not so sure).

The big, and destabilising, questions that hover over these ancient accounts and images are: what does the love between a father and daughter actually mean? What are the limits of love between the different generations of a family? Those are exactly the issues that are debated in many modern images of Cimon and Pero too, where the apparent innocence of the title 'Roman Charity' is often undermined by the details of the painting. Most modern artists avoided the problem of what to do with the father's hands (which awkwardly pawed his daughter's other breast in more than one ancient painting). The vast majority of images from the sixteenth century on, like Van Baburen's, show the father's hands in chains. But all kinds of other details point to the erotic character of the scene.

The puzzled beard-scratching jailer of the Boccaccio manuscript is a rarity in later art. The jailer usually appears, as in Van Baburen's painting, as a leering face (or faces) through the bars of the tiny window. In part, this was guided by the logic of the story. The whole point is that the daughter's devotion was discovered. But it adds an inescapable element of voyeurism to the scene, which has the effect of recasting it in erotic terms, while suggesting to the viewers of the painting that they see *themselves* as voyeurs too. And the figure of Pero straddles the line between devoted daughter, embarrassed participant and complicit partner. Van Baburen, as many artists do, makes her turn away. Again, there is a narrative logic here: she is startled as she realises that she has been spotted, but her pose also suggests

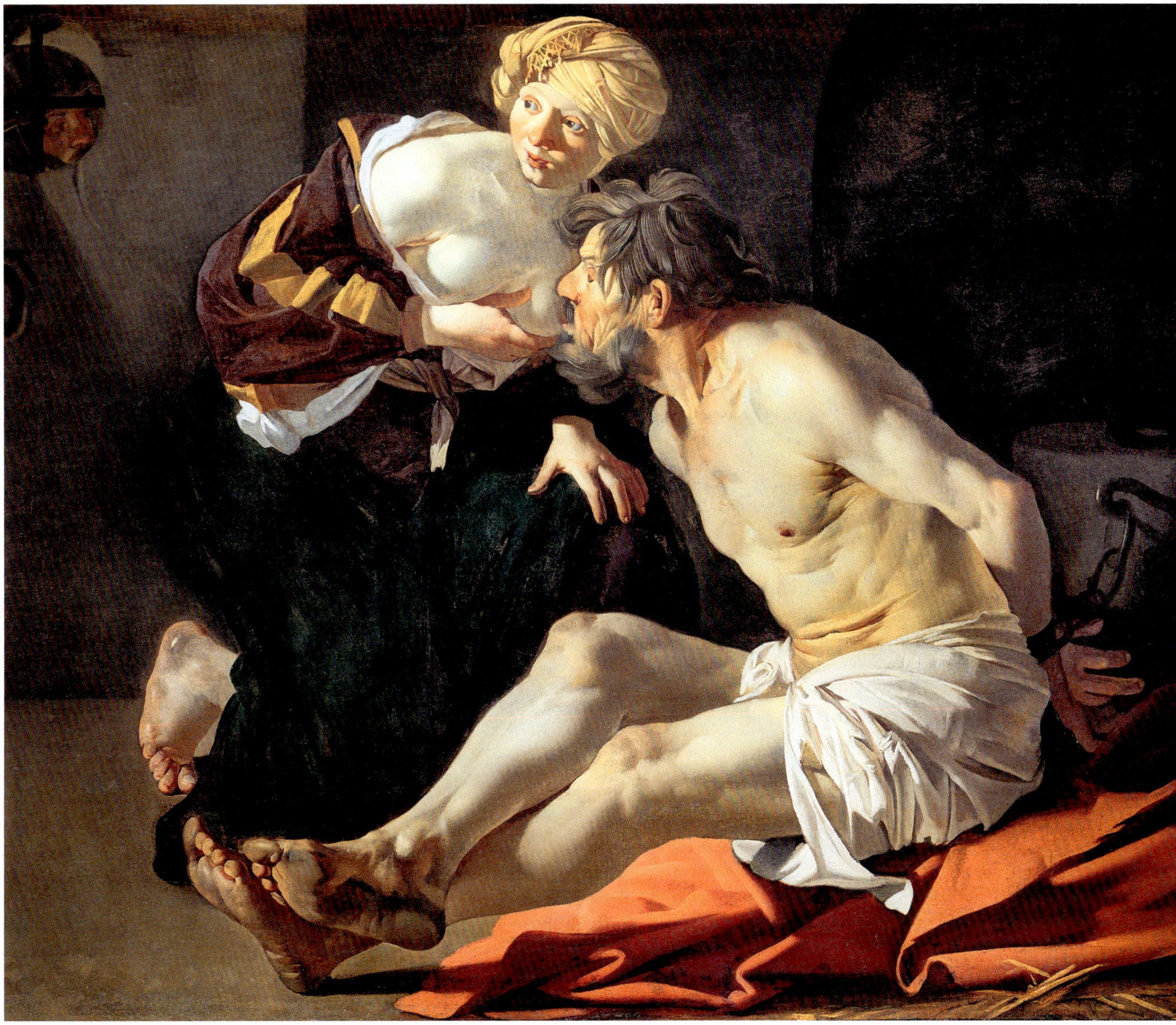

50.
Dirck van Baburen
Roman Charity, Cimon and Pero
1618–24, oil on canvas
147.7 × 171.5 × 6.5 cm
York Museums Trust
(York Art Gallery)
Presented by F.D. Lycett Green
through The Art Fund, 1955
YORAG: 788

that she cannot bear to look at what she is doing. In other paintings she looks directly at her father, tenderly embracing him (Rubens's first version of 'Roman Charity' is one of those), or her pose displays her breasts fully frontal to the viewer. From the father's side, the relief on his face, as he drinks his daughter's milk, could to some eyes looks as much like an orgasm as a welcome quenching of thirst and hunger (not unlike the 'swelling veins' of the poem in Pompeii, perhaps). In one or two modern versions (for example, a seventeenth-century design for a cup by Thomas de Bry) the veil of propriety was literally removed, and the pair appeared entirely naked. It was as a strong, but probably ineffectual, counter to this, that when Arthur

Murphy made a whole play out of the story in the later eighteenth century, entitled *The Grecian Daughter* and starring Sarah Siddons, he made sure that all breastfeeding took place off stage.

I admit that I find it quite hard to look at the images of 'Roman Charity'. It feels far too much like a ringside seat at incest or even child-abuse. All the same, it is important to try to explain their huge (albeit now concealed) popularity. What was driving the repeated return to this image, in the modern or the ancient world? Obviously, many different factors must have been involved. The sculpture at Ghent was presumably meant to say something about compassion to prisoners. In some paintings, the idea of celebrating *Roman* charity could have been a way of reflecting on the difference (or similarity) between pagan and Christian virtues. In the house at Pompeii, maybe it was a question of a debate about the nature of *pudor*. This is a tricky Latin word, which can mean 'shame' but also 'modesty' or 'decency'. On the façade of the same house a painted election slogan actually celebrated the *pudor* of the owner, who was standing for political office. Some classicists have seen a connection between the two uses of the word, inside and out. But what connection, and how awkward? And, overall, the significance of the much rarer images of the daughter and mother must have been very different from those of daughter and father (the slightly comic puzzlement of the observing jailer in the Boccaccio manuscript would not have fitted so well with *that*).

But the bottom line is that this story was one focus of a debate about the nature of the family, about how the erotic life within it could be (or should be) policed, and about the very nature of love between parent and child. There are lessons here for us. I do not mean that we ought necessarily to pay more attention to the story of Cimon and Pero and the issues that it highlights (though I suspect it would add usefully to our conversations if we did, unsettling as we may find it). The bigger point is that these texts and (especially) images are a wonderful antidote to the 'presentism' that can beset the history of the family, as it besets so many other histories. It is very easy to imagine that, before our own day, the family was a traditional, perhaps conservative but relatively uncontested unit; and that it is only now that we have questioned that or tried to change it. The fact is that Cimon and Pero were asking viewers and readers to think harder about what a family was and what its rules were 250 – and 2,000 – years ago. They are a useful reminder that the family has never been uncontroversial, has always been in flux.

There is, however, a sting in the tail. Paintings of Cimon and Pero may now be very largely forgotten, consigned to museum basements, hardly recognised, and certainly not popular. But the scene has a cameo role in a painting that is one of the best known in the world. That is Vermeer's *Lady at the Virginals with a Gentleman*, also now known as *The Music Lesson*, painted in the 1660s. Here a young woman sits playing the virginals, with her back to us, but her face reflected in the mirror above the instrument; to her right stands an older man listening and perhaps singing (though there is no reason to suppose that he is her teacher as the common modern title implies). Just behind his head, at the far right-hand side of the canvas, Vermeer has depicted a framed painting hanging on wall. Although only just under half of this is visible to us (we have to imagine the rest extending beyond the canvas's edge), it is absolutely clear that it is another known version of Cimon and Pero by Dirck van Baburen. It is very similar to the one in the exhibition, though in this case the father is on the left, the daughter on the right: we can make out the man's back and chained arms, instantly recognisable, and part of Pero's head.

Why did Vermeer copy this painting into *Lady at the Virginals*? We know that his family owned one of Van Baburen's versions of the scene. But we need a more driving reason than that he just happened to have the picture to hand. What is it saying about what is happening in the rest of the painting? Perhaps it is a hint that the listening man is as much a prisoner (of his desires) as Cimon. Is it only the young woman who will be able to sustain him (physically or spiritually)? Or is it a warning that what might seem at first sight to be an innocent relationship will turn out to be far less so? Whatever the answer, Vermeer and his audience were using this now largely forgotten story to think about their own personal and family dilemmas.

51.

Catherine Opie

Self-portrait / Nursing

2004, chromogenic print
104.5 × 81.5 × 5 cm
Private collection

The artist celebrates motherhood with a nod to a painful history, the faded scars of the word pervert scratched into her chest, reflecting the struggle for acceptance as a lesbian mother. The opulent backdrop references the cloth of honour hung behind the Virgin and Child in Italian Renaissance paintings.

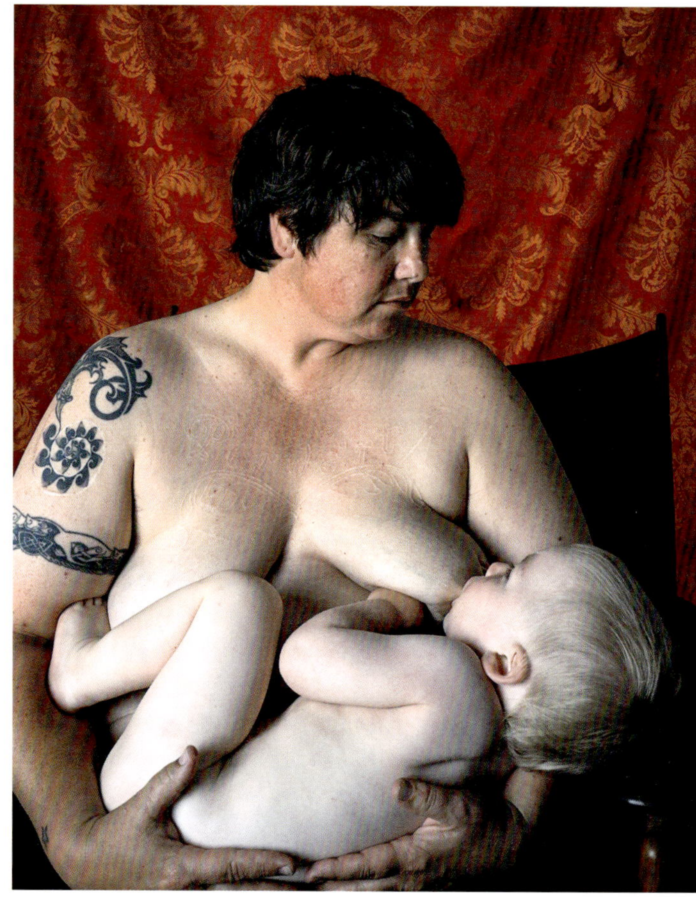

52.

Alice Neel

Nancy and Olivia

1967, oil on canvas
99.7 × 91.4 cm
Collection of Diane and David Goldsmith

Alice Neel's portrait of her daughter-in-law and granddaughter, Nancy and Olivia, illustrates the fierce protectiveness of mothers, and an infant's feelings of security in being held. Infants become attached to their mother, or main caregivers, through behaviours that keep them physically close, such as crying and smiling. This closeness protects and comforts the infant.

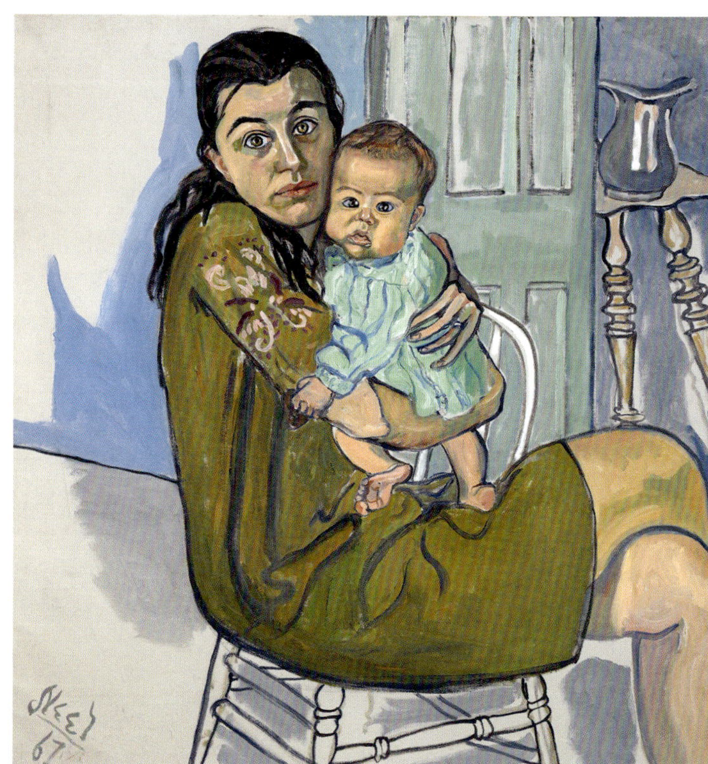

53.
Lena Cronqvist
The Madonna

1969, oil on canvas
122 × 108 × 3 cm (framed)
Moderna Museet, Stockholm
Purchase 1970
NM 6278

Lena Cronqvist's *Madonna* speaks to the stress and exhaustion that accompany early motherhood. Despite the greater involvement of fathers in parenting, most mothers remain disproportionately responsible for childcare, and experience a more dramatic change to their lifestyle and identity.

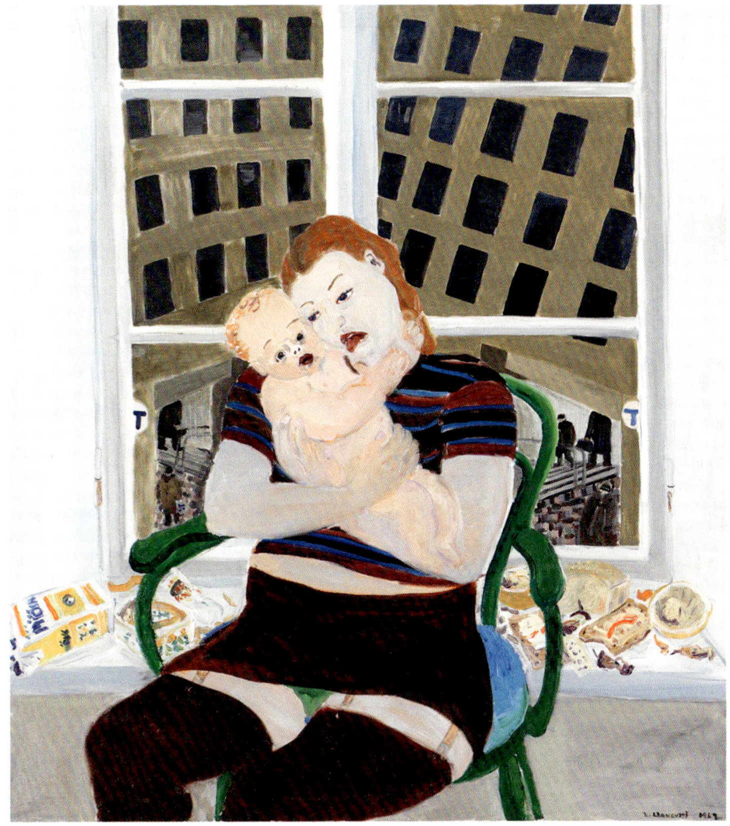

54.
Caroline Walker
Study for *Refreshments*

From the series *Lisa*
2022, oil on paper
55.1 × 51.5 cm (framed)
Private collection

Caroline Walker's *Refreshments* shows a joyful and engaged interaction between the artist's sister-in-law and her baby. All children form attachments, unless they experience severe deprivation, but they differ in how secure their attachments are. Infants whose mothers or caregivers are sensitive and responsive to them, and interact with them in a conversation-like way, are more likely to become securely attached.

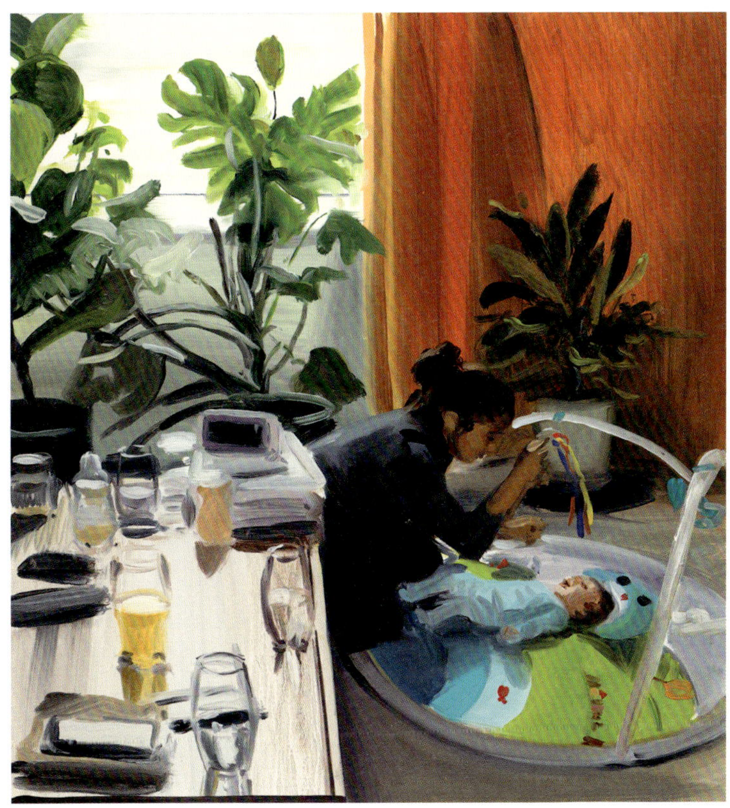

55.
Nicholas Nixon
Bebe and Clementine, Cambridge, Massachusetts

1990, printed 2006, gelatin silver print
35.6 × 43.2 cm (framed)

Nicholas Nixon's work shows his young daughter, Clementine, very much in charge while arranging her mother's hair. It used to be thought that parents influence the behaviour of their children, but research has shown that right from birth children also influence their parents' behaviour towards them.

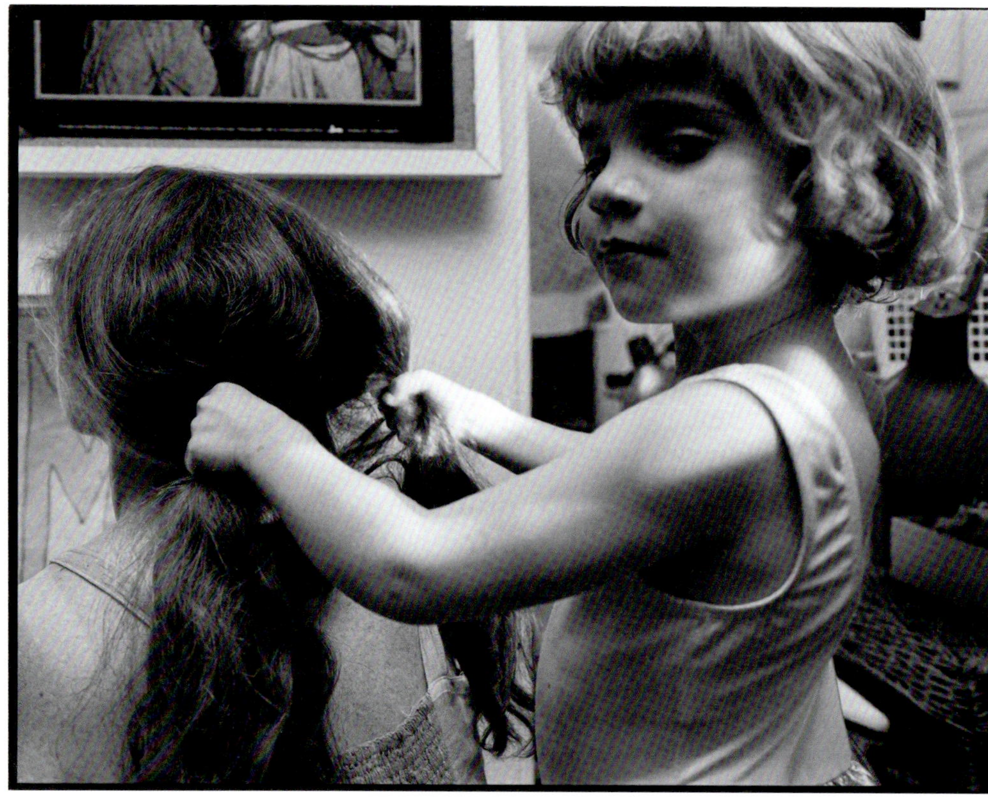

56.
Thomas Holton
Bored, 2011

From the series
The Lams of Ludlow Street
2011, inkjet print on paper
50.8 × 60.9 cm
Courtesy of the artist

Adolescents become focused on their identity – who they are and who they wish to be – and strive for greater autonomy from their parents, as alluded to in Thomas Holton's *Bored*.

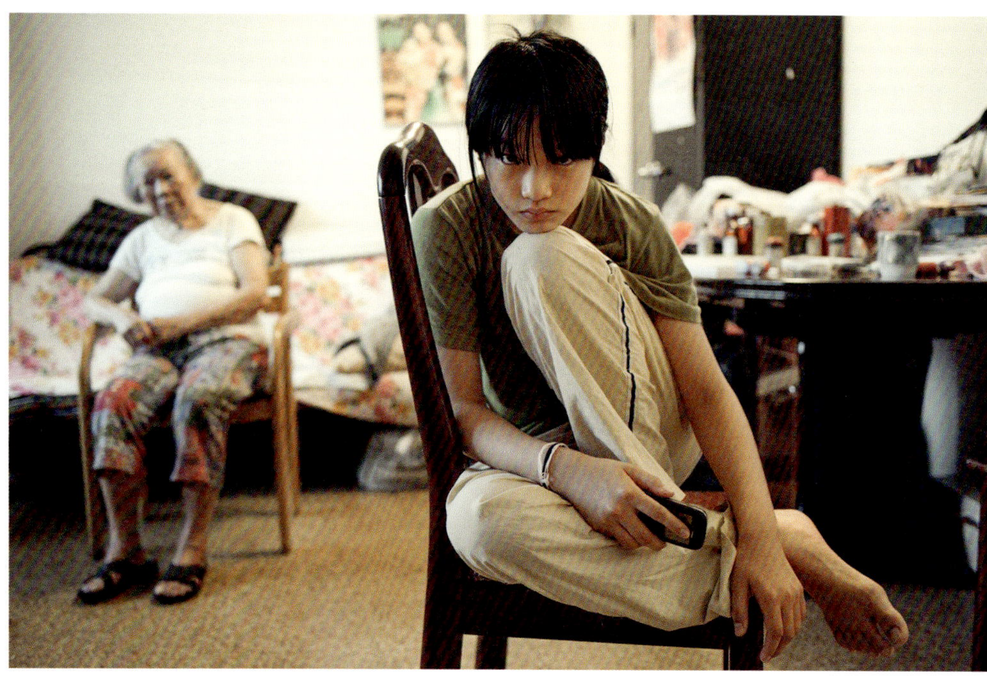

57.
Ishbel Myerscough
All

2016, oil on canvas
196.3 × 127 cm (framed)
Ishbel Myerscough / Flowers Gallery, London and Hong Kong

Ishbel Myerscough's portrait of her family shows a time when they were particularly close-knit. She reflected, 'I see my daughter growing into an uncanny reflection of my younger self, same hair, wearing my old clothes. Life is full of echoes.' Family ties remain important for adolescents, providing them with a foundation for entry into the adult world.

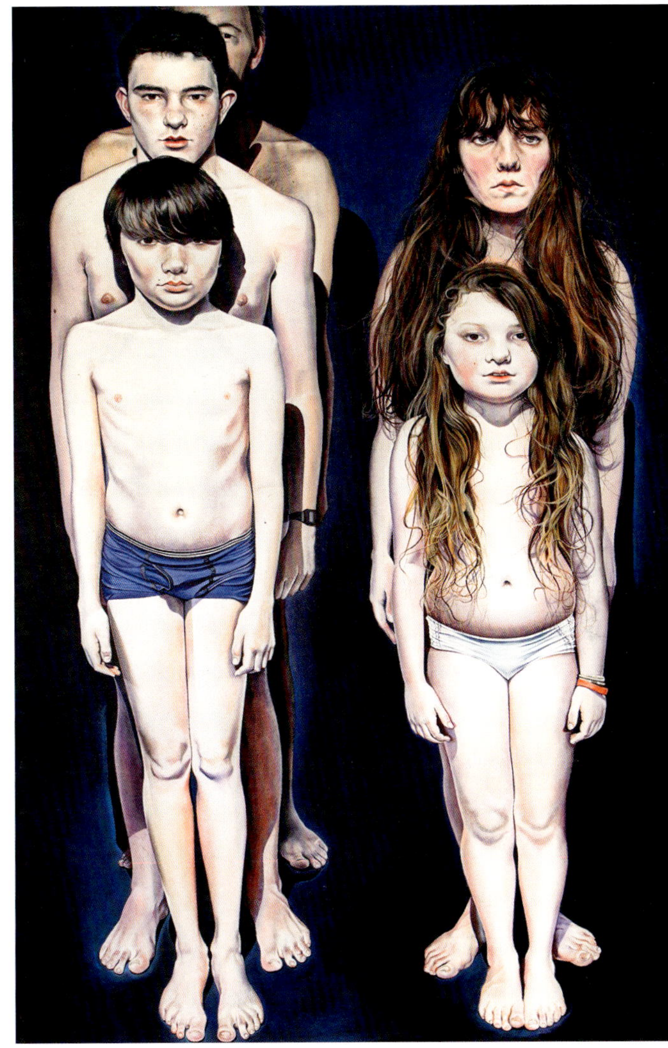

58.
Winifred Nicholson
Kate and Jake, Isle of Wight

1932, oil on canvas
67 × 75 cm
Bristol Museums:
Bristol Museum & Art Gallery
K4094

Soon after Ben and Winifred Nicholson separated, in 1931, Winifred rented a house on the Isle of Wight where she painted *Kate and Jake, Isle of Wight*, a portrait of her two eldest children.

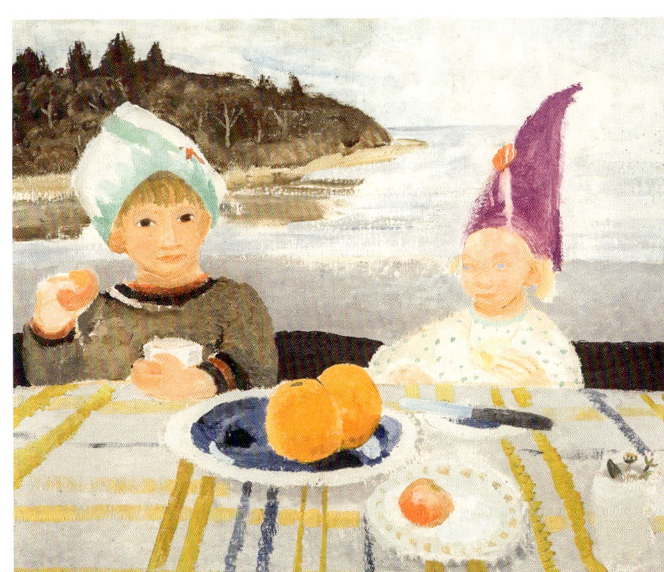

59–62.
Zun Lee

Billy Garcia and daughter Esmeralda sharing a tender moment at a gas station, Bronx, NY, September 2012

From the photographic project
Father Figure
2012–13, archival pigment ink on 100% cotton rag paper
33 × 48.2 cm
Courtesy of the artist

Bedtime shenanigans with Carlos Richardson and his daughter, Selah Harlem, NY, August 2012

From the photographic project
Father Figure
2012, archival pigment ink on 100% cotton rag paper
33 × 48.2 cm
Courtesy of the artist

Guy Miller surveying the playground whilst bandaging son Nijel's injured arm, Harlem, NY, July 2013

From the photographic project
Father Figure
2013, archival pigment ink on 100% cotton rag paper
33 × 48.2 cm
Courtesy of the artist

Zun Lee's photographs of black fathers and their children, taken in US cities between 2011 and 2015 as part of his *Father Figure* series, contradict the stereotype of black fathers as absent fathers. Describing his project, the artist said, 'Few of the men I met were in traditional relationships, but I observed these fathers interact with their children, and I saw that they were loving, present and responsible, and took their parenting role seriously, nonetheless.'

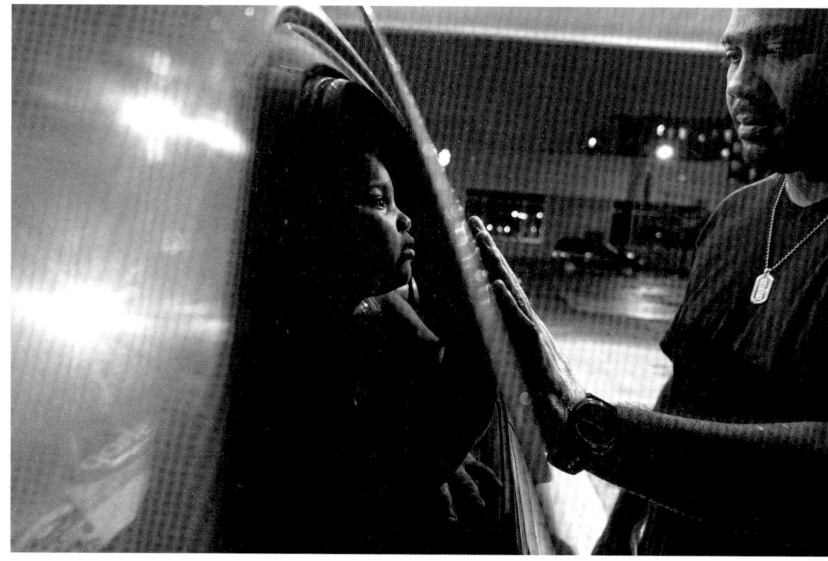

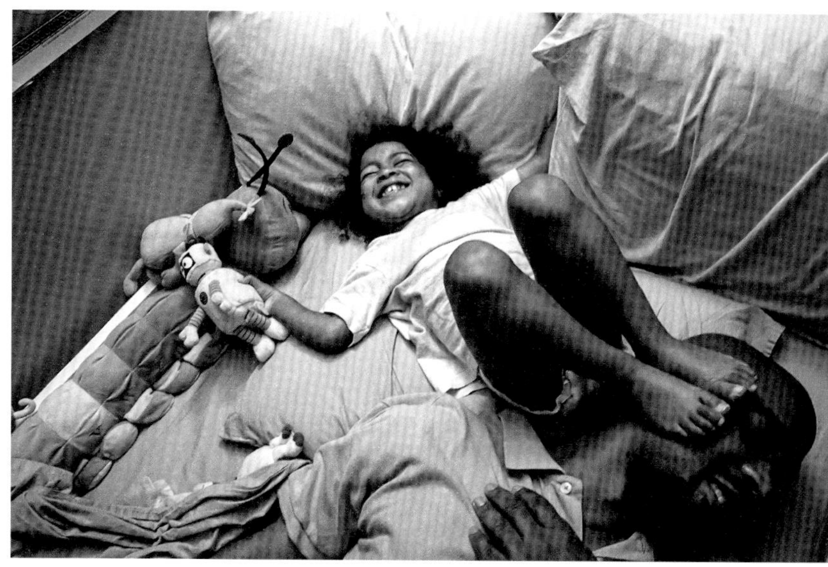

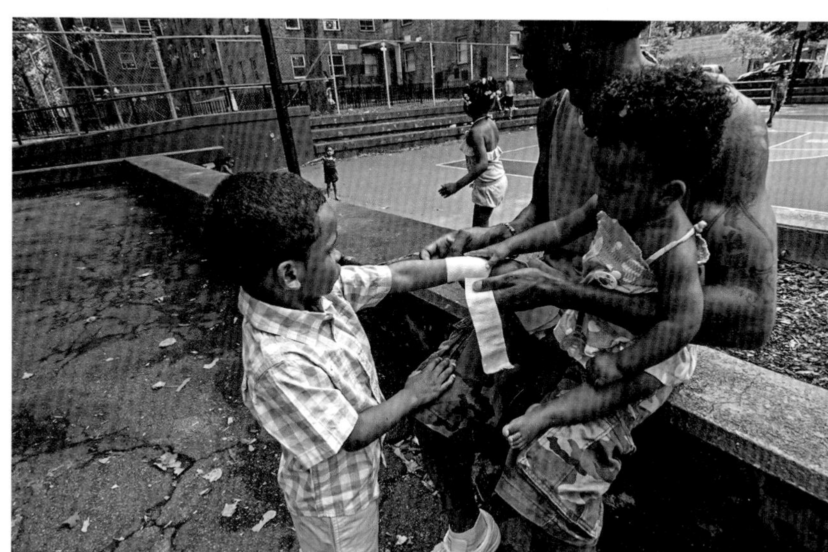

Guy Miller keeping an eye on all of his four children, Bronx, NY, December 2012

From the photographic project
Father Figure
2012, archival pigment ink
on 100% cotton rag paper
33 × 48.2 cm
Courtesy of the artist

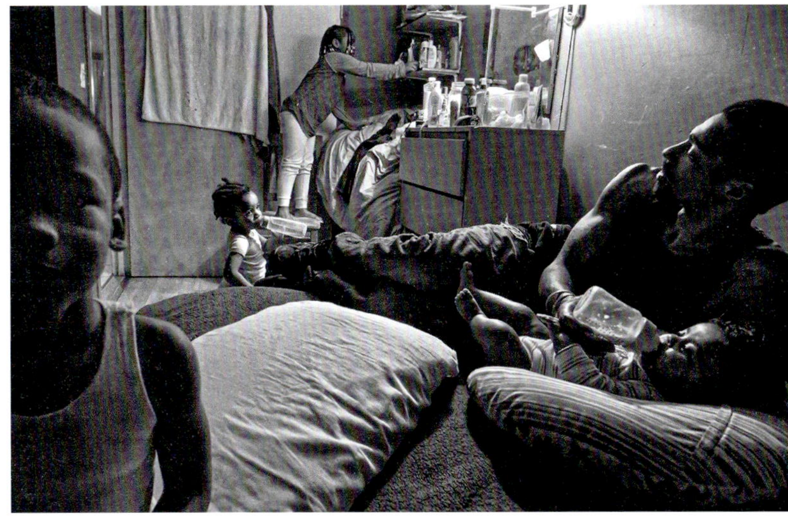

63.
Jean-Loup Cornet
Michael Andrews and his Daughter Melanie swimming in Glenartney, Scotland

1976, colour C-type print on paper
19.5 × 12.5 cm
Tate © The Estate of Michael Andrews
TGA 200025/3/9

This photograph of the artist Michael Andrews teaching his daughter Melanie to swim was taken by a family friend. It formed the basis for Andrews's painting, *Melanie and Me Swimming*, which shows an example of scaffolding, the process of helping children achieve what they can't quite do by themselves through instruction and support.

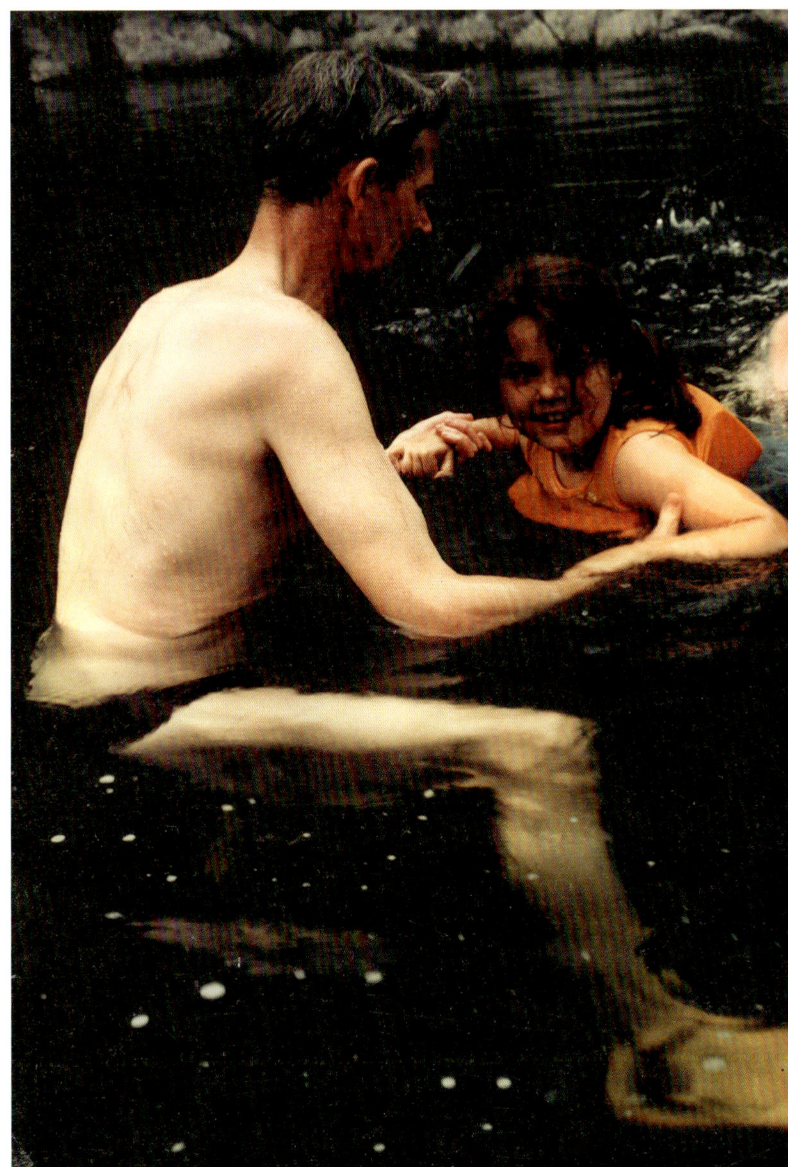

64.

Grayson Perry

Vase Using My Family

1998, glazed ceramic
60.5 × 32 cm
Lent by Stephen Kinder, Brighton

Vase Using My Family presents Perry's strong family unit. He found that being a father raised questions about his own childhood. Alongside photographs of his wife and daughter is a photograph of his childhood teddy-bear, Alan Measles, who Perry has described as a source of comfort in navigating his difficult relationship with his stepfather.

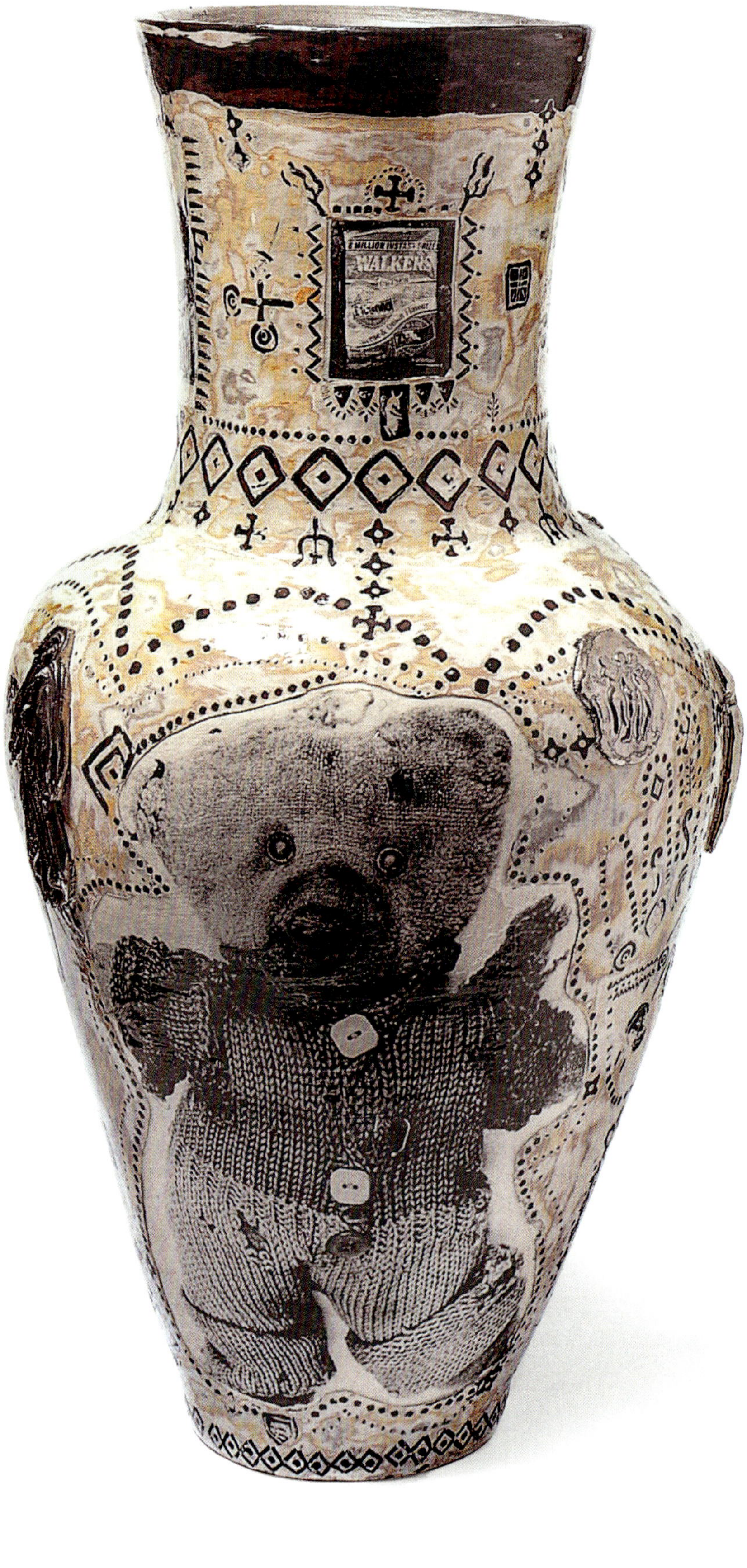

65.
Nicholas Nixon
Clementine and Sam, Cambridge, Massachusetts

1989, gelatin silver print
35.6 × 43.2 cm (framed)

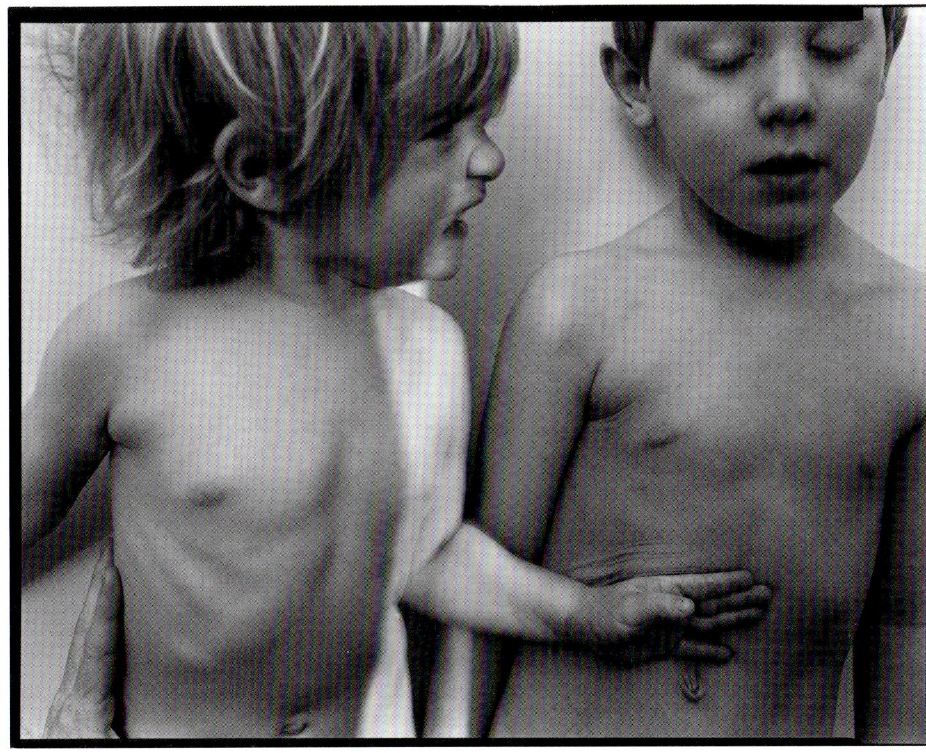

Nicholas Nixon's photographs of his children show the close, yet often aggressive, interactions that characterise sibling relationships. The photographs also highlight changes in these relationships over time. Siblings who get on well in childhood are likely to continue to do so as they grow up. If parents treat siblings differently, with one child being 'the favourite', this can have a damaging and long-lasting effect on the relationship.

66.
Joy Labinjo
Having the Conversation

2020, oil on canvas
180 × 200 cm
Private collection

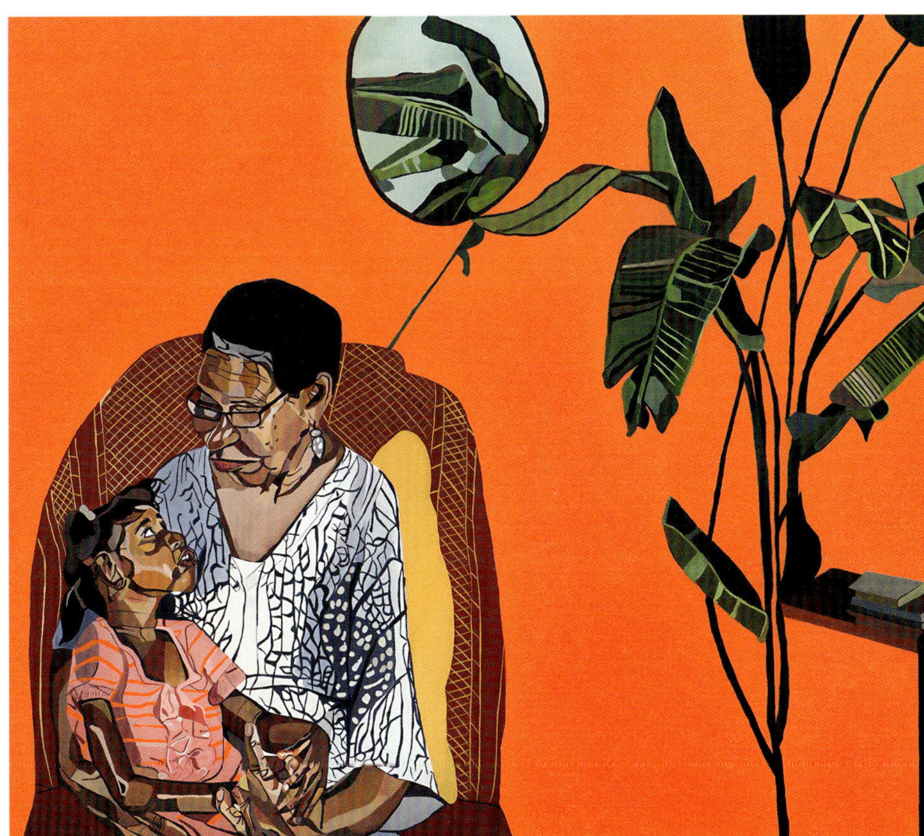

Joy Labinjo's *Having the Conversation* depicts a tender moment between a grandmother and her grandchild. The importance and involvement of grandparents in the lives of their grandchildren can vary across cultures. Multi-generational households are the norm in some parts of the world, while rarer in others.

67.
Tracey Emin
May Dodge, My Nan

1963–93, Memorabilia and text
(five parts) all framed
Overall: 16.2 × 18.2 × 18.1 cm
Tate: Presented by Tate Members 2004
T11886

May Dodge – My Nan She's 92 I call
her Plum She calls me
Pudding –
She made me the most beautiful
baby clothes – white crocheted
she made them for me a few
years ago – She said at the time
'I've made them for you now
because – by the time you have a
baby – I'll be making clothes
for angels.'
Dear Nanny I'm not afraid anymore –
Life's fantastic – who'd have thought
I could make angels –
for you –
They're waiting
xxx

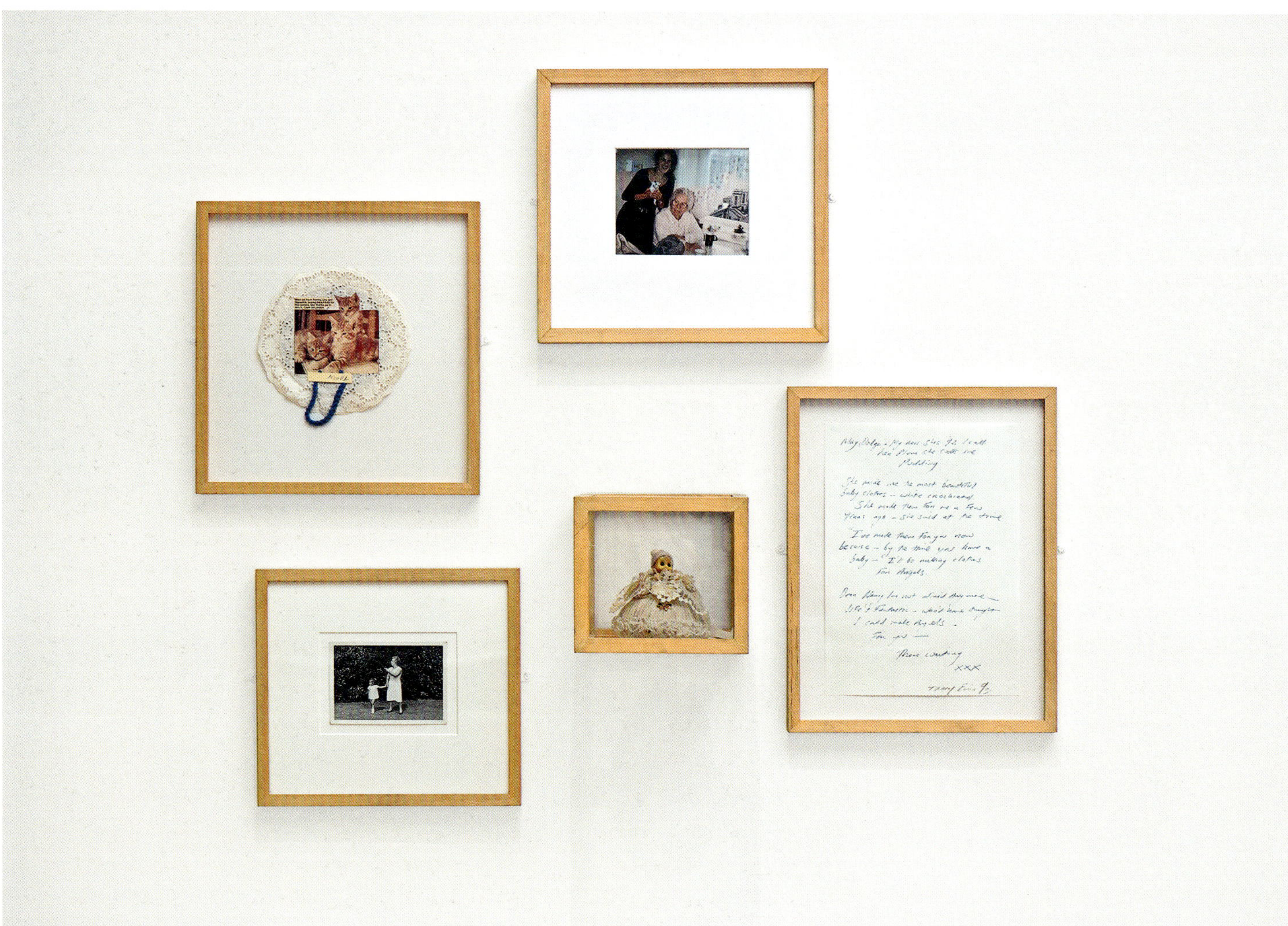

68.
Celia Paul
My Mother with a Rose

2006, oil on canvas
90.3 × 90.4 × 6.4 cm (framed)
Private collection

Celia Paul's piece reflects the altered nature of her relationship with her mother. The artist made many paintings of her elderly mother, who at first was a reluctant sitter, but then became dedicated to the project. As the artist described it, 'I was a bully at first, but it came to mean everything to her. It became her vocation.'

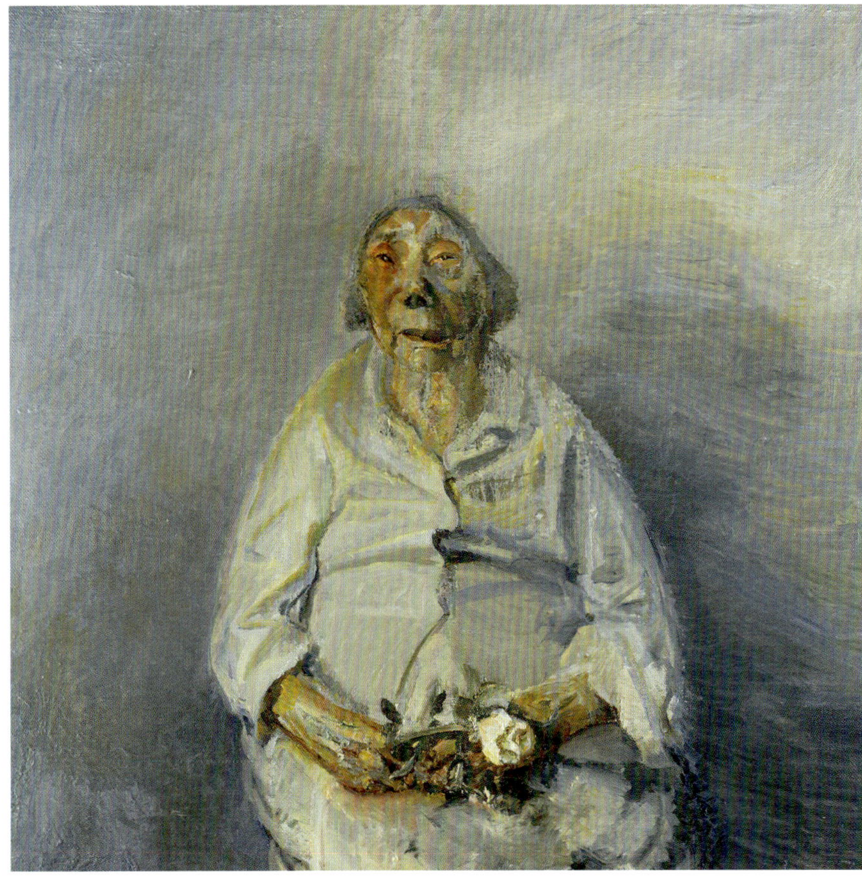

69.
Lucian Freud
The Painter's Mother Resting

1975–76, oil on canvas
105 × 105 × 5 cm (framed)
Private collection

Lucian Freud's portrait of his mother shows her looking away from his gaze, or asleep. He could only paint her when she wasn't looking directly at him. In Martin Gayford's memoir, *The Man with the Blue Scarf*, Freud said of this work, 'I was feeling sadder than I ever have before or since. I was painting the paisley patterns on her dress and remember worrying that my sadness would get into the paisley shapes and I suppose perhaps it did.'

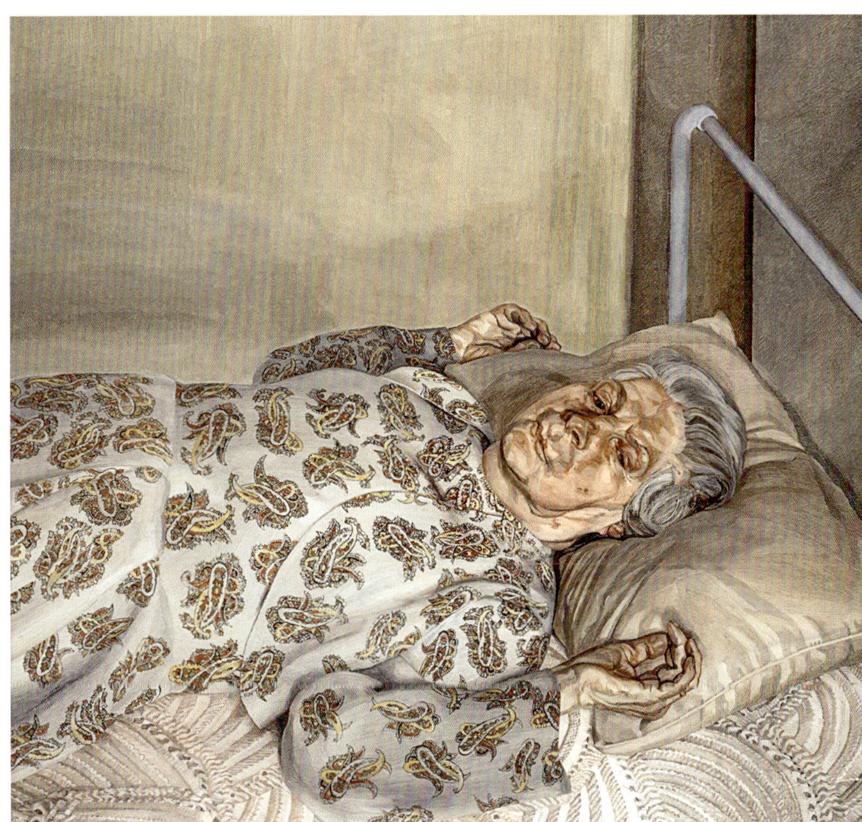

70.

Larry Sultan

My Mother Posing

From the book *Pictures from Home*
1984, chromogenic print
50.8 × 60.9 cm
© Estate of Larry Sultan.
Courtesy of Casemore Gallery, San Francisco; Yancey Richardson Gallery, New York; Galerie Thomas Zander, Köln; and the Estate of Larry Sultan

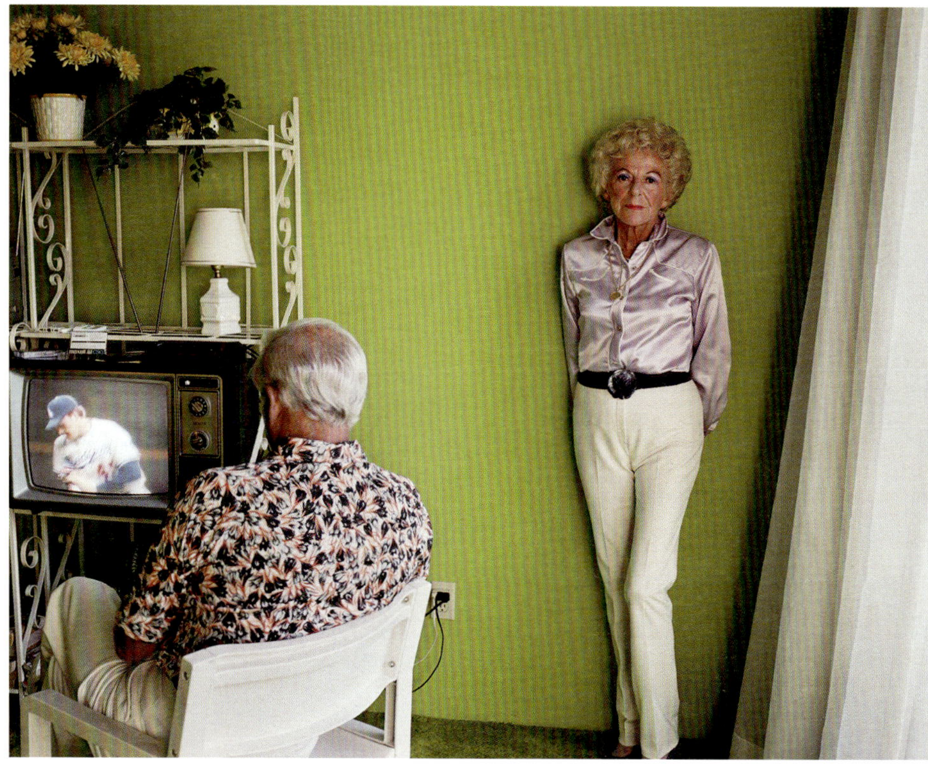

71.

Larry Sultan

Business Page

From the book *Pictures from Home*
1985, chromogenic print
50.8 × 60.9 cm
© Estate of Larry Sultan.
Courtesy of Casemore Gallery, San Francisco; Yancey Richardson Gallery, New York; Galerie Thomas Zander, Köln; and the Estate of Larry Sultan

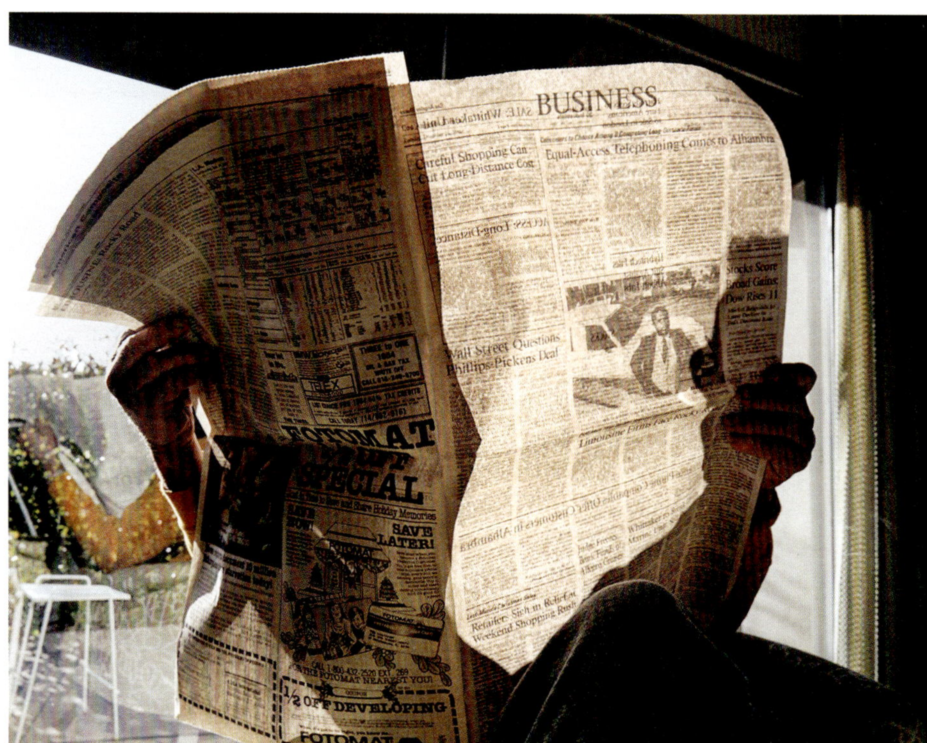

In 1982, Larry Sultan embarked on a ten-year project photographing and interviewing his parents at their home in California. Sultan's exploration of his mother and father's relationship with each other, and with himself, examined their vulnerabilities, what it means for a parent to age, and questioned how much a child can truly understand their parents.

72.
Nan Goldin
Lil Laughing, Swampscott, MA

1996, cibachrome
76.2 × 101.6 cm
Collection Fotomuseum Winterthur, Gift of Andreas Reinhart
1999-008-023

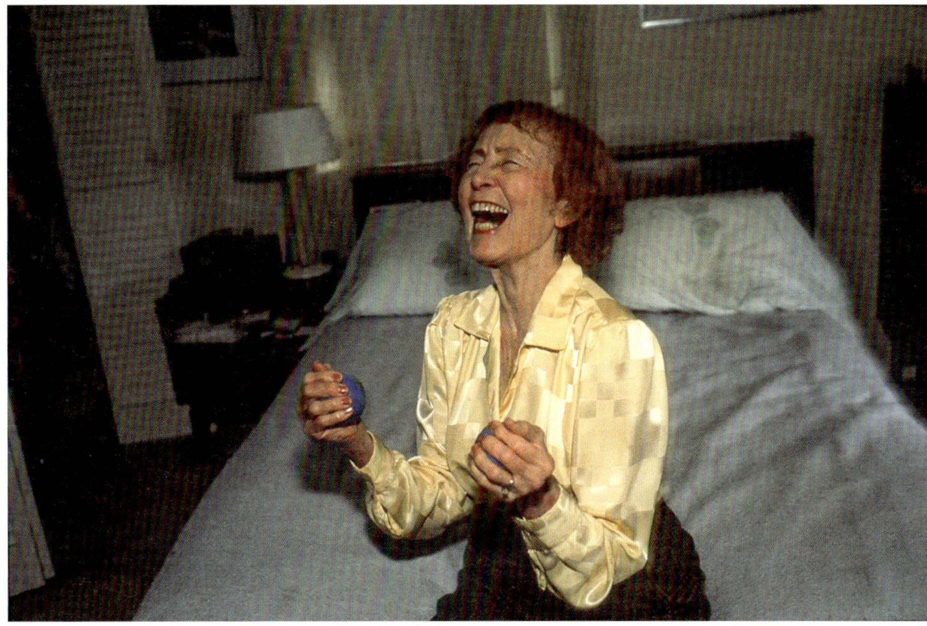

73.
Nan Goldin
My Father Shaving, Swampscott, MA

1997, cibachrome
76.2 × 101.6 cm
Collection Fotomuseum Winterthur, Gift of Andreas Reinhart
1999-008-022

Nan Goldin had a difficult relationship with her parents from childhood onwards, made worse by her older sister's suicide when Goldin was eleven. These photographs of her mother and father were taken when they were in their eighties.

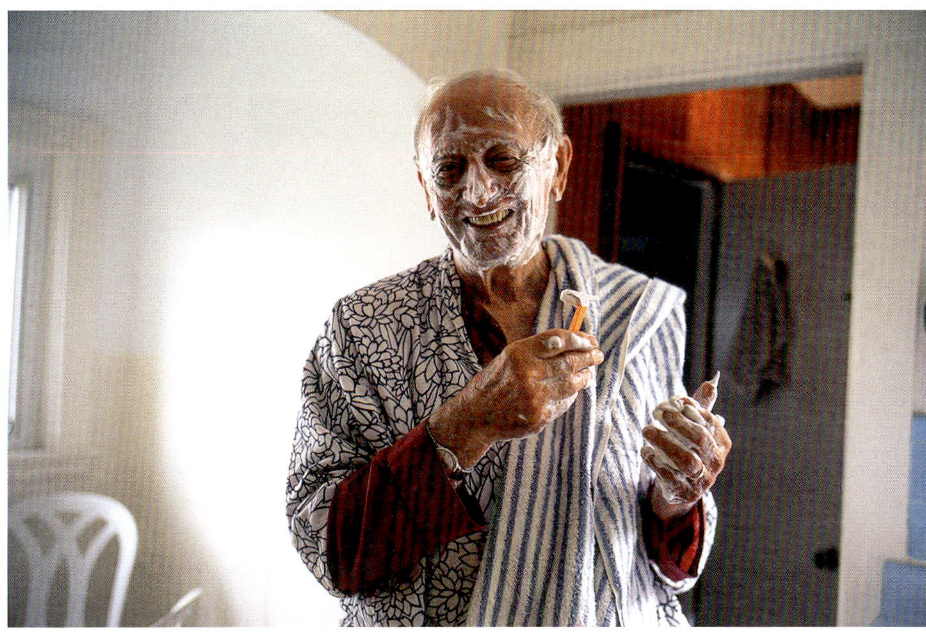

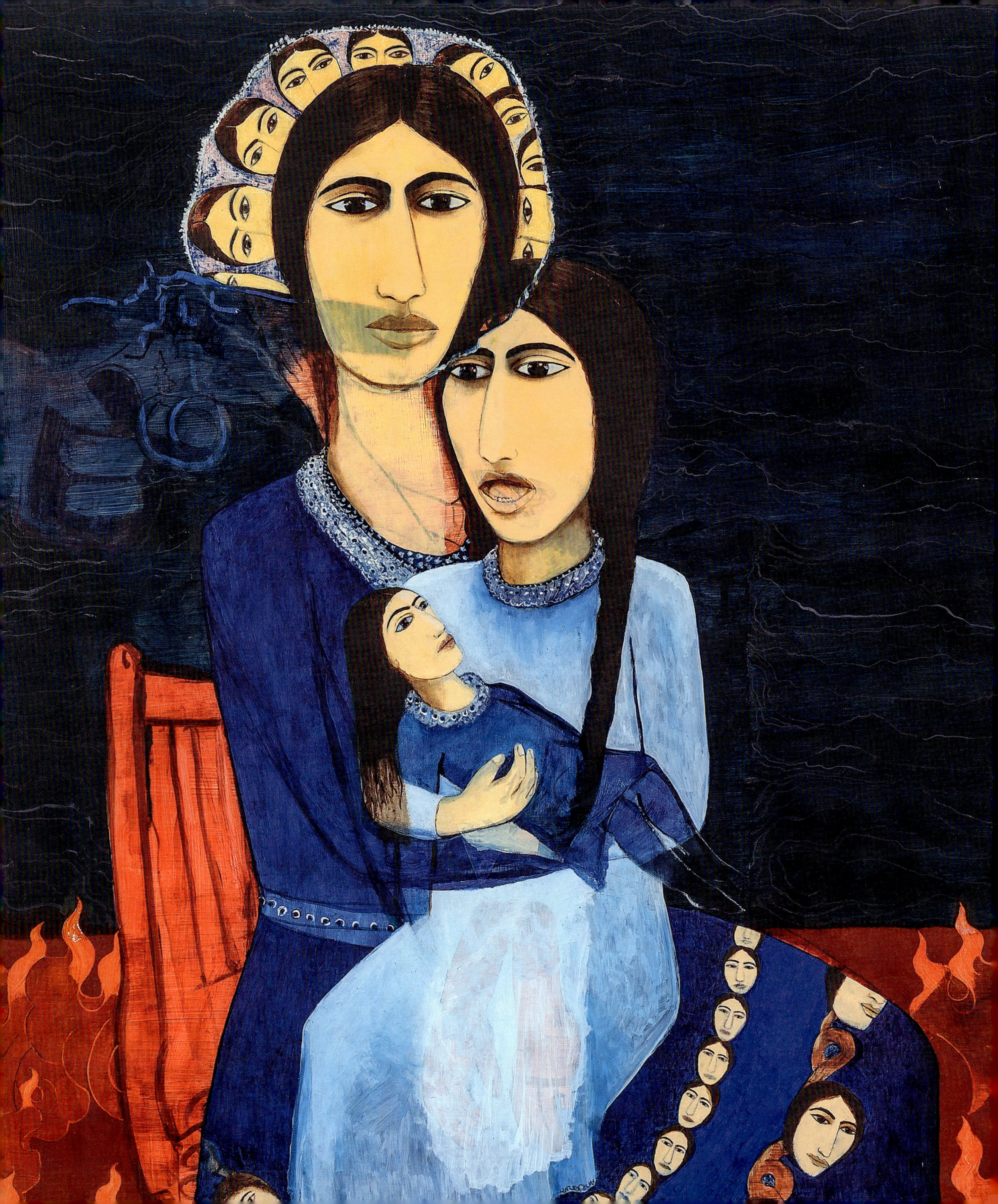

Families are often portrayed as extremely happy or deeply dysfunctional, but the reality usually lies somewhere in between. Based on our experiences from infancy onwards, we build up ideas and expectations of family relationships in our minds, especially those with our parents. This has an influence on how we interact with them, and how we come to see ourselves. Artists are uniquely placed to translate their internal representations of family to the outside world. By doing so, they can help us reflect on our own family relationships. The artists in this section explore positive and negative family dynamics between couples, parents and children, and extended family, with works that foreground affection and rejection, comfort and conflict, involvement and estrangement, and not fitting in. They also examine the wider social and cultural influences on family relationships.

Family Dynamics

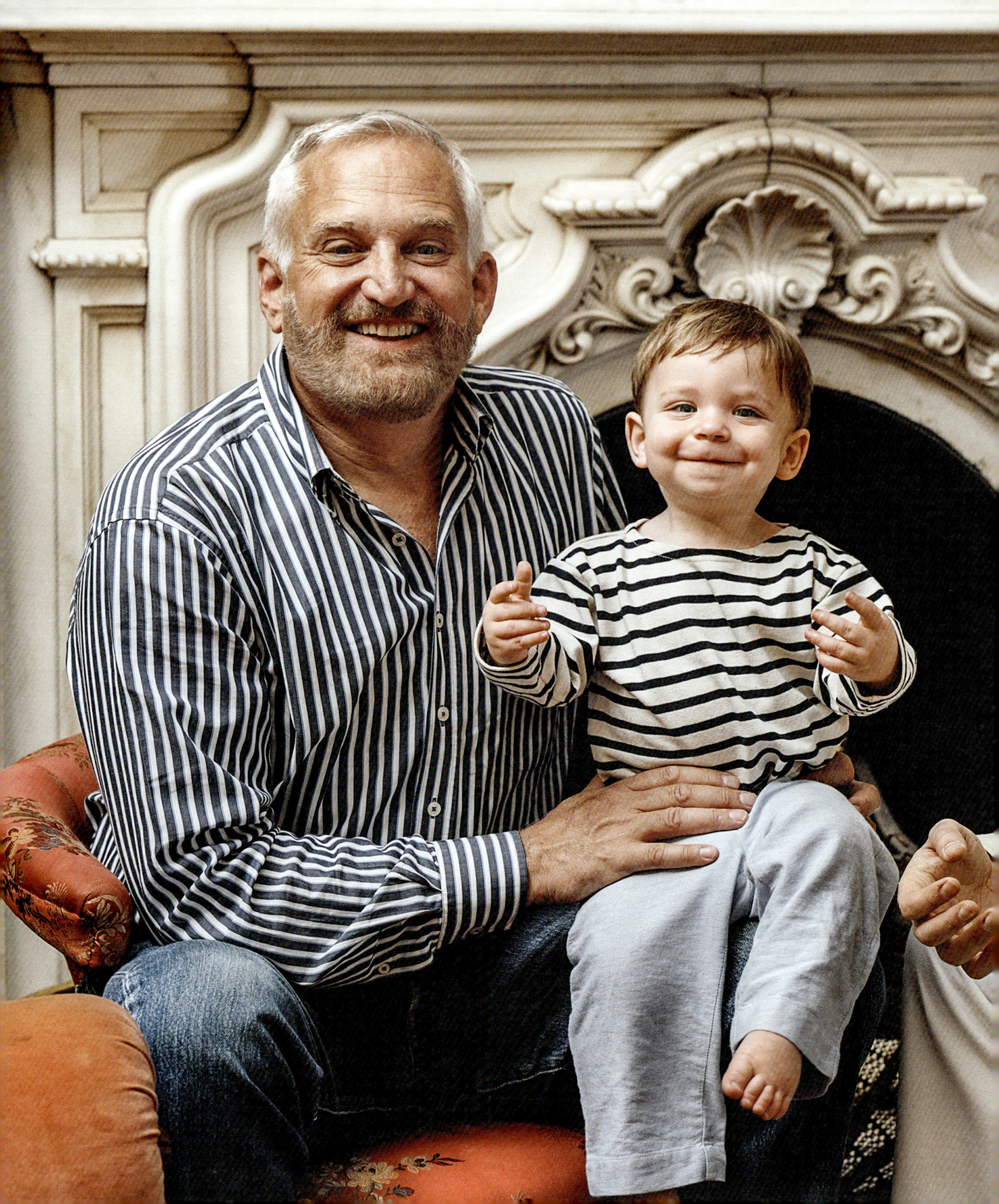

Much to Give Thanks For

Detail of **74**, Tina Barney, *Andrew, John and George*, 2011

When I heard that *The New Yorker* was sending Tina Barney to take a photo of my husband, John, our son, George, and me, I was bewildered. The image was to illustrate a piece I had worked on for two years in the hope of advancing acceptance of the new model of family we represented. I wrote a lot about love, and I had assumed the accompanying picture would be celebratory. I had long admired Tina Barney's work for its cool depiction of people whose affection is buried, awkward or inadequate, and for its intimate look at the stilted formalities of American WASPs and European aristocrats. In many ways, her usual subtext was the opposite of what my article required. On the other hand, she was a highly regarded artist, and, if she was willing to document our family, I didn't want to refuse the opportunity. I was bemused that the magazine didn't want to fly in my daughter and her mother, or my husband's two biological children and their mothers, but I suppose that a photo of us all might have seemed too anarchic, while a photo of the three of us would more obviously convey the notion that my family was recognisably a family. It is hard to remember that, not much more than a decade ago, a photo of two men with their child still seemed bluntly political. Families like mine were a relative rarity, and while images of activists at Pride marches with infants on their shoulders appeared with often cynical journalistic reports on the LGBT movement's agenda to undermine traditional values, a more intimate, mainstream portrait of a gay-parented family being simply a family was singular.

Any parent who has tried to achieve family portraits with young children knows how inherently stressful the experience is. You want your child to look happy, but being photographed does not make a toddler particularly happy. George's nanny stood behind Tina Barney and danced around hilariously. Many snacks were proffered. John jiggled George up and down as if he were a human basketball. George alternated between being amused by all this (briefly) and being impatient and miserable (less briefly). I heard the camera click on scenes that would have bolstered the notion that men don't know what to do with babies. I liked Tina Barney when we met; her personal affect was more forgiving than her lens. But she works on large-format plates and, unlike the shutter-happy photographers of the digital age, she does not take a thousand photos in the hope that a few will turn out well. Reflecting many of the people she documents, she is frugal, confident enough not to bother with second chances. She arranges her subjects formally, but she is seeking not your best moment, but your truest one, recognising that truth includes not only what you would like to disguise, but also the disguises you deploy.

Andrew Solomon

In the end, *The New Yorker* decided not to run the piece, and when Tina Brown, then the editor of *Newsweek*, picked it up for that magazine, she headlined it 'Meet My Real Modern Family', and wanted just the kind of photos I had originally envisioned, with all of us crowded around the kitchen table, with all four children playing raucously on a bed; we looked exuberant in our affections. The photos, by Michael Sharkey, captured frankly the tension between the fun we had with one another and the idiosyncrasies of our set-up. Brown ran an adjacent chart to explain the parental interrelationships among our three separate households. Sharkey has repeatedly documented our family in the decade since. He has celebrated the chaotic nature of our family, making us look both good and exceptional. In this regard, his photos are the opposite of Barney's. They bedeck my social media pages, our various mantelpieces and the pages of sundry publications. We have made ourselves an adequate curiosity.

Photographers from around the world have made images of us since; one was deployed in the campaign for gay marriage in Taiwan, another displayed at the Hermitage in St Petersburg. The London photographer Hugo Burnand has repeatedly made us look better than we do in real life, not through digital retouching, but through the exercise of his charm during sessions. Chuck Close revealed an unsettling darkness in his daguerreotype; Annie Leibovitz photographed the three of us with her fastidious attention to detail and painterly lighting. But George had by then lost his primal innocence and his smile looks slightly forced.

I did not see the Tina Barney photos after she took them; when my article was cancelled at *The New Yorker*, I was too disappointed to give them much thought. I had hoped that my writing would inspire more gay men to have children, and would lead people whose definition of family was narrow to appreciate a wider construct. Most of my work springs from a sense of mission, but this story was vested with my most fundamental reality and my dreams for that reality. Perhaps it was too lyrical for *The New Yorker*, at once too agenda-driven and too mawkish. I had imagined that my lyrical sentimentality was a political statement, but, in 2010, that was still an obscure view. There was something unseemly about the fuss and high poetics; if we gay people wanted to have families like everyone else, we should have them and be done with it. As for the photos, the years when your children are entirely dependent occupy the present so completely that documents of the past count for relatively little. We had some baby pictures of our children here and there, but most of our burgeoning collection of frames received new images as we revelled in the excitement of each stage of the children's development.

It was only four or five years later that I admired a large photo by Tina Barney in the apartment of good friends, taken for her book *The Europeans*. I mentioned that she had taken our photo, and our friends asked how it had turned out; I had to confess I didn't know. After I inquired, Barney's studio assistant sent us some images to review. We pored over the contact sheets, then found out what a print would cost and decided we could manage without. But, as George grew up, representations of his earliest years took on a new value. So, one Christmas, I ordered a print (in her usual gigantic format) and had it wrapped under the tree for John. I had faced a difficult choice: there were several photos in which I looked suave, while in this one I look startled and bug-eyed, but the one shown here was by far the best of George and it was good of John, too (**74**). Artists tend to want to capture your vulnerabilities, while parents tend to want to recall moments of perfection. This was as close as we had come to achieving both at once. Two men and a baby: it had been an almost inconceivable idea when I was growing up, and it mattered more to demonstrate that it was possible and had happened and was good than to assuage my personal vanity.

I do not know which photo the editors at *The New Yorker* would have selected. Tina Barney herself had given us a limited selection among which to choose, and her studio assistant assured us that she was happy with each of the ones we were examining. In a strange way, her picture of us is as contrarian as her pictures of her own family, including *Thanksgiving*, which appears beside ours in this exhibition. To demonstrate the inherent discomfiture and haughty disconnectedness of the traditional aristocratic family is a slap at hackneyed ideas of their enviable privilege. To demonstrate a fleeting moment of grace in a non-traditional family delivers a comparable slap at notions of convention, even though we are, as are most of her subjects, nicely dressed and positioned in our own home like figures in a Victorian portrait, our drawing room observed so carefully that it looks almost like a stage set.

We ourselves were at a cusp, then. We had sworn a lifelong commitment in a civil partnership two years earlier in Northamptonshire, and had designed our wedding to resemble a traditional ceremony (with a few flamboyances for good fun) because, in 2007, the more conventional our wedding, the more radical it was. Assuming the style and rhetoric of a heterosexual wedding when gay marriage was not yet legitimate struck us as a conquest of forbidden territory. George was born in 2009; Barney's photo was taken in 2010. Soon thereafter, aping convention ceased to feel liberating and became oppressive; gay activists looked to establish totally fresh forms of celebration, dispensed in many cases with the affective binary, and in radical instances decried marriage entirely.

Many aspects of ordinary, traditional life, however, are winning. As the victim of a rather happy childhood (aside from the problem of my being gay), I am content to echo, even recreate the systems of affection that were so potent in my family. But, as social acceptance has surged, I have had the leisure to understand the ways that our experience lies outside the conventional social fabric. I have ceased to believe that equality can

74.
Tina Barney
Andrew, John and George

2011, chromogenic colour print
122.4 × 155.6 cm (framed)
Collection of Andrew Solomon and John Habich Solomon, Rhinebeck, New York

come only at the price of equivalence – that respect for my family hinges on its similarity to other, more 'normal' ones. I have an increasingly playful relationship with convention. Yet even as I acknowledge the pressure to keep up with activist viewpoints and respect the wilder shores of sexual freedom, even as I acknowledge that our primary obligation is just to be ourselves, I am always aware of being an emissary whose success in making a gay family work has social implications. Tina Barney is famous for probing advantaged lives, and her photo captures both our poise and our anxiety – our effort to be truly authentic while looking our best.

As I write this, George is about to enter high school, and we have just endured the gruesome process by which children are admitted to private

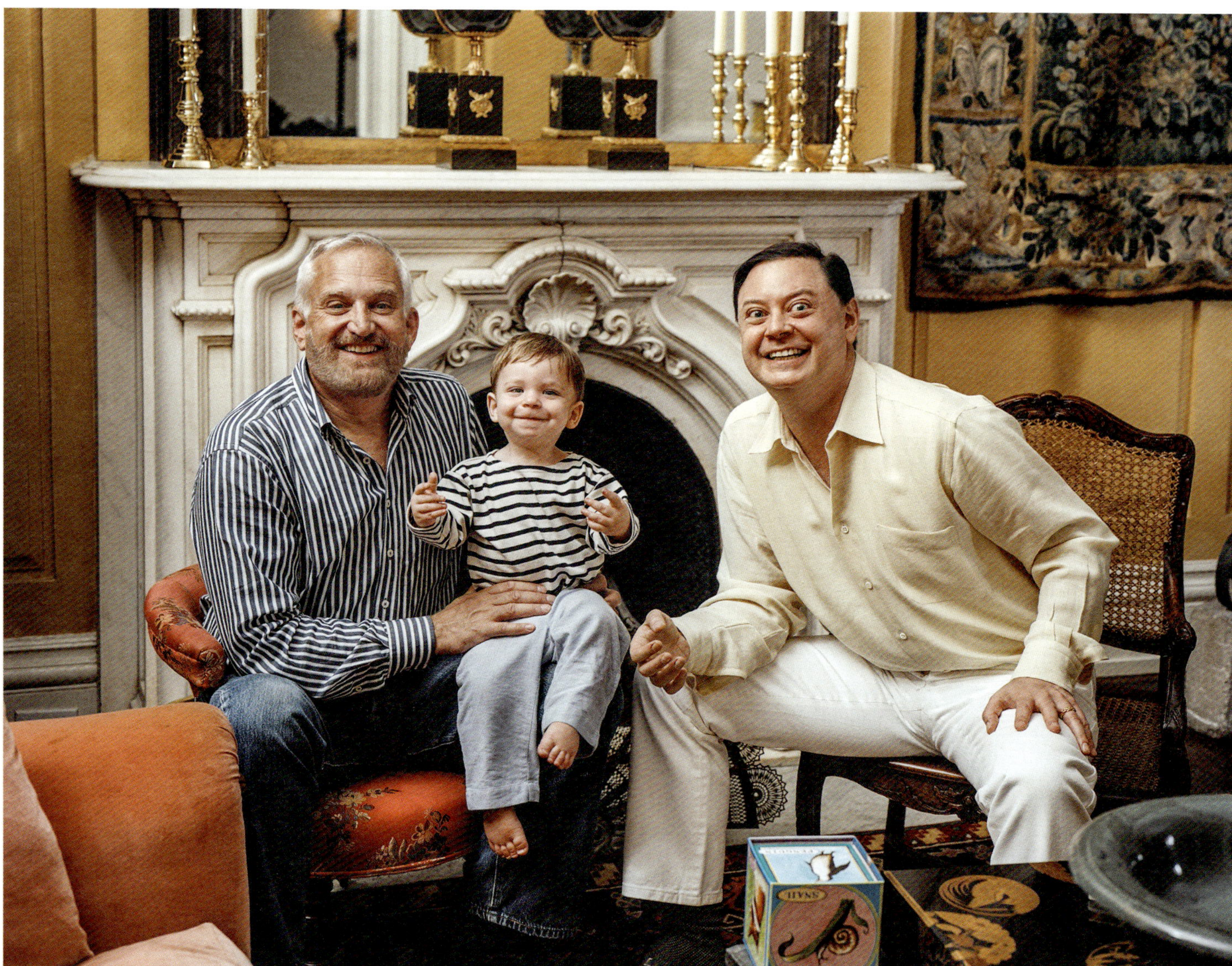

75.
Tina Barney
Thanksgiving

From the series *Theater of Manners*
1992, chromogenic colour print,
from an edition of 10
121.9 × 152.4 cm
© Tina Barney. Courtesy
Kasmin, New York

schools in New York City. He had to write fourteen essays; John and I had to write eight. One school asked him to describe his identity and explain how his presence there would strengthen the diversity of his class. George shook his by then weary head and said, 'I am white and straight and privileged, and I don't really have an identity that will contribute to their diversity'. I responded brightly, 'You could write about the fact that you have gay parents'. He cast me a withering look. 'What is interesting about that?' he asked. When I was growing up, it would have been more than interesting to come from a family such as ours. Now, it seems to him banal, perhaps because all thirteen-year-olds find their families banal, but perhaps because parameters of family, at least in the liberal New York and London where we

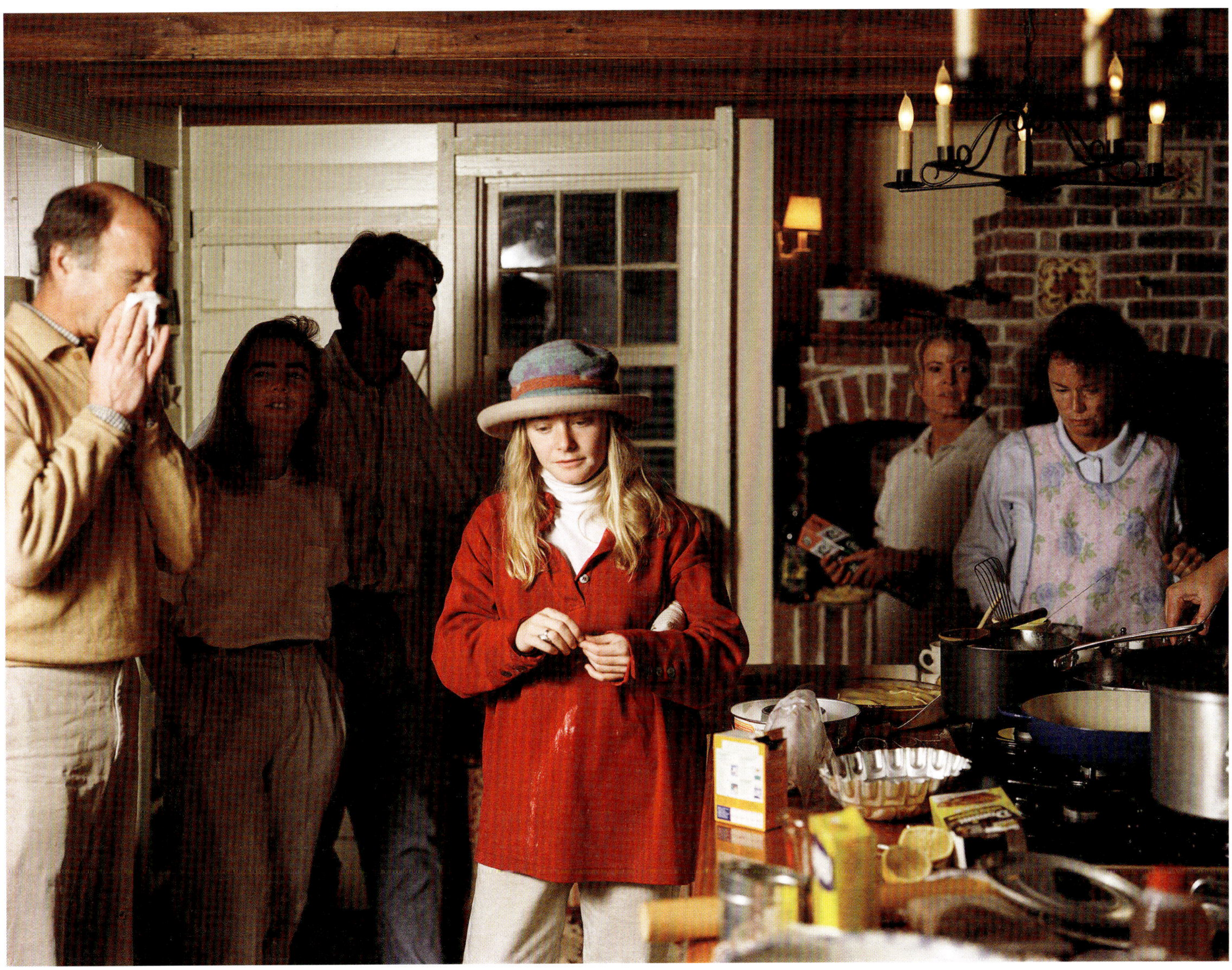

live, have changed so profoundly and fast. George does not see Tina Barney's photograph as anything more than a record of his early childhood. For him, it has no greater political overtones than a picture I took of him at about the same age on a park swing. He acknowledges John's and my stories of bygone struggles with a kind ear, but also with some boredom, much as children of yore responded to their elders' tales of a five-mile walk to school.

This photo, then, has shed some of its meaning because it has been outstripped by recent history; like any artefact, it requires an essay and a wall label lest its cuneiform be discounted as gibberish, its iconography mistaken for mere decoration. Barney's cheerful picture was, at least for me, a tiny part of the movement to make marriage and family available to LGBTQ people. That battle is not yet won, but its propaganda has come to seem mundane. Of course, this is a photo about love, an eternal topic, but it doesn't matter as much as it did that John and I transgressed by loving each other and by making and loving George. At the same time, Barney's artfulness is apparent. Her image's spirit is classical and deliberate, with echoes of Renaissance portraiture. The composition is meticulous. It is intimate, yet also a formal picture, not altogether dissimilar to the studio photos of my great-grandparents, who held long poses to achieve stern, sepia representations of their relationships. George's moment of exuberance was as transient as any baby's is, but this photo suggests that it was the fundamental truth about that day and, by implication, the days before and after it. It conveys a serenity we seldom felt at the time, but which has proved consistent with his developing personality and our developing relationship. It is an image of us as we were – such analogue photos do not lie – and of us as we wished to be. Tina Barney had the skill to capture only our shortcomings, but she chose to do this instead.

Barney's photograph *Thanksgiving* (**75**) is also about love – about an essential embarrassment that can hamper or define it when it is required of people. It is about the obligation inherent in traditional celebration and how inadequately it aligns with the actual emotions of actual people. Thanksgiving is a holiday ostensibly devoted to recognising all that we have. At the mythic 'first Thanksgiving', the Pilgrims sat down with the Indians and everyone overflowed with appreciation for everyone else. In reality, Thanksgiving initiates the American winter holiday season that begins on the fourth Thursday of November and ends on 2 January. It involves mixing people who have not chosen one another (i.e. one's family) yet are all obliged to seem glad to see one another. Everyone eats too much, because this national holiday has food as its theme: the menu is more rigid than for any other occasion and the purveyors of decorations mostly sell inflatable or paper turkeys. There is no babe in a manger, no fireworks, no charismatic bunny: there is just this extraordinarily effortful meal. Norman Rockwell portrayed the Thanksgiving table as the epitome of an American dream, but it is seldom dreamlike; in fact, the rate of suicide escalates at Thanksgiving (an increase that persists throughout the festive season). There is nothing less cheering than the obligation to be happy. Upper-class Americans have too much to be thankful for and yet it's hard to be appreciative at an appointed time. People who love one another are confounded by having suddenly to manifest that love; people who don't love one another are equally strained by having to pretend to like particular people more than they actually do.

In this image, the woman in the foreground holds casual claim to the upper-class style that those who sell the American dream tend to imitate. Her father, who is blowing his nose, exercises the prerogative of privilege; he does not turn away and his stance contains no air of polite apology. His other daughter and her new husband, behind him, are in shadow, a mysterious subplot of their own. On the right side of the picture and slightly anxiously towards the back are his ex-wife and her sister, who are making the meal. They look busy, tired and shy, their work central to this food-focused holiday but their presence distinctly secondary. The other figures are crowded into the kitchen even though they are not helping; they seem to appreciate the cosiness of the room rather than its function. It is widely held that the kitchen is the heart of any household, but most of these figures have an oblique relationship to the hearth and the cooking pots; their fondness for the kitchen does not extend to making use of it, at least on this exhausting day. As so often in Barney's work, the lighting is particularly dramatic: the front figure looks as though she could have been pasted on top of the scene; her father, to have plunked himself there; her sister in shadows and thus downgraded. And the women who are cooking are half-lit, half-seen, their expressions indicating their concern that everything turn out well – and perhaps their discomfort with having so many people crowded for recreational reasons into the space where they are working.

The representation of family dynamics is difficult even in extended literary narrative; it is nearly impossible in a single photo frame. Yet it is part of Barney's brilliance to capture the complexity of human relationships in photos that often bear the scrupulous conventions of paintings. In Barney's tableaux, captured on an obtrusive large-format camera, nothing is incidental – and yet her subjects are relaxed, unintimidated, unabashed. Like James Abbott McNeill Whistler or John Singer Sargent, she catches the flickers of humanity in people whose general objective is to project a controlled image of themselves. She is deadpan but omniscient, wise to every situation's complexities, which she highlights without intruding into them. The people who have gathered in this kitchen have meaningful relationships to one another, but no one is embracing; in fact, no one appears to be engaged in conversation. They are in proximity, but show no sign of relating to one another. There is something lonely about even the central figure; she embodies a careless elegance but seems unaware of anyone else in the room. Barney up-ends the fantasy that people of privilege spend their lives at ease in like company; here, the family seems more comfortable with the photographer than with one another. The charm and problem of holidays is an equal-opportunity one, and nothing can resolve the painful separateness of family members.

George is older now and so are my daughter and my husband's biological children, and the bullish confidence with which I helped launch our variously connected lives seems naïve. If I had total regard for my children's privacy, I wouldn't have allowed this photo to go into the exhibition and the catalogue. George said he was quite pleased for it to be included; he is proud of what we represent even if it's too boring for a school application essay. As for me, I am not prepared to forsake the symbolic value of our family. I am aware that the pleasures we enjoy simply in having a marriage and family are inaccessible to the majority of LGBTQ people, who in much of the world are more likely to be murdered than to find their unions blessed. I feel a kind of modernist *noblesse oblige* to share our sexuality-based privilege as widely as I can. From the hundreds of grateful letters I receive from LGBTQ people telling me how images of my family have given them hope, I feel as though we have accomplished something more than personal fulfilment.

But George is no longer an idea; he is a boy. Perhaps his contention that the structure of our family is boring provides him with a way to rebel against my proposition that it is fascinating. He does not always want to be avatar of an admirable new politics, although he gamely plays along at least some of the time. He wants the same things other boys want at fourteen, and, insofar as he wants to be interesting, he wants to be interesting on his own terms, not because of some idea that his parents had before he was born. When George was six, John asked him one night, 'Do you ever wish you had a more ordinary family with a mother and a father instead of two dads?' George said, 'No, because then I wouldn't have one of you'. It was immensely touching to me at the time and it made me feel that our experiment had been a success. Looking back on it, I see that our family was a success, not our experiment. George didn't say that he loved having two dads because he believed that the existence of our family would expand the scope of human rights, or because he felt conceptually enriched by our unorthodox set-up; he merely expressed affection for his parents, as six-year-olds are wont to do.

We all reflect our parents and likewise see ourselves through their eyes. We echo them even when we resist them. My parents were well-educated, Jewish, relatively comfortable, clever, kind. They produced a family organised around some of those characteristics and I am partially a product of who they believed themselves to be. George is the product of a gay union and has to endure the concomitant particularity as well as my enervating narrative of glory. Parents' hopes, whatever they may be, cling to their children like muck. Tina Barney captured a precognisant rapture in George. If she came for a follow-up shoot, we would be a bit more like *Thanksgiving* – loving, very much a family, but also awkward, complicated, ambivalent, unknown to one another and ultimately unknowable.

We have an abundance of later holiday snapshots in which we all look as good as we did when Tina Barney came by the house, but whatever it is we show in those is deliberate – not necessarily posed, but generally self-aware. You can be deliberate and still be real, I suppose, but that deliberateness masks the secrets we keep as soon as we learn lies, tact and self-image. I adore my children and hope they reciprocate; I have, nonetheless, betrayed them by treating them (or designating them?) as archetypes. There was a moment before that betrayal crystallised, and Tina Barney captured it.

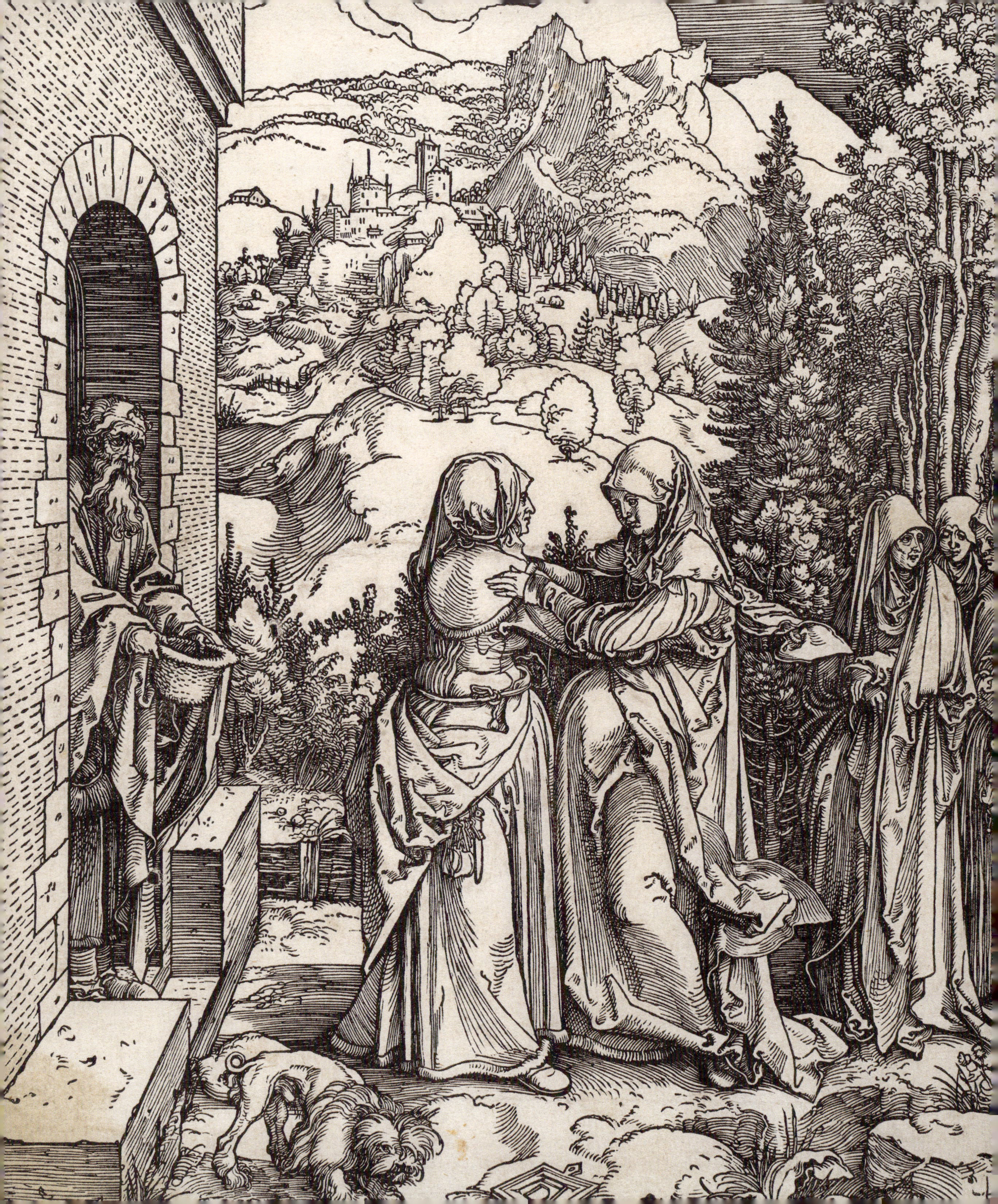

The Visitation

76.
Albrecht Dürer
The Visitation (detail)

1503, woodcut
29.9 × 21 cm (image)
42.7 × 33.4 cm (sheet)
The Fitzwilliam Museum, Cambridge
Bequeathed by the Rev. R.E. Kerrich
1872 (received 1873)
P.3418-R

No exhibition about the family would be complete without a depiction of the most famous family of them all – the Holy Family.

The Visitation highlights the moment when Mary, who has just discovered she is pregnant with Jesus, visits her aunt Elizabeth. Elizabeth, an elderly woman, is also miraculously pregnant. It has always been a popular subject with artists.

Let's imagine this moment as if it was a scene in a family reality show.

Mary: Hi, Auntie Liz. You're never going to believe this. You know I'm a virgin. Well, I'm pregnant!

Elizabeth: Ha! If you want some really amazing news, I'm eighty-eight years old and I'm going to have a baby!

Mary: So? I'm giving birth to God!

Elizabeth: Silence.

This story particularly interests me because I'm the nearest thing you get to a Virgin Mother nowadays. When I was forty-four, I announced to my mother that I was five-months pregnant by an anonymous sperm donor. She was a lot more surprised than Mary's auntie looks in these pictures. Indeed, her horror was so great that she asked the most terrible question a mother can ask a daughter, 'What will the neighbours say?' Not something which had been at the forefront of my mind when I decided to have a baby, I admit. Fortunately, when the neighbours eventually met my daughter, they thought she was wonderful. The queen neighbour, for there is always one, pronounced, 'If this had been available when I was young, I wouldn't have bothered with a man'. And, of course, the moment my mother saw my baby daughter, she loved her completely.

I like to think news of Jesus's impending birth was welcomed in Nazareth. When I was a small child I accepted completely that Joseph didn't mind his wife being impregnated by God. Let's imagine this scene in the family reality-show format:

Mary: You'll never guess who came by today! I'd just put the washing in to soak and who should turn up but the Angel Gabriel?

Joseph: That's nice dear. Bearing any news perchance?

Mary: Yes! I'm going to have a baby! God is the father. And my future son. And, if I understand it right, some sort of dove that hovers above you is also God, and was the one who implanted the seed. Isn't that great?

Joseph: Lucky I'm a carpenter. I can start work on the crib right now.

Dorothy Byrne

On the face of it, the Visitation tells a ridiculous story and the only reason I accepted it as a child was that I had no idea how a woman became pregnant. But I love this beautiful tale about the relationship between an aunt and niece and its depiction is an opportunity for the artist to show tenderness between women.

In the Bible story, the Visitation followed the Annunciation, when the Angel Gabriel had told Mary of her pregnancy through the good offices of the Holy Spirit. At the same time, he (we should say 'they', since angels have no gender; so modern!) had announced to Mary that her elderly aunt Elizabeth was six months' pregnant. Despite the turmoil she must have being undergoing because of her own pregnancy, Mary felt compelled to travel from her home in Nazareth to visit Elizabeth, who lived in the Hebron area. Hebron was about 130 kilometres away, a huge distance at that time. Mary's decision to visit is seen as an early sign of her goodness and compassion. She wanted to help her aunt in the later stages of the older woman's pregnancy and with what might be a very difficult birth.

Joseph is assumed to have travelled with Mary on her potentially perilous journey. Contrary to the impression I was given as a Roman Catholic little girl, the New Testament tells us that he had been tormented by doubts when Mary told him of her pregnancy. The couple were 'espoused' but had not yet had sex. Matthew writes, 'Joseph her husband, being a just man and not willing publicly to expose her, was minded to put her away privately'. Mary must have been distraught. But, luckily, when Joseph went to sleep, an angel appeared to reassure him that it was the Holy Ghost who had done the deed, not a mere mortal, and he was happy.

And so they arrived at Elizabeth's house to be met by her heavily pregnant aunt and her husband Zechariah. The Bible doesn't say how old Elizabeth was but the Mandaean Gospel of John the Baptiser (the Mandaeans were followers of a gnostic religion of the region) gives her age as 88. In Dürer's version (**76**) we see Zechariah on the left. He had earlier been visited by the Angel Gabriel and informed of his wife's pregnancy but refused to believe it, so was struck dumb temporarily as a punishment for his lack of faith. Perhaps this is why he is holding out some form of receptacle; maybe he is asking for forgiveness. He certainly looks miserable.

Zechariah also looks his age, which was 92. But Dürer's Elizabeth looks more like a middle-aged woman. In most paintings, Elizabeth is depicted as merely middle-aged but in the print by Sadeler after Maarten de Vos (**77**) Elizabeth looks very elderly indeed. Elizabeth had suffered greatly because of the fact she was 'barren', the stark word used in Matthew. Luke tells us she was overjoyed to be pregnant because God 'had taken away my disgrace among the people'. Even today, difficulty having a child can be a source of great pain and humiliation. What must it have been like for a woman more than 2,000 years ago?

77.
Jan Sadeler I after Maarten de Vos
The Visitation

From the series *The Youth of Christ*
1582, engraving within an album of prints
18.2 × 12.5 cm (image)
Sheet trimmed within the platemark
The Fitzwilliam Museum, Cambridge
Bequeathed by Richard, 7th Viscount Fitzwilliam, 1816
23.I.2-403

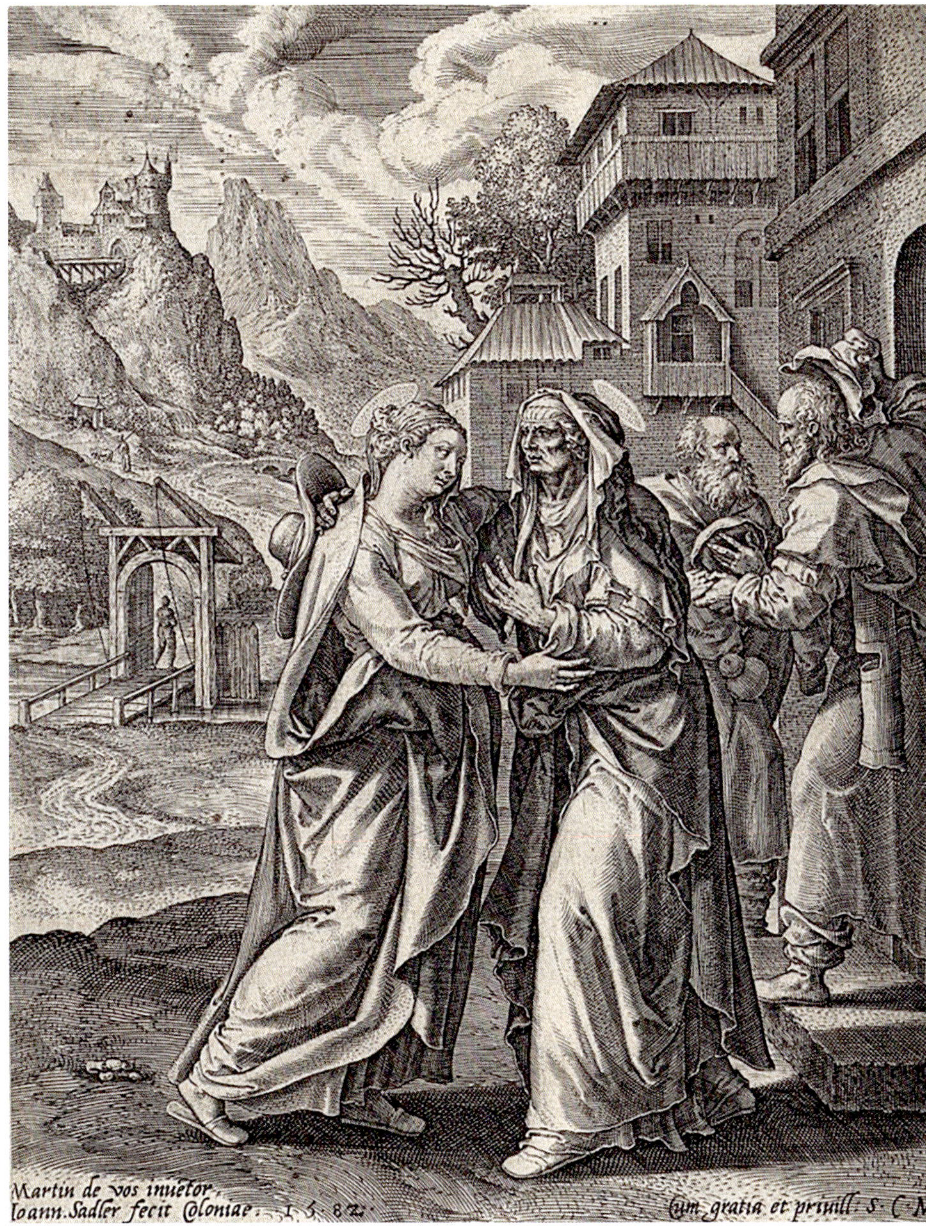

Most people looking at this picture now won't know the back story but in Europe hundreds of years ago it would have been a familiar tale. Elizabeth was in fact pregnant with the prophet John the Baptist, who would later go on to baptise Jesus himself. We are told in the Bible that John leapt for joy in the womb when Mary arrived and his original sin was washed away. Some depictions of this scene show the babies exposed in their mothers' wombs. Elizabeth, too, the moment she laid eyes on Mary, knew the truth and said the words which are now in the prayer called the 'Hail Mary', 'Blessed art thou among women and blessed is the fruit of thy womb.'

Mary's reply is one of the most beautiful canticles in Christianity, the Magnificat.

This is the traditional Roman Catholic version I learned as a child:

> My soul doth magnify the Lord,
> And my spirit hath rejoiced in God my Saviour
> Because He hath regarded the humility of his handmaid: for behold from henceforth all generations shall call me blessed.
> Because He that is mighty hath done great things to me, and holy is His name.
> And His mercy is from generation unto generations to them that fear Him.
> He hath shewed might in His arm: He hath scattered the proud in the conceit of their heart.
> He hath put down the mighty from their seat, and hath exalted the humble.
> He hath filled the hungry with good things, and the rich He hath sent empty away.
> He hath received Israel His servant, being mindful of His mercy.
> As He spoke to our fathers, to Abraham and his seed forever.

A pregnant woman's expression of great joy as she greets a beloved relative celebrating her own miraculous pregnancy. This should be a happy painting. But church worshippers of the past would have known that this story ends in a double tragedy. John will be beheaded when he is only thirty on the orders of the ruler of Galilee Herod Antipas. Three years later, his cousin Jesus will be crucified. The three women on the right in Dürer's depiction are allegedly Mary's sisters, although there is nothing in the Bible to say Mary had three sisters. They are there to remind the viewer of the three women who supposedly joined Mary at the foot of the cross as Christ was crucified and died. There is a terrible poignancy to the scene. Both the unborn babies are doomed.

The Visitation celebrates love between women. Although they are aunt and niece, they remind us of the love between a mother and daughter. Often, Elizabeth is kneeling before Mary because she is carrying the Holy Child. But in both these versions the women are equal. Dürer's Elizabeth seems to be smiling as she grasps Mary firmly. The younger woman bows her head slightly, with the humility often shown by the Virgin in art. Perhaps she is looking down at her womb. Dürer had travelled through the Alps on two journeys a few years before and he places the women in a beautiful Alpine scene.

In Sadeler's version, it is Mary, plump and blooming, who encircles her aunt in an embrace, looking at her with great concern. Elizabeth looks deeply worried and even older than her eighty-eight years. There are heavy clouds in the sky and looming mountains. This is not a happy scene at all. If you asked someone to guess what was going on, they would never think both women had had good news. Joseph and Zechariah appear to be in a state of shock, which is understandable.

So what should a feminist make of this story?

We should be glad the two women are clothed. So many paintings of women show us naked. And if there is more than one woman in a picture, it's often some ghastly gang rape, using a classical story as an excuse for violent pornography. The women are also at the centre of the pictures, which is another tick. But their key role is as baby carriers; the people in this picture who really count are the unseen foetuses.

Catholics are taught that motherhood is a sacred calling. But if it's really good for a woman to be a mother, which means you must have had sex, why did Mary have to be a virgin? The whole story is so negative towards women and indeed many Christians reject the idea she was a virgin and say the word in Hebrew should have been translated as 'young woman'. Some Christians who believe she was a virgin when Christ was born say she and Joseph went on to have normal sexual relations and several children. However, the Roman Catholic Church subscribes to the Doctrine of the Perpetual Virginity of Mary which states that Mary was a virgin before, during and after her pregnancy. So she and Joseph are denied all sexual relations. No wonder he is looking so grim. In paintings, the young Mary always looks peaceful and happy, as though giving up sex didn't bother her at all.

In contrast, the Catholic Church celebrates 'the Heroic Chastity of St Joseph'. Joseph's consolation was to be declared Patron Saint of Virgins. I know, a man being patron saint of virgins just feels weird. I bet you are also wondering what the job entails. Saint Anthony is the Patron Saint of Lost Things so he can help you find your car keys. My own namesake Saint Dorothy is the Patron Saint of Pregnancy and Gardening and therefore doubly useful. I surmise that, for most people reading this, the boat has already sailed on what St Joseph has to offer. Here is his traditional prayer:

> Saint Joseph, father and guardian of virgins, to whose faithful keeping Christ Jesus, innocence itself, and Mary, the virgin of virgins, was entrusted, I pray and beseech you by that twofold and most precious charge, by Jesus and Mary, to save me from all uncleanness, to keep my mind untainted, my heart pure, and my body chaste; and to help me always to serve Jesus and Mary in perfect chastity. Amen.

Of course, until very recent times, neither motherhood nor virginity was a great option for a woman. Not that you had the option of choosing for yourself. If you married, you could end up having a baby every year and it was highly likely either you or they would die, or both would. Or you could be shut up in a convent. I very much admire Catherine of Siena, the fourteenth-century Italian saint. Her mother had 22 children, half of whom died. Catherine's favourite sister perished in childbirth. A lesser girl would have accepted that this was her fate too but, when Catherine reached fifteen, the marrying age, she declared she had married Jesus Christ in a mystical marriage and had a mystical wedding ring made of his foreskin to prove it. She told her family that, as she was already married, she couldn't marry anyone else. Nor could she go into a convent because she was a married woman. Genius. All over Europe women popped up who were mystically married to Jesus.

The virgin thing was big in medieval times. Stories of the virgin martyrs of early Christianity were very popular and uncannily similar to each other. The victim was always from a wealthy family and beautiful. Even then, men were promulgating the myth that women get attacked for their looks. The lovely virgin would catch the eye of the local Roman governor who would ask her to have sex or marry him. When she refused, terrible things happened to her, some pretty similar to pornography of today. She would be thrown into a brothel to be raped but God would save her because you couldn't die as a virgin martyr if you were not a virgin. Obviously. She would be paraded naked through the streets and pelted with awful things. Then she would be boiled, stabbed or otherwise mutilated before finally dying and ascending into heaven.

Catherine of Alexandria was an unusual one. She beat 50 pagan philosophers in argument in defence of her Christianity so was tortured horribly and thrown into prison to starve, but every day a dove flew down from heaven to feed her. The Emperor begged her to marry him but she refused because she was already married to You Know Who. In fury, the Emperor condemned her to death. As lovers of fireworks will know, the Catherine wheel is named after the spiked wheel on which she was tortured before being beheaded. Milk rather than blood flowed from her head.

I loved these stories as a child. We had a huge collection of them in my convent library and they were my equivalent of boys reading adventure stories.

When I was growing up, Mary was obviously Top Woman. We learned that women had two roles: to be a chaste virgin and then to be a mother. And Mary was both at the same time! Beat that! Well, of course you can't. We were told constantly that motherhood was the expectation of us. One teacher, a single woman, told us that babies were up in heaven waiting to be born, like parachutists waiting to jump out of a plane, so it was our duty to have as many as possible. I wish I had been the daring girl who put her hand up and asked, 'In that case, Miss, why don't you have any?'

Funnily enough, my convent was run by The Society of the Holy Child Jesus. Bizarrely, it was founded by a woman, Cornelia Connelly, who took vows of chastity as a nun despite having a living husband and several children. One fell into a vat of boiling sugar and died and another expired of yellow fever. These incidents sounded to me suspiciously like a punishment from God for child neglect, but apparently I was wrong because in 1992 Pope John Paul II proclaimed her as Venerable, just two down from being a saint.

Cornelia is a one-off in the world of nuns. The other nuns in our order were, as far as we knew, virgins but one did run off with the lesbian games teacher. I'm not sure if she counted as a proper virgin after that. If waiting for babies to launch themselves from heaven into our bellies seemed unappealing, being a virgin nun was even less so. We definitely had no desire to join them.

Clearly the subject of sex didn't come up much. In fact, we didn't even discuss periods. When, every now and then, a huge van rolled up and disgorged vast numbers of boxes of Dr White's sanitary towels, we used to giggle because the nuns got embarrassed. When we were about thirteen, we were told in a Religious Education class that French kissing was a mortal sin. A girl burst into tears. We were all jealous. Then when we were about fifteen, we were suddenly taught how rabbits procreate. At the end of the lesson, the nun said hurriedly, 'It's the same for people but with people the Holy Ghost is involved'. The bell went, and she went pink and rushed out of the room. 'That's called troilism,' a girl declared confidently.

The school library had a very good collection of art books but an elderly nun had been through every single one sticking small black rectangles of paper on all the naughty bits, including women's breasts. I thought the breast censorship was particularly pointless as we all had breasts but a girl told me the nuns washed in some strange shift thing so they never looked at themselves. Maybe that was why they smelled. We were told we had to sleep on our backs with our arms crossed over our chests so we were in the right position if the Lord struck us dead in the night. But another girl told me it was so we wouldn't be tempted to touch ourselves.

It was the late 1960s and it felt like everyone else in the world was having amazing sex except me; they must have been because they were always being condemned in *The Daily Telegraph*. I wrote a story about a woman who lost her virginity at the sweet counter in Woolworth's but a sharp-eyed pensioner spotted it and handed it into the police. Unfortunately for the woman, she got her virginity back again. I was desperate to rid myself of my virginity but I was too shy to tell the boy I fancied that I was mad about him. He even tried to ask me out and I jumped on a bus to escape. He wore pink shirts and a silk cravat and I thought he was gorgeous. Most of the other boys had social attitudes that would not have been out of place in ancient Galilee. If you refused to have sex you were a 'lessie' and if you had sex you were a 'prossie'.

Eventually, I managed to free myself at university but only after I had been to the university GP for advice on exactly what happens in sex. I realised my random readings from the copies of *Forum* magazine which my friend occasionally purloined from her brother had provided insufficient information. And so, I said farewell to my virginity.

I taught my daughter Bible stories because you need to know them if you are to understand references in literature and art. But I never mentioned that Mary was a virgin. To this day, I think my daughter's unaware of it. I think I'll hide this catalogue at the back of the bookcase so we can keep it that way.

78.
Richard Billingham
Untitled

RAL 25 (top) and RAL 27 (bottom)
1994, C-type prints mounted on aluminium
50 × 75 cm; 80 × 120 cm
Copyright of the artist,
courtesy of Anthony Reynolds,
London

Richard Billingham's photographs of his parents provide intimate and expressive examples of conflict and joy. These works reflect research findings that warmth and affection, as shown by the artist's parents, are protective against the negative effects of conflict, perhaps explaining why the couple stayed together despite their differences. What matters is not whether couples argue, but the frequency and severity of their arguments, and how quickly and easily they make up.

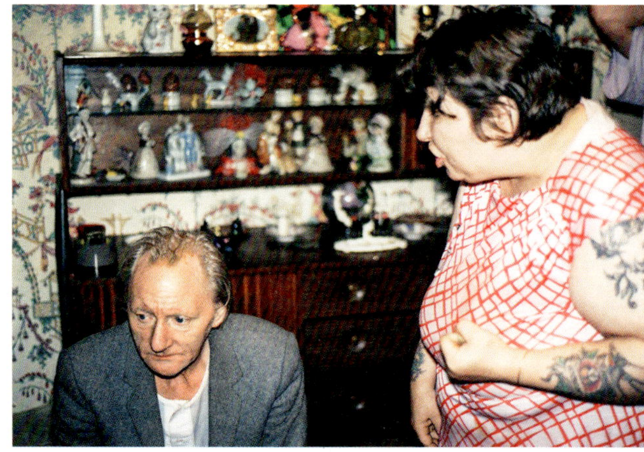

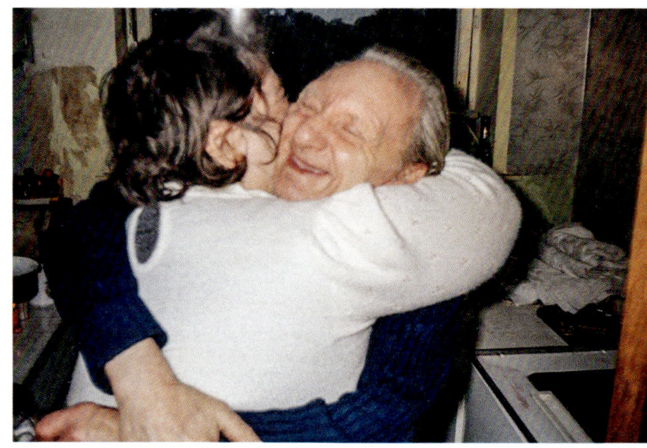

79.
Samira Abbassy
Reincarnated Fears

2017, oil on gesso on birch panel
122 × 91.4 cm
Courtesy of the artist

Reincarnated Fears speaks to the transmission of trauma and anxiety from one generation to the next, with the hidden gun at the mother's head addressing the destructive impact of external and domestic violence. As the Iranian-born artist described it, 'It comes from the geopolitical all the way down into one room where there is a fire'.

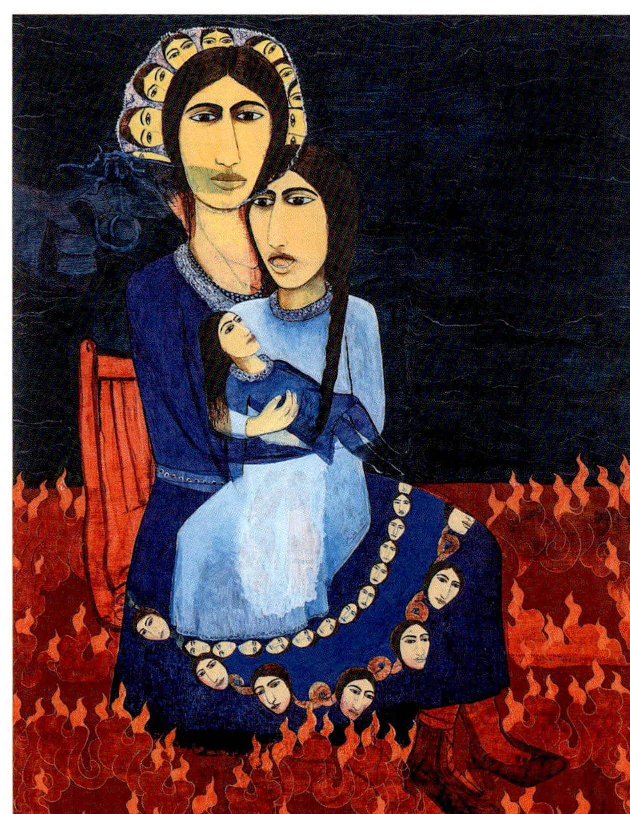

80.
Zoë Buckman
When She Had a Black Eye

2018, embroidery on vintage
linen tea towel
71.1 × 41.9 cm (framed)
Bill and Christy Gautreaux
Collection, Kansas City, Mo.

Buckman embroiders textiles that have a history of use in the home and suggest a connection to the stories of the women who owned them. This work is from a series that examines the universal female experience of violence and loss of power, based on real or imagined encounters, reflecting on the strength and resilience it takes to endure them.

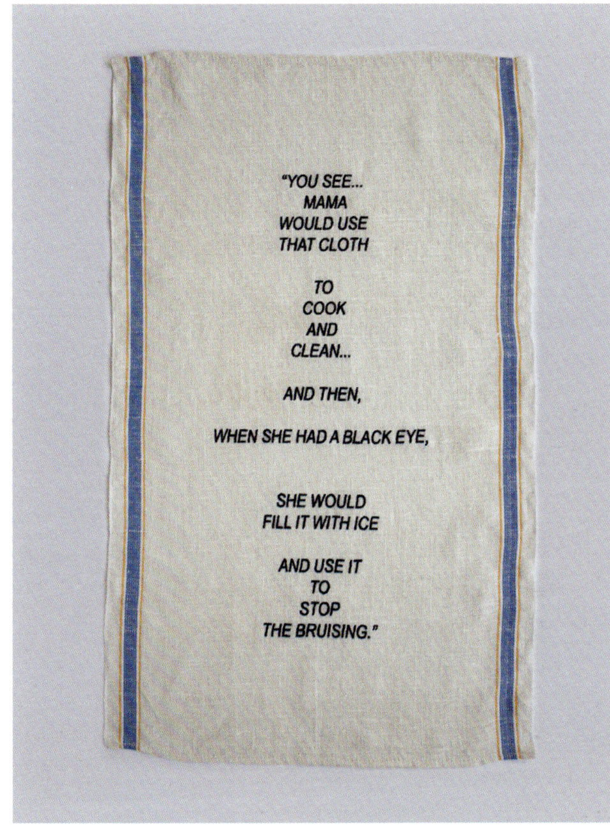

81.
Paula Rego
Split

2017, pastel on paper on aluminium
102 × 67 cm
Anne Wilkening Collection

Paula Rego's works relating to the family are both subversive and insightful. *Split* evokes the dysfunctional alliances that can occur in families, and which can have a damaging effect on family relationships. Here a child appears as an outsider plotting to split the others apart. This drawing was inspired by the French children's book *Sophie's Misfortunes* (*Les Malheurs de Sophie*) written by the comtesse de Ségur in 1858.

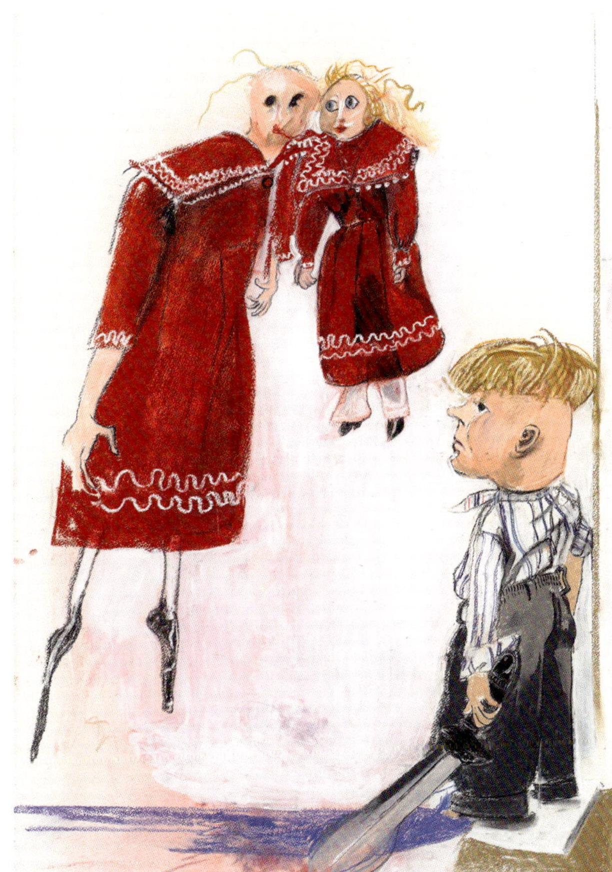

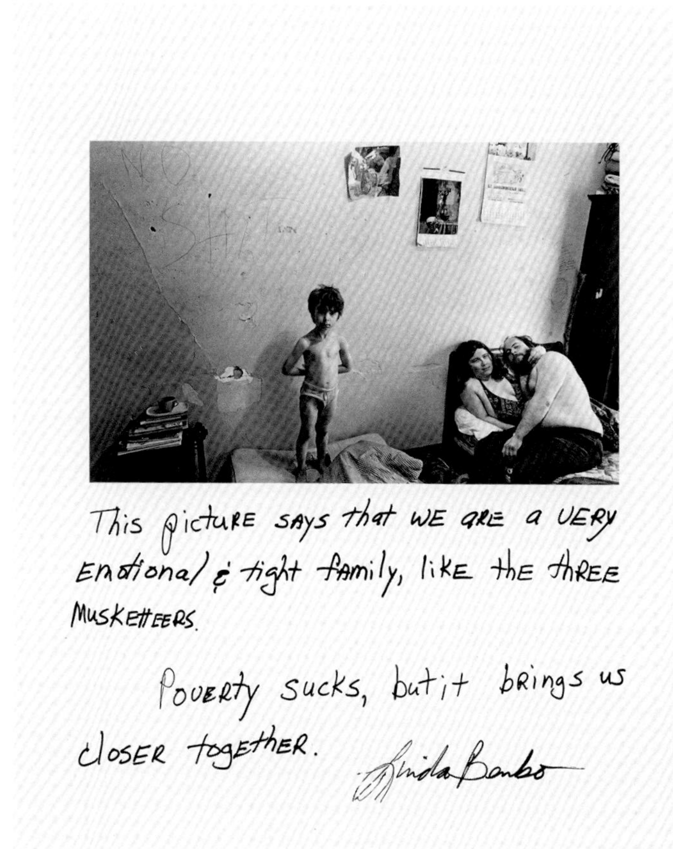

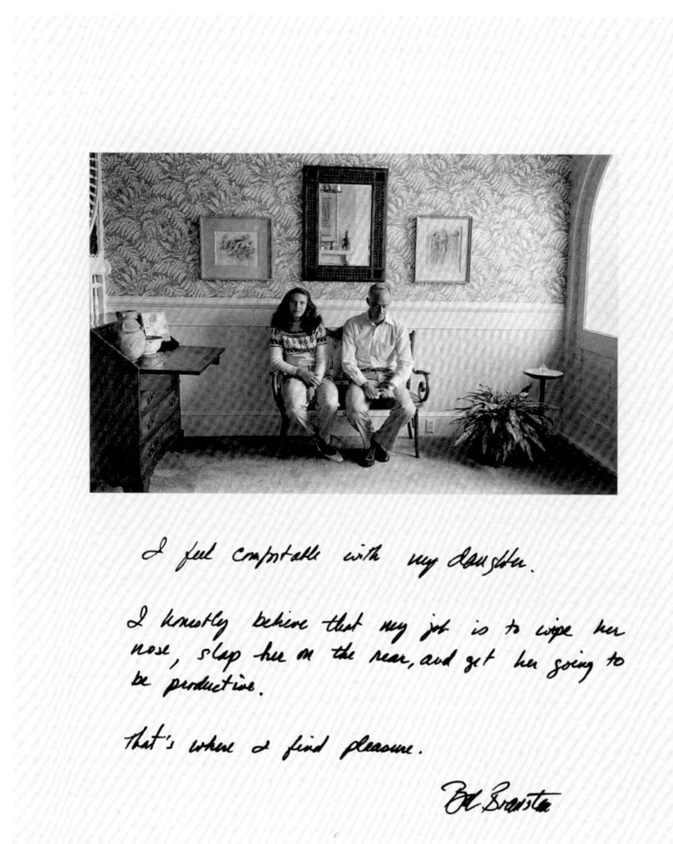

82–85.
Jim Goldberg
Untitled

From the series *Rich and Poor*
'This picture says that we are a very emotional & tight family, like the three musketeers. Poverty sucks, but it brings us closer together. Linda Benko'
1977–85, gelatin silver print
27.9 × 35.6 cm
© Jim Goldberg. Courtesy of the artist

Untitled

From the series *Rich and Poor*
'I feel comfortable with my daughter. I honestly believe that my job is to wipe her nose, slap her on the rear, and get her going to be productive. That's where I find pleasure. R. Bransten'
1977–85, gelatin silver print
27.9 × 35.6 cm
© Jim Goldberg. Courtesy of the artist

The photographs from Jim Goldberg's *Rich and Poor* series speak not only of the devastating impact of social inequality on family life, but also of resilience in the face of adversity. The voices of the families show that close and affectionate bonds can prevail despite economic hardship, and that affluence does not guarantee warm family relationships.

Untitled

From the series *Rich and Poor*
'My family is o.k. I think Im stupid I always do something wrong Lonnie Lynch
Lonnie Me Mom Wayne
This is my Family I love them I like moms dress the Hotel is rotten I want to move Roy'
1977–85, gelatin silver print
27.9 × 35.6 cm
© Jim Goldberg. Courtesy of the artist

Untitled

From the series *Rich and Poor*
'To my discomfort, I am often considered a grand dame. I know how to behave in most circumstances whether with inferiors or superiors, without attracting attention. I was properly brought up. To the manor and manners born. Katherine Cebrian'
1977–85, gelatin silver print
27.9 × 35.6 cm
© Jim Goldberg. Courtesy of the artist

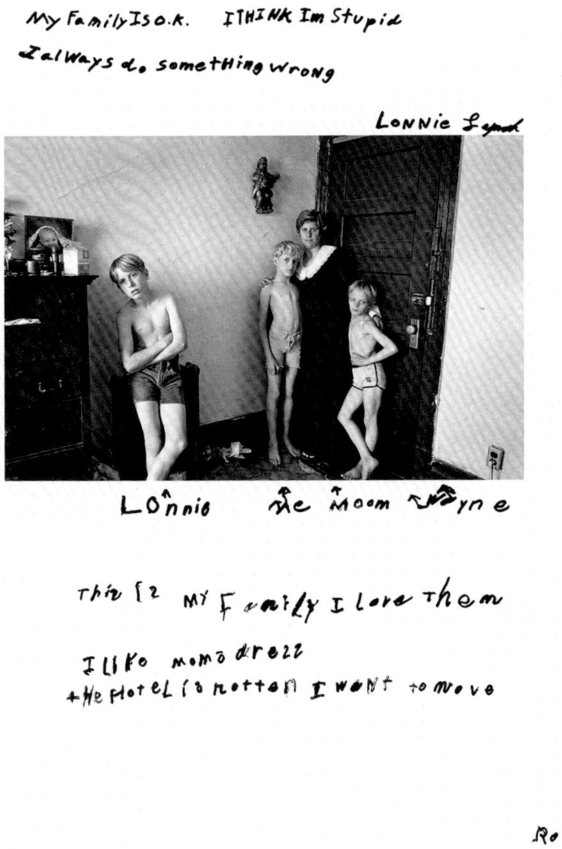

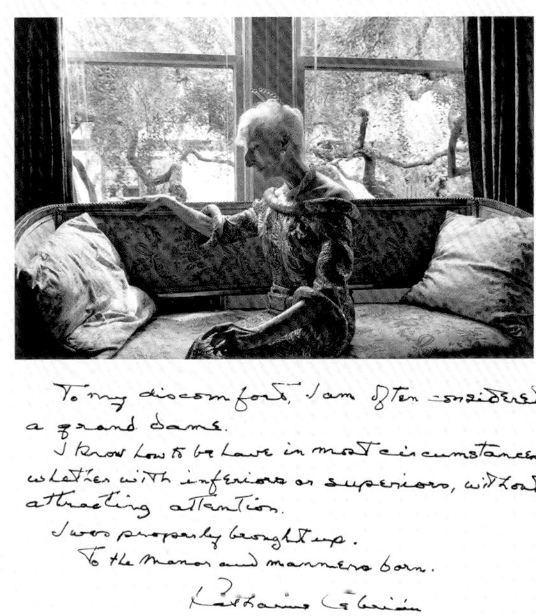

86–87.
Caleb Cole
Stripes

From the series *Odd One Out*
2018, inkjet print made with
Epson's archival ink
61 × 76 cm
Courtesy of the Artist and
Gallery Kayafas

The Big Day

From the series *Odd One Out*
2018, inkjet print made with
Epson's archival ink
61 × 76 cm
Courtesy of the Artist and
Gallery Kayafas

Caleb Cole's works from his *Odd One Out* series express the uncomfortable sense of not belonging in one's family. Sometimes children feel that something is amiss, like the boy in *Stripes*, perhaps because they don't meet parental expectations, or they feel different in some way. Adults who don't fit in, sometimes because of their gender identity or sexuality, may feel under pressure to conform, as depicted in *The Big Day*.

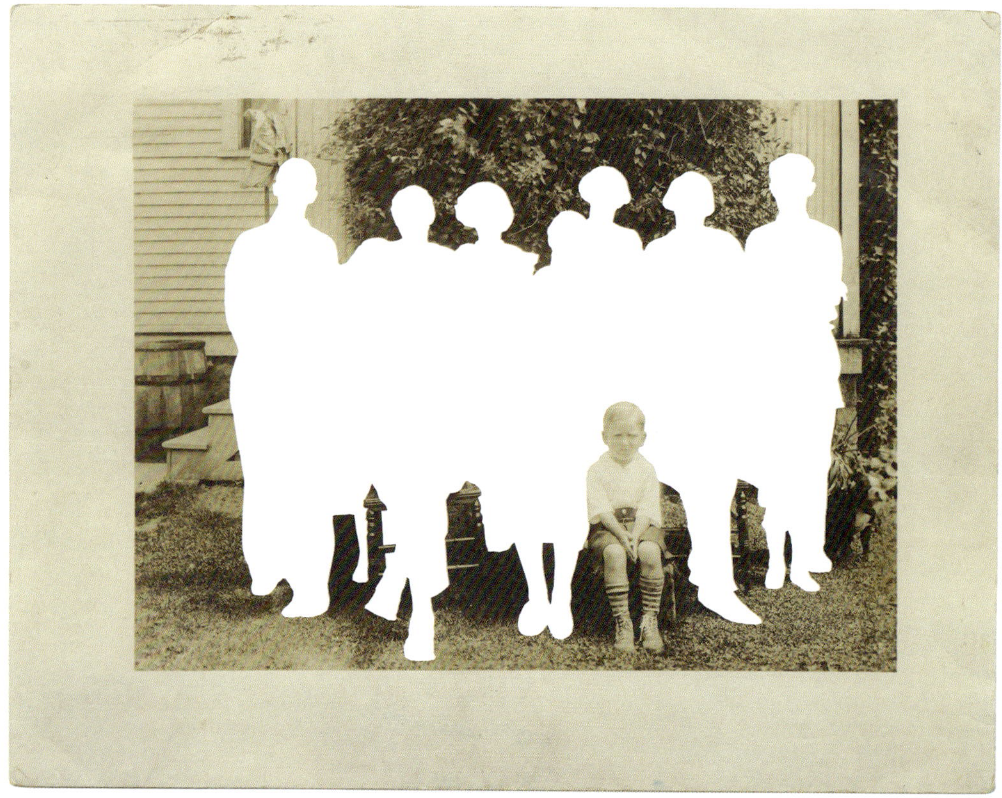

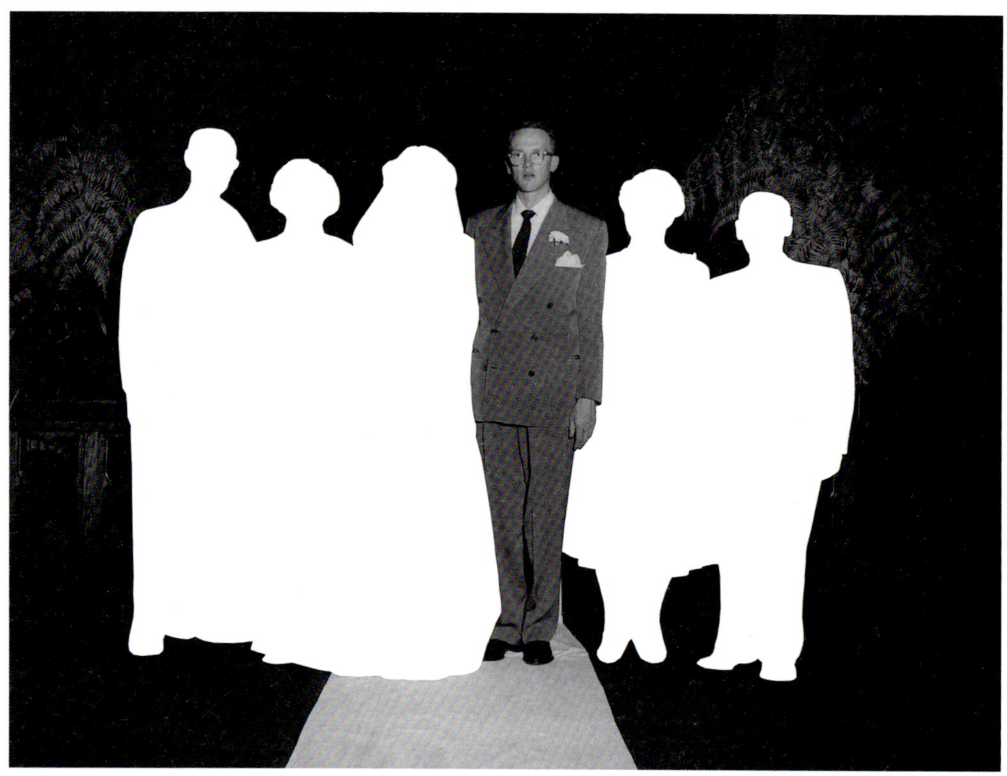

88–90.
Tracey Moffatt
Birth Certificate, 1962

From the series *Scarred for Life*
1994, lithograph on paper
80 × 60 cm
Tate: Purchased 1998
P78101

The Wizard of Oz, 1956

From the series *Scarred for Life*
1994, lithograph on paper
80 × 60 cm
Tate: Purchased 1998
P78100

Useless, 1974

From the series *Scarred for Life*
1994, lithograph on paper
80 × 60 cm
Tate: Purchased 1998
P78105

Tracey Moffatt's *Scarred for Life* series, based on stories told to the artist, speaks of the adverse impact of rejection and trauma on mental health and self-esteem.

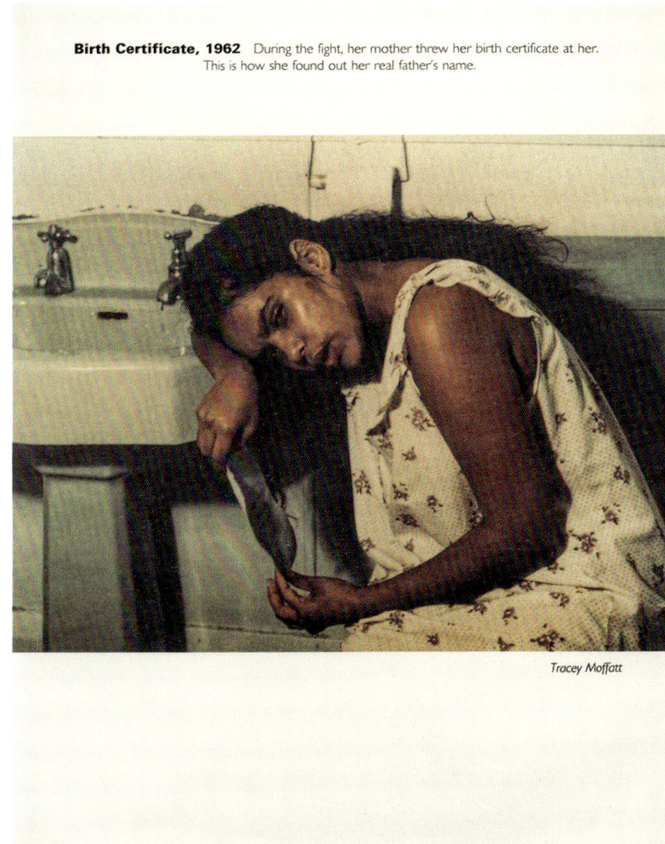

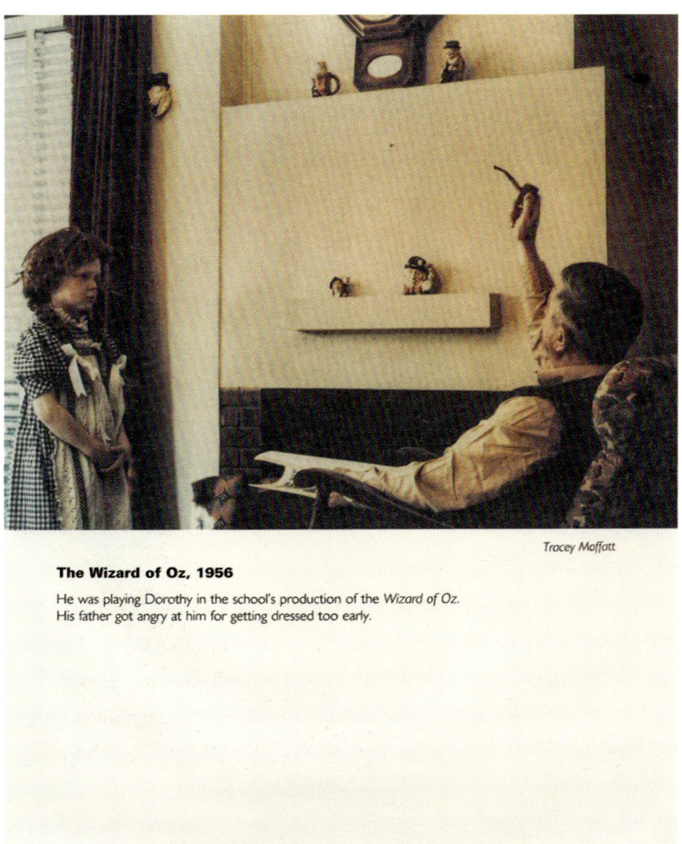

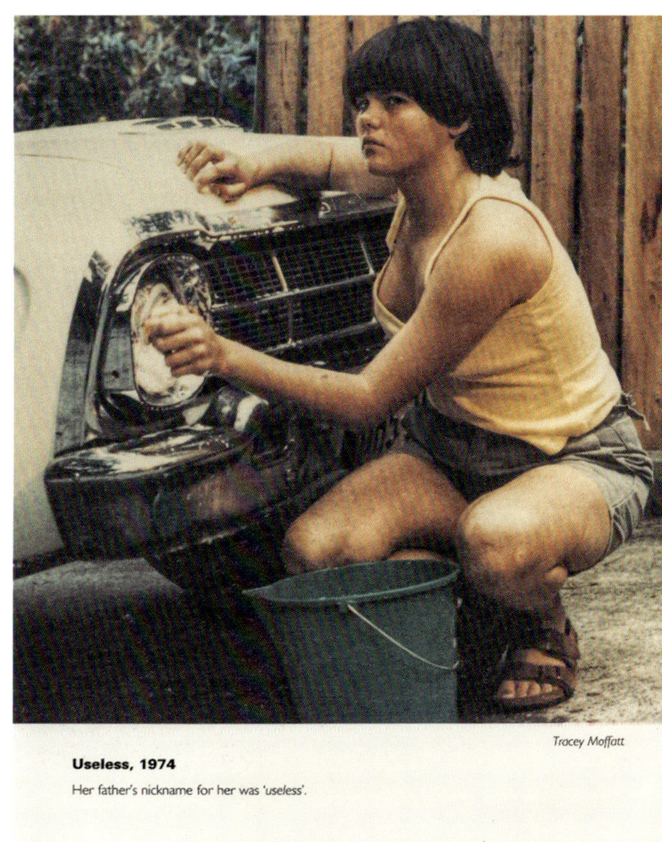

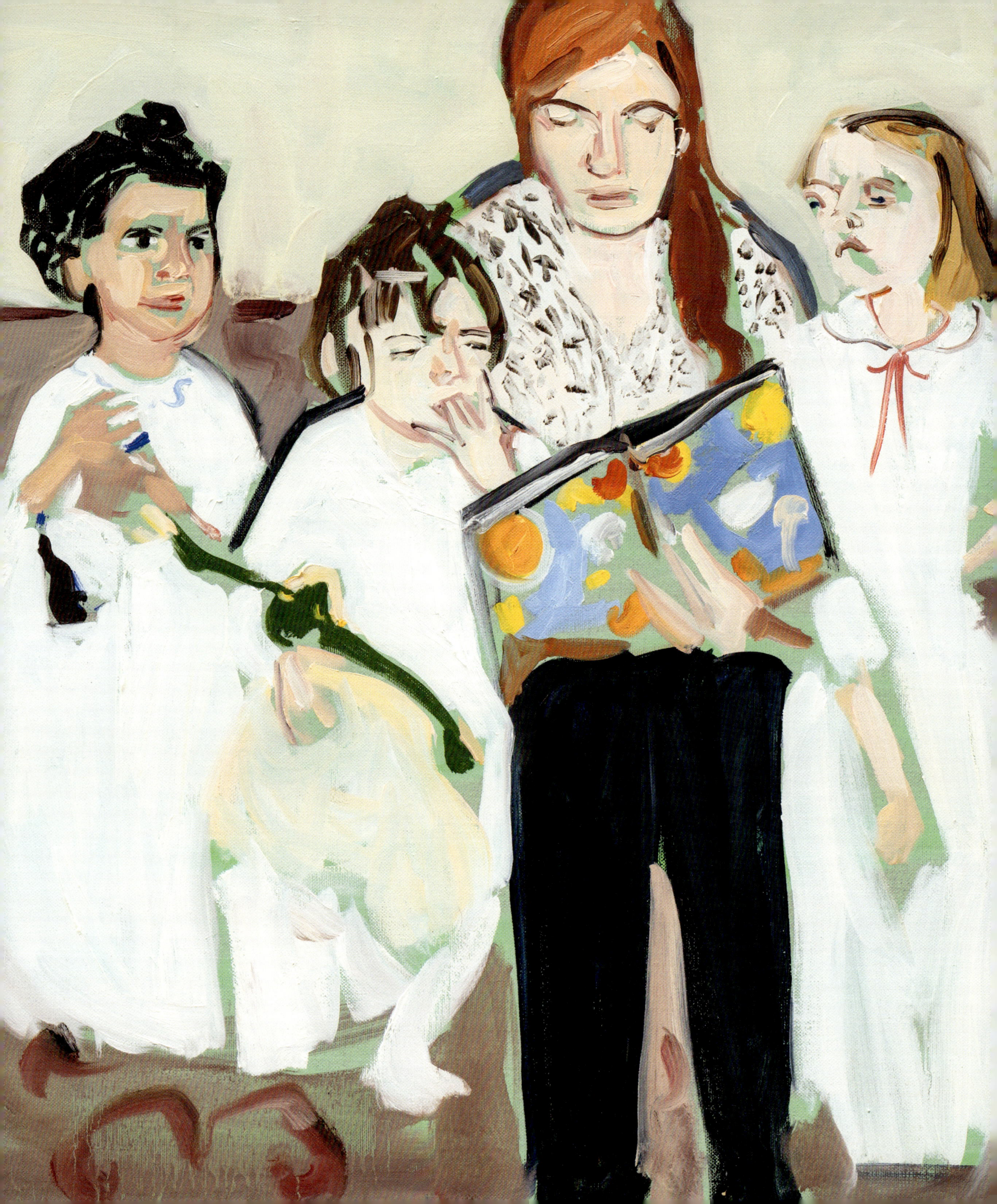

The huge popularity of television shows that explore ancestry, such as *Who Do You Think You Are?*, and the enormous number of people who are signed up to family tree databases, highlight the importance to many of a sense of connection and belonging. Sometimes we uncover family secrets in this way. All it can take is a saliva sample to find out online whether we are genetically related to our parents, and, if not, who our genetic parents are. This section of the exhibition explores the transmission of family from one generation to the next through genetic inheritance, social and cultural practices, language and objects, and how these can forge emotional connections and give rise to family memories.

Family Legacies

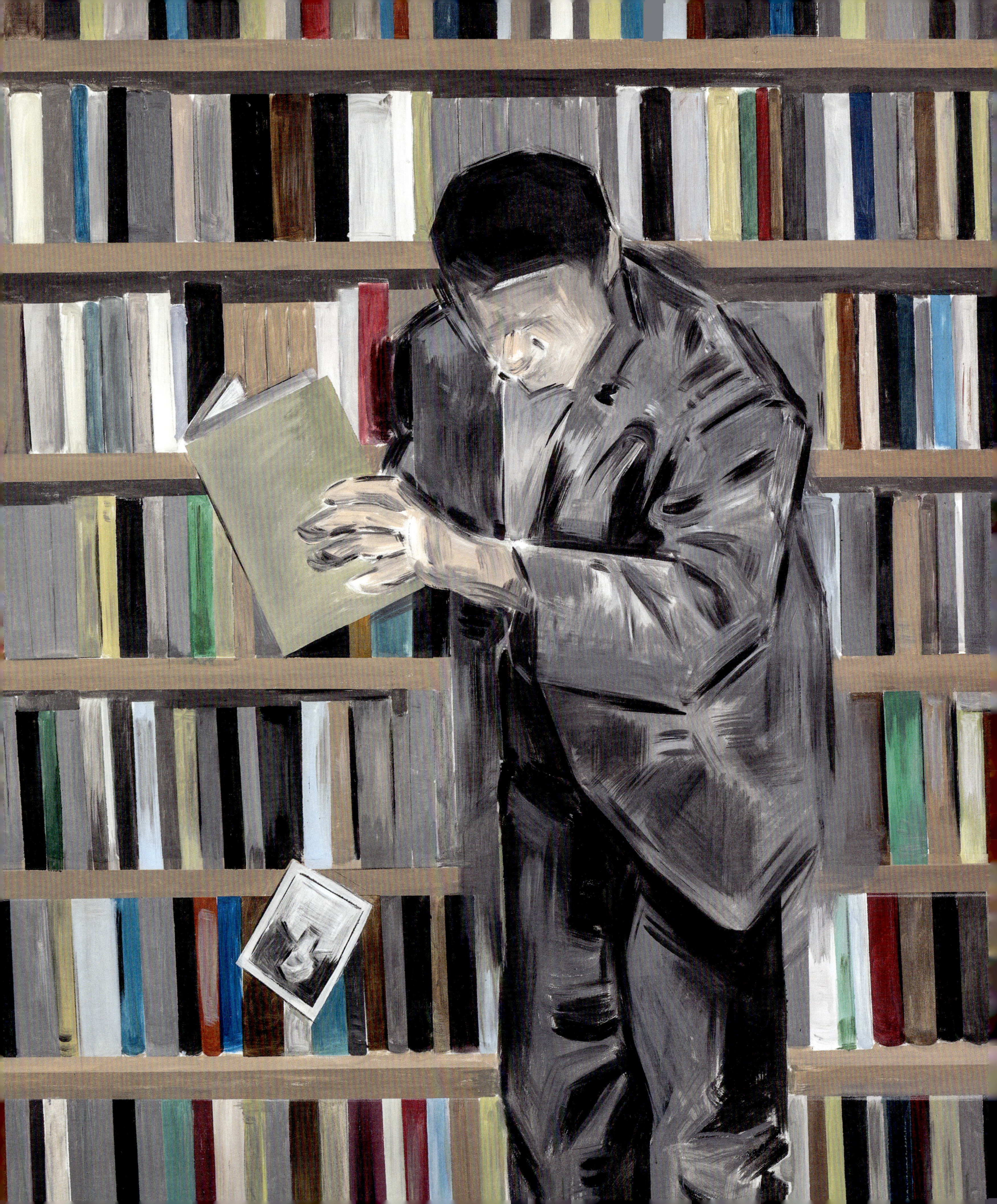

Who You Think You Are

Detail of **96**,
Apostolos Georgiou,
Untitled, 2019

There was a shudder of recognition when I first saw this painting, painted in 2019 by Apostolos Georgiou (**96**). Twenty years ago, the BBC commissioned an idea from me for a new television series. We would take famous Brits on a journey to explore their family tree. Genealogy was shaking off its reputation as an arcane pursuit for history buffs and entering the mainstream. It occurred to me that family history had the capacity not only to provide a window to social history but also to be a great leveller. While I could never aspire to be Stephen Fry or Dame Judi Dench, it was likely that Fry or Dench's parents were not so different from mine, or anyone else's.

The idea was that *Who Do You Think You Are?* – as our series came to be called – would take our celebrities on a magical mystery tour. While the production team would know how the story ended, our protagonists wouldn't. The audience would thus get to share that moment of discovery with them – on camera and in the moment. By the end of Series One we had demonstrated that even people who thought they absolutely knew their roots almost certainly didn't. At least not until we had taken them on a journey full of twists, turns and copious amounts of tears.

So, when I saw Georgiou's man-in-a-crumpled-suit (a familiar figure in his work, it turns out) flick through a book and discover a mysterious photograph between its pages, the painting made perfect sense to me. Or so I thought.

Apostolos Georgiou was born in Thessaloniki in 1952 and studied architecture in Venice and Florence. He likes to work on large canvases – this one is almost six feet square – and he paints his figures with a monumental volume. Their smudgy anonymity recalls some of the work of Francis Bacon. But whilst Bacon worked and reworked his layers of oil in a domineering, impasto manner Georgiou's work is resolutely in acrylic. The palette he prefers is pale, considered, almost translucent, perhaps connected to the light of his native Aegean. Acrylic is a challenging medium for a painter. It dries quickly, leaving little scope for re-working. But it seems to suit Georgiou. He captures the outline of his characters, but little in the way of detail. His work is clearly influenced by photography and cinema. The fleeting nature of his paintings recalls the words from the great photographic artist Henri Cartier-Bresson; 'Within any event there will always be a peak moment, the perfect moment, the decisive moment to press that shutter button'. In the moments when Georgiou chooses to press his shutter button, his grey-clad characters find themselves falling out of windows, draped over mantelpieces, tripping over a brood of chickens or dangling a fish from the window of a car. They seem to be channelling their inner Buster Keaton, or Luis Buñuel.

Alex Graham

Georgiou also acknowledges his debt to abstract painting. Discussing his work, he has said: 'My paintings are stories, but they can be liberated by the fact that when I see something is too much, then I think of an abstract painting which lets [the painting] go loose, lets it be finished in the most simple way, not just following the dogma of the story'.

This is a 'liberated' painting. It's as if Georgiou acknowledges the narrative power of his work but he also sees it as a kind of trap. Story can quickly become dogma. And – for Georgiou at least – that is to be resisted.

With that in mind, let's look at the painting again. I had assumed I recognised this scene. We're in a library, aren't we? Well, maybe. Georgiou is deploying what he has termed the 'logic of abstraction' to keep his options open and to play with our expectations. The spines of the books are blank blocks of random colour. Like the painting itself, the books are 'untitled'. The shelves stretch to all four edges of the painting and beyond. The background could easily be a piece of furniture or abstract art.

Something else struck me when I looked more closely at this painting. This contemporary work depicts a world which is resolutely analogue. No screens; no phones; no clues as to when this scene is set. The more I looked at it, the more it began to resonate in a quite different way.

My love affair with libraries began when I was not quite nine years old. My father had died young, leaving my mother to find a job and bring up my brother and me. We became what were known as latch-key kids. At eight and five, we were deemed too young to go the funeral and so never got the opportunity to grieve. At first, my father's parents were supportive, doing the after-school shift while my mother was at work. But when she fell in love with another man, their grief, still raw from the loss of their son, turned to anger. There was a falling out and I never saw my grandparents again.

I felt angry. But being uncertain at whom I should direct my anger (my grandparents? my mother? my father for having the bad grace to die in the first place?) I chose instead to retreat. I might have chosen delinquency or drugs. Perhaps fortunately, I didn't have the social skills to navigate these exotic worlds. I was extremely tall for my age, a gangly awkward young man and painfully shy. The library became my refuge. I started going there every Saturday morning. Books became my family. Every week, there they were, in the same section, on the same familiar shelves, exactly where I had left them. You couldn't say that about people, as I had discovered to my cost. Even now, I find libraries places of greater safety. And so, I find something comforting about the immersive quality of the books in Georgiou's painting.

But, as we've seen, the books, if indeed that's what they are, are just a backdrop. In front of them, a drama is being acted out. There's surely little doubt where the not-so-still centre of this painting lies. It's the photograph. It's the only moving object in an otherwise static composition. The gaze of the man-in-the-crumpled-suit leads our eyes to it. Georgiou clearly wants it to be our focus. But what does it mean?

I first pitched the idea which became *Who Do You Think You Are?* in 1989. But, back then, nobody was interested. Genealogists were anorak-clad obsessives haunting graveyards in much the same way as trainspotters frequented railway-station platforms. But just a year after my idea failed to sell, a revolution began. In Provo, Utah – just an hour's drive south of Salt Lake City – two young men began selling floppy disks from the back seat of their car. Provo is home to Brigham Young University, whose sponsor is the Church of the Latter-Day Saints and whose student cohort is 98% Mormon. One of the peculiarities of the Mormon Church is that it permits dead ancestors to be posthumously baptised provided living members of the church can prove a connection. The car-boot disks contained genealogical records which could provide that proof and they proved to be incredibly popular. In the years that followed, the internet allowed the young men to find a market way beyond their fellow Mormons. By 1994, their business had become one of the 500 fastest growing companies in the US. In 1997, they launched a website which they called Ancestry.com.

Suddenly, it became possible to research one's ancestry from the comfort of one's own kitchen table. By the early 2000s, genealogy had shaken off its nerdy origins and was entering the mainstream. The BBC woke up to its potential and, fourteen years after I had first pitched it, finally commissioned my idea. In 2007, the series launched in the US with Ancestry as the major sponsor. Now, sixteen years later, driven by the power of network television, Ancestry.com is the largest genealogical website in the world, with a database in the region of 30 billion records and counting. The company was recently valued at around five billion dollars.

But there's the paradox at the heart of this story, captured brilliantly in Georgiou's painting. Digital technology has made genealogy accessible to millions. But the emotional power of family history remains resolutely analogue. The dopamine rush can't be found sitting at your laptop. It's the thrill of finding that crucial letter, signature or photograph.

Some genealogists remain trainspotters at heart, ticking off ancestors and filling in the infinite jigsaw that is their family tree. But most – at least in my experience – want more than that. They are amateur detectives. They want to put flesh on the bones of the census records and certificates. They are looking for evidence which might prove or disprove stories that have been passed down through the generations or which might reveal secrets which have been kept from them.

Our very first *Who Do You Think You Are?* protagonist was former Goodie and Springwatch presenter Bill Oddie. Bill was very specific about why he wanted to make the programme. His mother had been strangely absent from much of his childhood, hospitalised with a mysterious illness. Much later in life, when he himself confronted depression, he began to wonder whether his mother's affliction might have been mental rather than physical. Our researchers helped Bill access his mother's medical records, which not only proved Bill's hunch to be true but uncovered a tragic tale of the older sister he had never known. She died in her cot when just five days old and the subsequent grief and guilt which his mother felt overwhelmed her. She never properly recovered. She spent years in and out of psychiatric hospitals, and Bill was never told.

My experience as creator and original producer of the show, now in its eighteenth season, has revealed that secrets and lies run through the lives of the rich and famous as much as they do the lives of anyone. Sometimes people keep secrets to protect the people they love. Sometimes they tell lies, for the same reason.

Comedian Griff Rhys Jones came to us with a tale of high drama. His grandmother Louisa, or so he had been told, was orphaned when her parents were killed in a train crash. We set off to investigate but within a few weeks it was obvious the incident never happened. Louisa's father Daniel (Griff's great-grandfather) had indeed been a train driver, and he had been killed when she was a girl. However, not in a train crash, but in a street brawl in Llanelli. To make matters worse, the jury decided that Daniel had started the fight and acquitted the man accused of his murder, on the grounds of self-defence. Louisa's mother – unable to cope alone – farmed her children out. We'll never know who invented the story of the train crash, but it's clear the myth was constructed to protect the children. Anyone could have tracked down Daniel's death certificate, which would have revealed the truth, but it was in nobody's interest to do so.

This year the scientific journal *Current Biology* published a remarkable paper – the result of a collaboration by more than thirty scientists from more than twenty institutions spread across Europe, Australia and the USA – which set out to analyse the DNA from the hair of Ludwig Van Beethoven. They tracked down eight locks of the great composer's hair and subjected them to genomic analysis. The object was to throw light on Beethoven's health and try to explain the deafness which plagued him for much of his life. But the researchers got more than they bargained for. First, the most celebrated lock of hair – believed to have been clipped by Frederick Hillier, a fifteen-year-old acolyte of the celebrated composer, which had been the subject of a book and a television documentary – turned out not to be Beethoven's at all. Instead, it belonged to an Ashkenazi Jewish woman. No-one knows exactly how this deception happened, but one explanation is that the original lock had been lost or destroyed, and, rather than admit the calamity, Hillier had decided to replace it with a lock of his daughter-in-law's hair.

Not everyone, however, has a secret to uncover or a lie to be exposed. Sometimes people are simply looking for a connection. My mother was fond of speculating that we were descended from James Graham, the 1st Marquess of Montrose, the legendary seventeenth-century Scottish aristocrat who was painted by Van Dyck, immortalised by Walter Scott and eventually hanged, drawn and quartered by order of the Scottish Parliament. Given the slightest encouragement, she would produce a photograph of a distant great-aunt and invite people to comment on her resemblance to the Marquess. She was convinced that somewhere there was a snuffbox which, if found, would prove our right to inherit the marquessate. If only she were around today, to harness the awesome power of Ancestry.com.

I have come to believe this desire for affinity is closely allied to a crisis in identity. It's not an accident that we ended up calling our show 'Who Do You Think You Are?'. One of the things which took me by surprise while making the show was the powerful emotional connection people feel to sometimes very distant ancestors. Jeremy Paxman captured this very well when he discovered his great-grandparents died of tuberculosis 'and exhaustion', a revelation which famously reduced the hard-bitten scourge of politicians to tears on screen. Reflecting on this moment, he went on to say: 'I don't know these people. I mean, I wouldn't know them if I fell over them in the street. Thousands, hundreds of thousands of people must have lived like this and died like this. And yet, I'm connected to them. It's that possessive thing – my great-grandparents.'

'That possessive thing' becomes more important as the old collective forms of identity melt away. In the absence of guilds, trade unions and churches, we need new ways of making sense of ourselves and our place in the world. Family history gives us the tools to do that. It provides a worm's-eye view of the world. It is history lived not objectively, but subjectively. Genealogy isn't about looking at history. It's about being part of that history. And for many, that is comforting.

Identity played a large part in persuading Paxman to take part in our show in the first place. He was a reluctant protagonist, equally suspicious of genealogy ('I've always believed you should life your life forward, not backwards') and popular television ('Most of what you see on television these days is rubbish'). After we had endured several months of negotiations with his agent, Paxman was presenting 'Newsnight' one night and became embroiled in an argument with Tony Blair's health secretary, John Reid. Paxman accused the pugnacious Reid of being Labour's 'attack dog'. Reid counter-punched, accusing Paxman of patronising his Glaswegian accent, and went on to taunt Paxman as a soft, Southern public schoolboy.

On screen, Jeremy was as combative as ever. But the following day, talking to us, he seemed shaken. The encounter had made him think more deeply about his roots. He said he had decided to do the show and was looking forward to the seeing the research. He signed off with a jokey aside: 'Of course, what would be really interesting is if I turned out to have roots that were

Glaswegian and working class'. We laughed. Little did we know at that point that one side of his family indeed came from the slums of Glasgow.

For so many of our protagonists on *Who Do You Think You Are?* their journey into their family history is a cathartic one but also revealing and closely entwined with their identity.

Sue Johnston, the much-loved star of *Brookside* and *The Royle Family*, captures this perhaps better than anyone: 'It's really strange because you know these conditions existed and you've studied history, but it really is extraordinary when it's your family. It doesn't just bring history to life, it personalises it. It makes it very real. It's almost like you feel that as your history is revealed, you think that makes sense, that's where I've come from, that's why I react to things the way I do, that's my history. Do you know what I mean? It's me, this route. It's all about what's handed down; what comes through not just genetically but – I don't know, it maybe sounds crass – but I feel that, because I'm a socialist and because I've always cared about the injustice of the working-class, and always had a love of Scotland, [that] maybe that's what my past is revealing.'

So perhaps that's what the photograph means. I'd assumed it was a relative or an ancestor that the man-in-the-crumpled-suit was searching for. But perhaps it's something closer to home. Maybe it's himself he's found between the pages of the book.

And yet ... I wonder if Georgiou's story painting has one final twist. Let's take one last look at it. At first, I assumed the face of the-man-in-the-crumpled-suit was just another smudge, like the faces of so many of Georgiou's characters. But, on closer inspection, this smudge has a very definite shape to it. It is, unless I'm very much mistaken, the shape of an open book, a deliberate reflection of the shape of the book our protagonist is holding. Again, my first thought was that that was just the artist's little joke, the sliver of surrealism which seems to lurk in so many of his paintings. But I think there's more to it than that.

While writing this essay, I have been spending some time with my brother in Glasgow. Partly inspired by our show, he has started digging into our family. Sadly, so far at least, there is no evidence of that snuffbox, but we have found our own share of secrets and lies within our recent family history.

When my father's parents cut off ties with my mother, she was devastated, not least because she was already the product of a fractured family. Her own father had walked out on her mother and her when she was just fourteen and she never saw him again. She would tell the story that, some twenty years after her father disappeared, two policemen turned up at her mother's door. My mother's father had been found dead in a boarding house in Blackpool, with their address on a slip of paper in his jacket pocket. Guided by this piece of paper, the police had tracked them down and they now wanted to know if his long-estranged wife and daughter would take care of the funeral arrangements. My mum enjoyed telling us how her mother had sent them packing with some choice words.

Well, that was her story. But what my brother uncovered was that this missing man, our grandfather, did indeed die in Blackpool but he wasn't found by the police. He died in hospital, of pneumonia, and what's more, he died six months after the death of his estranged wife, our grandmother. The conversation with the police on the doorstep simply could not have happened. The whole scene had been invented by our mum.

But why? Perhaps she needed to close off the story of her own father's disappearance to her two curious sons. Maybe the story of him carrying his grandmother's address was consoling as it seemed to prove that they had not been forgotten. And maybe their refusal to pay for his funeral was just a bit of wishful thinking on her part – a fantasy of what she would have liked to have said.

So, ultimately, Georgiou's painting is about the photograph and about the books. He's saying that, in discovering our family history, we are discovering ourselves. But he's also saying that our identity is not simply constructed of names, and dates and places, but of stories. Ultimately, we're the stories we tell about ourselves – some true, some outright fiction. It doesn't really matter whether they are true or not. What matters is that they make sense of who we think we are.

Yet, even as I write this, I fear I am descending into dogma and that A.G. (that's him, not me, by the way) would not approve. Let's just say this is one reading among many of Georgiou's fleeting, witty and translucent painting. You will no doubt have your own. Let's invoke the painter's 'logic of abstraction' and liberate this essay from the 'dogma of the story'.

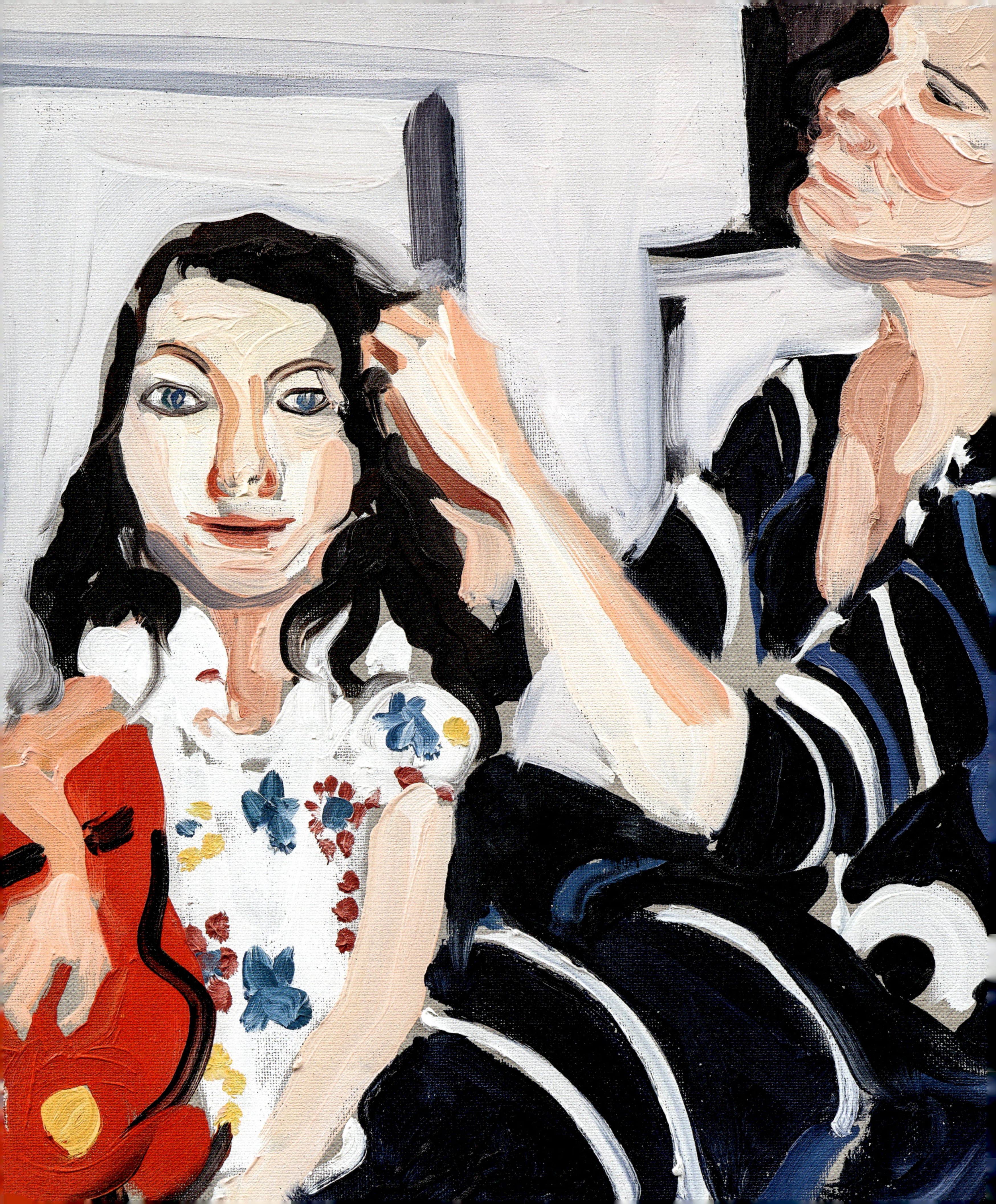

There Will Be Blood

Detail of **94**, Chantal Joffe, *Self-portrait combing Esme's hair*, 2009

I've been reading Ivy Compton-Burnett. Strange novels from the 1930s, set fifty years earlier, almost entirely composed of dialogue. Often you don't even know who's talking, or you think you've grasped who's in the room and then realise someone else must have slipped in unseen, which means they potentially overheard a skin-scraping sentence. The most shocking things keep happening. A nephew/foster son impregnates his uncle/foster father's much younger wife and then marries his daughter from a previous marriage, who later pays a servant to murder the child. Now I'm making it sound like melodrama but what's really shocking is the ordinary things they say to each other, the polite weaponry of people confined hierarchically in a household, the words designed to dismantle a psyche, to detonate on impact and spatter the walls. Family as blood sport, though the first time I typed that I wrote *blood support*.

While I was talking to Chantal Joffe about her family paintings, she detoured into an anecdote about a stint the Joffes spent in Yugoslavia in 1982, when she was eleven. Her father Justin, a Jewish academic, had won a Fulbright award to spend a research year working in the psychology department at Zagreb University. Her mother Daryll (**91**) was keen for the four children to immerse themselves in local culture, but Chantal and her sister Nat spent most of the year obsessively embroiled in a game they'd invented. They made paper dolls modelled on two sets of neighbours back home in America, the Lipkes and the Spaffords. They gave the dolls enormous paper houses, laid out like blueprints across the bedroom floor, and provided them with elaborate outfits and meals.

The point of the game, its deep and compulsive pleasure, was the exactness of reproduction. The devilish fun was in the details. One of them would decide to make a patchwork quilt for the parental Lipke bed; another would hit on the idea of the dolls having roller skates. They were both good at drawing. Nat was particularly skilled at making very exact renditions of outfits: white Oxford button-down shirts, khaki trousers, jumpsuits, denim skirts. It was an orgy of nostalgia – for American suburbia, for lost connections – and also an enjoyably transgressive way of entertaining adulthood, trying it on for size, sampling its moves. By the end of the summer, the dolls were having affairs. The men acquired paper penises, which could be removed when prying adults came into the room.

Daryll had told the children about the Brontë sisters and Gondal, the imaginary world they invented, but the fun of playing Lipkes and Spaffords was that they were chasing down reality, not escaping it. They were

Olivia Laing

91.
Chantal Joffe
Beach Hut
2018, oil on board
41 × 51 cm
Private collection

somewhere else and wanted to go home, not stuck at home and longing for adventure, though their uncertainty about how well they actually fitted into the adorable suburb of Burlington, Vermont, also drove their obsessive concern with what people wore and ate and said. The nostalgia encoded in dinner at a Howard Johnson or a pair of Calvin Klein jeans was both about wanting to go home to a specific place and, more trickily, wondering how to be at home when you got there.

Neither of Chantal's parents were American. Both grew up in South Africa. They met at university and left the country for England after Daryll was arrested protesting apartheid. For the next two decades they had the peripatetic life of the academic family, moving from London to Birmingham,

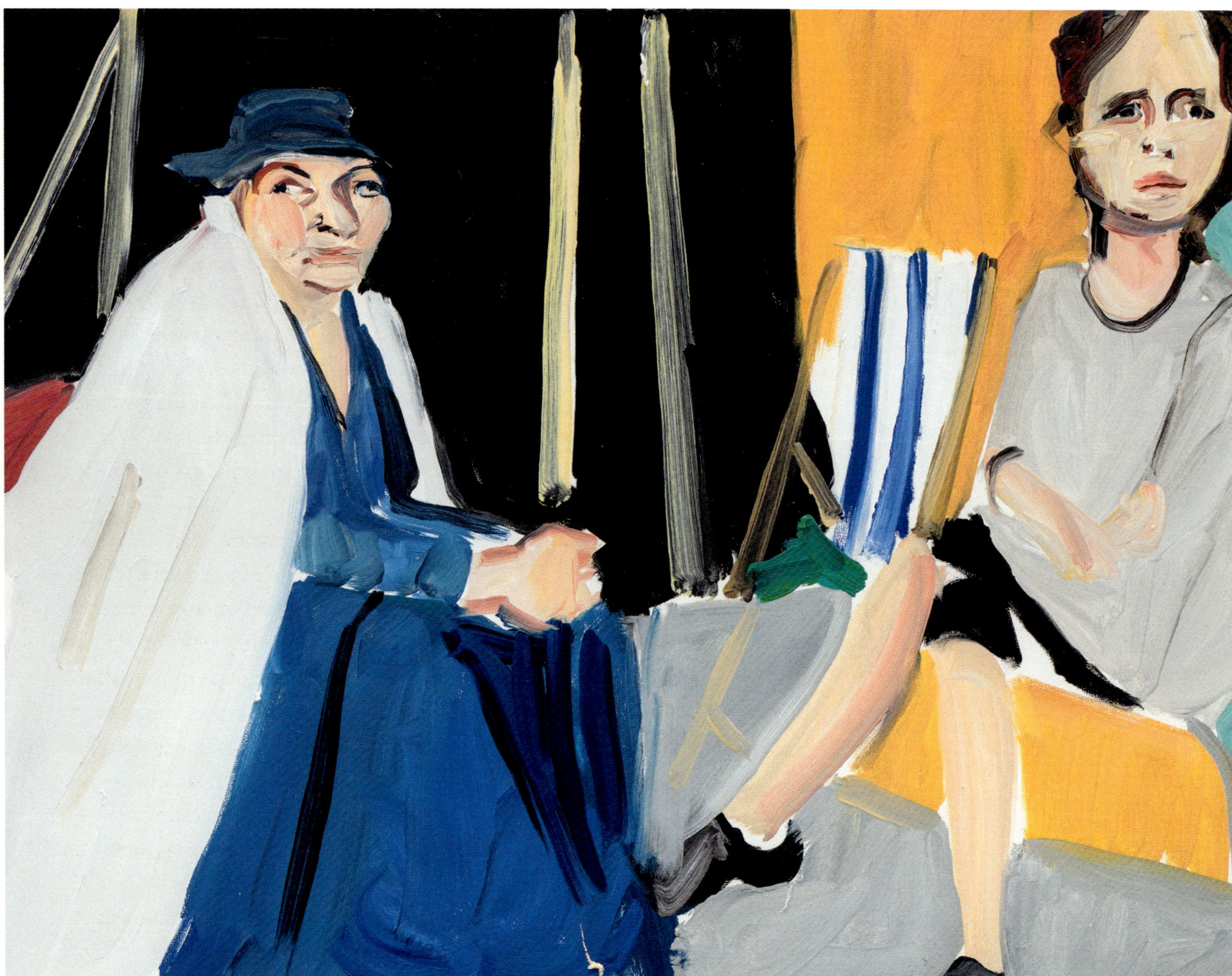

where Emily was born, then to Palo Alto in California, birthplace of Nat, followed by Burlington, birthplace of Chantal and her younger brother Jasper. The dolls at once encapsulated and dispersed anxieties about belonging – the immigrant's or outsider's need to observe and mimic local customs precisely, the child's fascination with how other families operate and function. 'Some of them,' Chantal added, 'caught the essence of the person and some didn't. It taught me a lot.'

This is a great origin story for a painter of family: head-down with scissors and glue, pasting a new face with a new expression on to a cardboard doll. It's easy to see it as a juvenile entry point, an antechamber to the adult domain of the artist. There's the high of getting it right, making something that really did reduplicate the original's talismanic power, like the pink ruffled peasant blouse that one of the Lipke daughters described in a letter and which Chantal created, right down to the monogrammed L embroidered on the pocket. This paper blouse is one of the only remnants of the dolls' existence to have survived into the present day, by the way, pasted into a childhood diary alongside a sticker that said *Smurfy*.

Even the game's residual excitements were the same as in adulthood: a thick plenitude of material, i.e. lots of felt-tip pens and crayons with their delectable/frustrating specificity of shades, training wheels for the oils of the grown-up painter. You could destroy things that didn't work out or try them again. You could loll about in old memories like an inflatable pool on a summer lawn, or else snip them up into new formations and make something else altogether. The Lipkes are getting a divorce! Mr Lipke has to live in a tent in the garden! I want to add at this stage that very few of Chantal's family paintings are ever made from life. They're nearly all recreations of photographs, which is to say also engaged in a reclamation project with things that are definitively no longer happening and people as they were days or years earlier.

In one sense, the word 'family' is a matter of descendants and heirs, though not all of us have both, and they aren't necessarily present at the same time. In another sense (and I'm speaking as the kid of a gay family myself) family is a matter of deliberate associations: liking or love or need set above blood. Chosen family, that fist-pumping aspiration for undermining the bad spell, the unlucky fate of reproduction. Nurture doesn't necessarily follow genetic lines and inheritance is not the same thing as provision.

But looking at Chantal's paintings of her mother and her daughter Esme in particular is a bit like looking at Russian dolls, all these people popping out of each other. It might not be the intention of any individual picture, but the accumulated effect is blatantly strung up with time. Little girls in red sandals become mothers, mothers go grey and lose their sight, the wobbly amphibious version of Esme as a toddler in nappies reappears lissom and wary as a fox in her red prom dress.

92.
Chantal Joffe
Esme on the Sofa 1

2022, oil on board
61.4 × 45.8 cm
Courtesy the artist
and Victoria Miro

Looked at through a Lipke lens, the *thisness* of fabric emerges in a way I'd never quite noticed before. Instead of being simply what someone has on, a suffused source of pattern or colour, fabric becomes a gateway to memory, a portal. It's not a green hoodie, it's the green hoodie that Es was wearing in 2022 (**92**), a transitional year between lockdown and life, when everyone was emerging wild-eyed from the isolation chamber of the pandemic. She looks literally like a chrysalis in it, top half still caterpillar green, the rest of her body pupating, wrapped very tightly in the snaggly weave of a throw. Mother as stalker, just ever so slightly, the voracious gaze on the girl who's getting away simply by living inside time, riding its wave. Nothing you can do to freeze this frame except paint it, though inevitably the face is out of date before it's even dry. Lipke situation all over again.

Our conversation about the dolls was rapidly invaded by a connected conversation about *Spare*, Prince Harry's detailed accounting of all the familial injustices he'd suffered, some major and some absurdly small, which Chantal had been insisting for weeks that I read. Harry's brother pushed him in a fight and he fell over and broke the dog bowl. Harry's brother had a bigger bedroom, with a bigger, nicer bed. Harry hadn't cheated on his A-level coursework. Harry's aunt had once given him a Biro for Christmas. The pettiness of these complaints, the way they still smarted, was very close in atmosphere to Ivy Compton-Burnett. You can't talk to me about hormones, we don't know each other well enough, says one duchess to another. It's every family, Chantal texts. All that pawing over old slights.

One of the things that made the book feel sad was that it was so heavily, hopelessly invested in a child's version of truth. It hadn't been able to separate experience from fact. Harry, also known as Harold, Hazza, Spike, was completely sure that if he could only get his witness statement down straight the judge and jury would be convinced. The idea that other people might have competing perspectives that were equally true seemed not to have occurred to him. Willy pushed me. Harold pushed me first. Only one version could be correct. The book offered up an uncomfortably cartoonish version of the artist as plaintiff – permanently speaking in their own defence, trying to get the last word on the true configuration of the family.

That's not the only available approach, of course. It's also possible to come to the past in the spirit of witness to a mystery, intent on analysing its constituent parts without necessarily having a dominating agenda that must be proved right. I do think that's the main spirit of Chantal's family paintings, even if she might spot the odd Harryish tendency to control the narrative or reshape the story. Curiosity and tenderness are the uppermost moods, for all that other less palatable desires might squirm away underneath.

I'm looking now at *Me, Em and Nat* (**93**), a painting from 2019 of a scene from the early 1970s. All three Joffe girls are piled on to a striped couch, sitting on the laps of their father, the figure on the right, and their

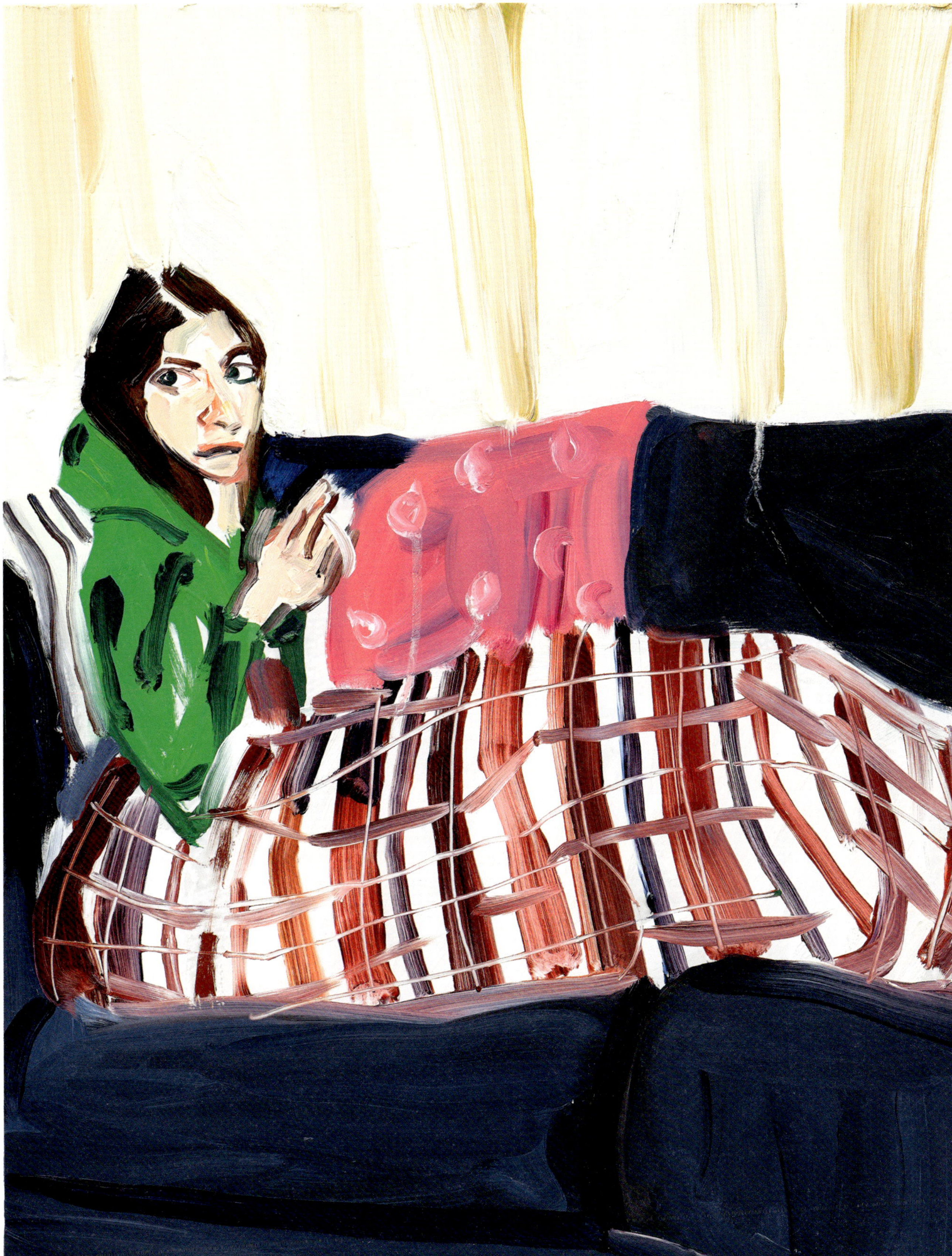

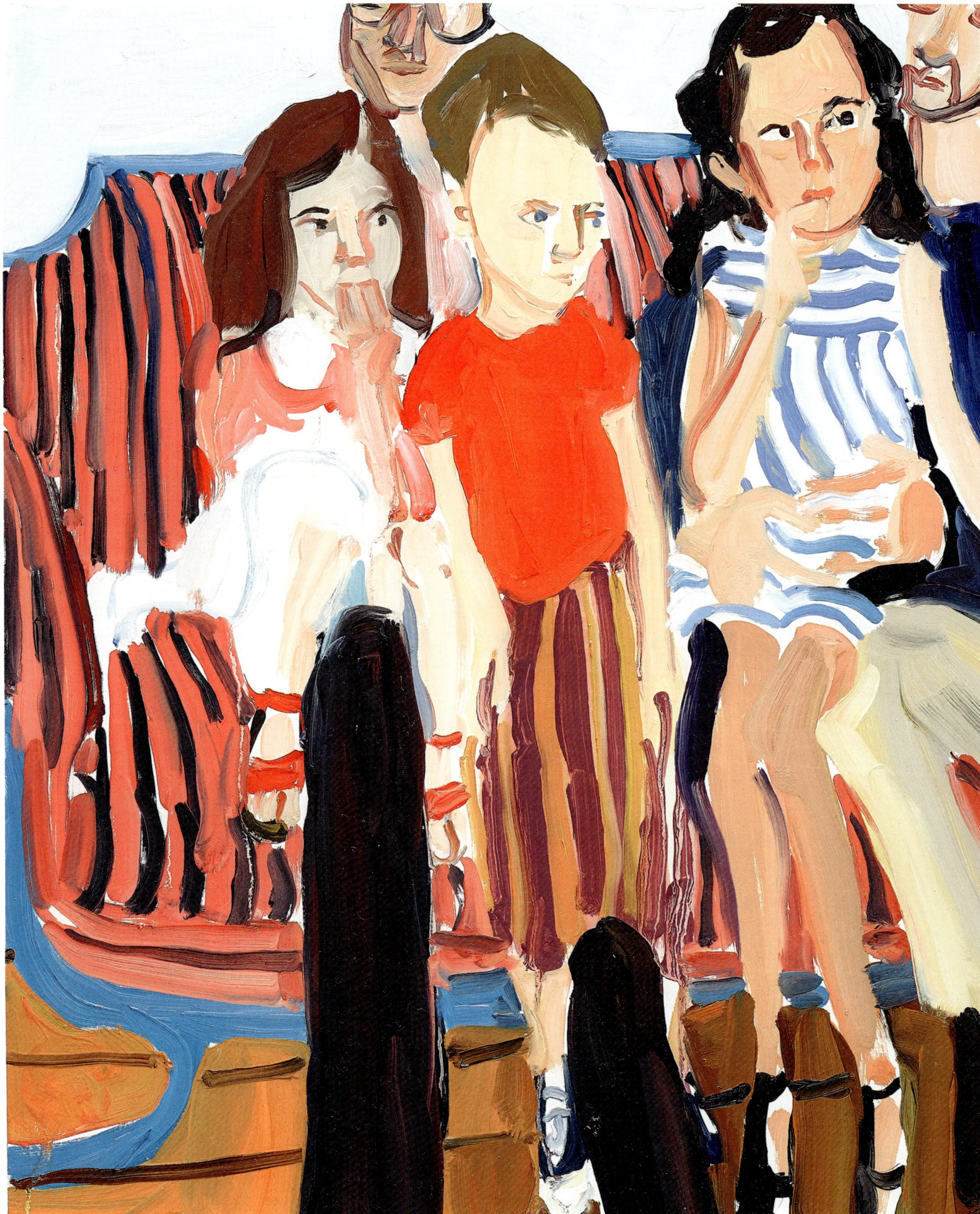

93.
Chantal Joffe
Me, Em and Nat

2019, oil on board
40 × 50 cm
Courtesy the artist
and Victoria Miro

uncle Eddie. Neither of the adults are fully visible. Their heads have been chopped off at the eyeline, like boiled eggs, and so have their feet. Each of the girls seems sunk in their own dream, though I suppose it's not implausible they're watching television. Chan, the littlest, is sucking her fingers and clutching a white blankie, dressed daintily in white and pink. Em is boyish with cropped hair, arms at her sides, her orange and purple skirt vibrating uneasily against the navy and pink stripes of the couch. Nat is long-limbed and tightly held, her father's hands making a belt around her middle. She's dressed in stripes too, crisp blue and white, the colour drawing her into allegiance with the adults.

They look like a masque representing three stages of dependence, three positions in a child's life. Then again, they're ultra-specific. This is the year that mum reupholstered the couch and painted the wood bright blue. This is the year that Uncle Eddie came over from London. This is the year I got the red shoes. The painting's ready fascination lies in the fact that no one is looking at the viewer, giving it the atmosphere of an off-moment, not quite camera-ready despite the camera's snap. What is everyone thinking about, with their dreamy, distant gazes? Is someone pondering a resentment or cooking up revenge? Is this a moment that will resurface in scalding future scenes?

Now switch to Chantal at forty, combing the hair of her own daughter (**94**). Esme looks straight at the viewer with the faint smile of a kouros, calmly holding her red guitar. Chantal's body is all around her, in fluid blue zones, the oceanic mass of motherhood. She looks concentrated, abstracted, a bit beatified by care, not a million miles from a Raphael Madonna in a wrap dress. There are a few wriggly yellow lines in the corner suggesting a chair, but otherwise the room they're in is a white chapel, stripped of accoutrements.

The last painting is my favourite. It might even be the same room, painted thirteen years later. Chantal is on the sofa, older, shoulders hunched, a cushion in her lap (**95**). Sleeping beside her, long legs slung over the arm of the couch, is her new partner Richard, his head like a lima bean cradled in her lap. I remember walking into the studio and seeing this huge painting a few days after it was finished and, technical term, losing my mind. It's so sleek, so effectively reduced to its essential cargo.

There's still the Lipke fascination with things: Evian bottle, suntan lotion, Chantal's beloved Birkenstocks, locating us securely in a twenty-first-century object world. But whole regions of the painting have escaped into abstraction. Peach and green. Cool blue. Slabs of white. Reservoirs of black. These coloured shapes directly convey a feeling of spaciousness, expansion, ease. The family configuration appears to have undergone another shift, and only Chantal's face, her body, betrays any lingering shards of worry.

Does the painting change if you know that it was made in the immediate aftermath of Chantal's mother's death? The soft peach and green squares are signifiers of a painful summer – a window looking out onto a garden, the

94.
Chantal Joffe
Self-portrait combing Esme's hair

2009, oil on canvas
40.7 × 51 cm
Courtesy the artist and Victoria Miro

reflected particles of an evening sky, suffusing the room with rosy light. Black regions of absence, white slabs of unaccustomed space. It's a painting full of hope and love, assembled around an infinite gap.

That's the way families roll, after all, the bloodiness of blood ties. Love equals loss and other undesirable equations. If people are too close they drive you mad, and when they go you find yourself tumbling through free space. At the end of *Spare* Harry decides to see a psychic. She tells him that his mother is nearby, and passes on an anecdote about a Christmas ornament that Harry seems to regard as definitive proof: Diana is still watching over him and his two children from beyond the grave. An enormous longing lifts from the page. To be seen, to be lovingly witnessed, is every child's most anguished wish.

No painting, no book can make up for actual lack, but it introduces a extra loop of time. The artist can voyage back, encounter scenes of care as well as its absence or distortion. Lost parents don't have to be hovering around us as ghosts for old parcels of love to be delivered. Nor, on the other hand, does the revelation of paucity and cruelty have to be permanently destabilising. I think the most powerful thing about Chantal's family paintings, taken as a set, is the case they make for moving on, inevitably departing from the primal scene, inhabiting a multiplicity of roles, shifting perpetually between positions of vulnerability and power, victim and perpetrator, lover and object of love.

Blood ties are static, the result of relationship. Mother-daughter is a blood tie, as is sister-brother. The term's essentially fixed nature fails to convey

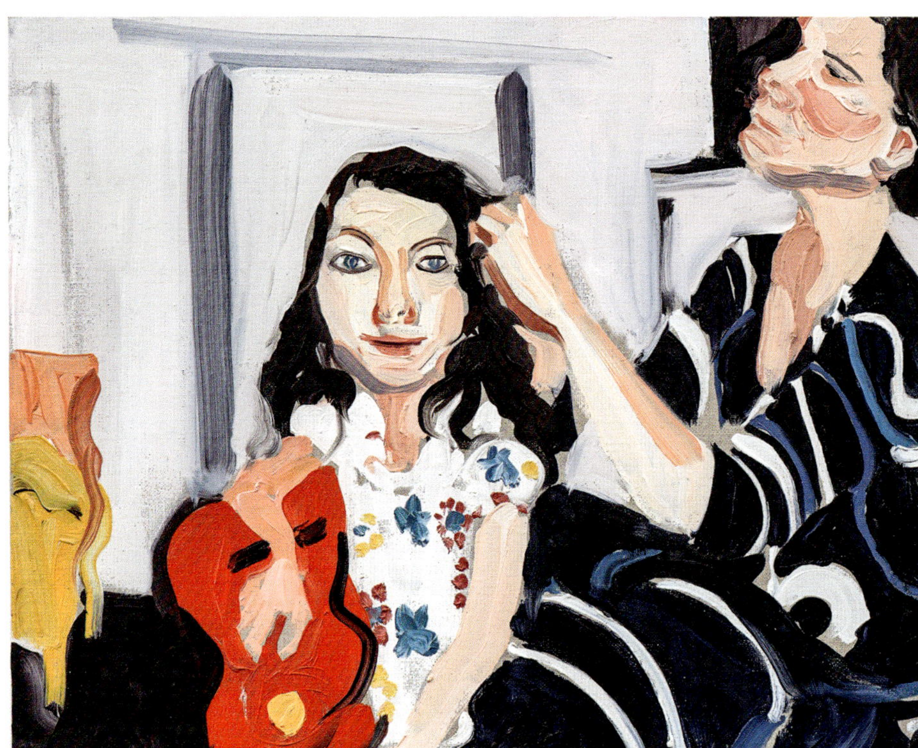

95.
Chantal Joffe
The Living Room 2

2022, oil on board
with collage
203 × 280 cm
Courtesy the artist and
Victoria Miro

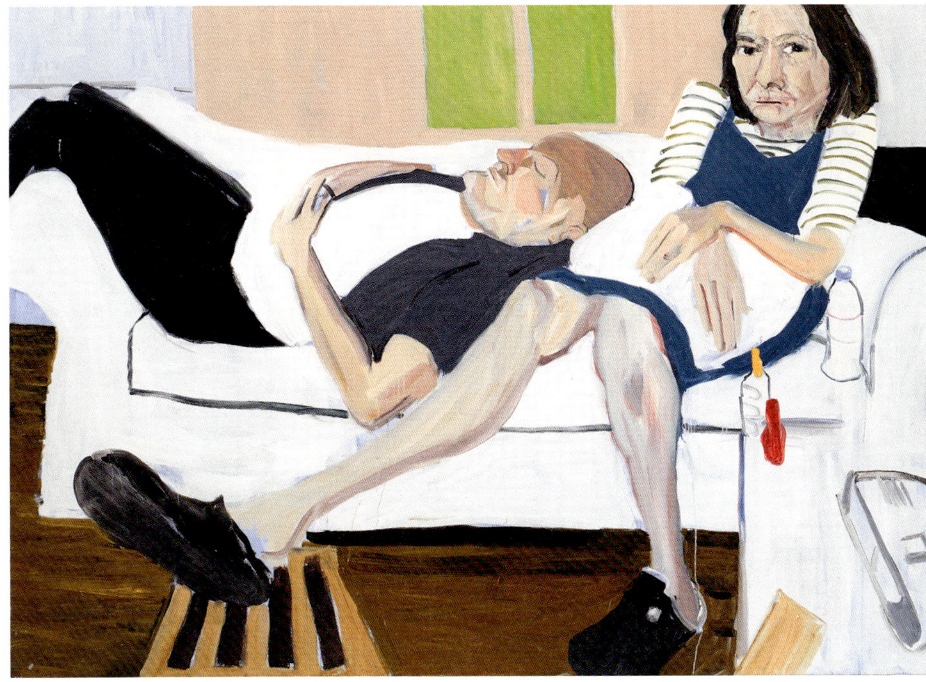

how these relationships morph and change. I wonder if it would make more sense to think of blood time, the way each of us moves through the matrix of family, sometimes at a distance and sometimes clutched very close. Blood time for those moods of hot-faced anger that Harry calls 'red mist' – he pushed me and I fell and broke the dog bowl! – but also for the scenes of calm and care, the daughter slumped in her father's arms, the mother combing her daughter's hair.

Blood time is a hellish Christmas, is being stuck together in the back of the car. Blood time is too much closeness and not enough privacy. You don't know me well enough to talk about hormones, said one duchess to another. Blood time is like a paddling pool on the lawn, like a shared single bed, hot stinky breath, a foot in your back. The inescapable intimacy of family, the rage it induces. Blood time is a game that everyone's playing – the essential struggle to get your version verified and notarised before it's too late. And blood time is the painful, liberating knowledge that the configuration will have changed and changed again before the ink is even dry.

96.
Apostolos Georgiou
Untitled

2019, acrylic on canvas
170 × 170 cm
Haidas Collection

Family secrets can have far-reaching consequences for family relationships, interfering with communication between those who know the secret and those who don't. The accidental discovery of a family secret, suggested in Apostolos Georgiou's *Untitled*, may be illuminating, but may also be deeply shocking and disturbing, causing those affected by the revelation to feel angry and deceived.

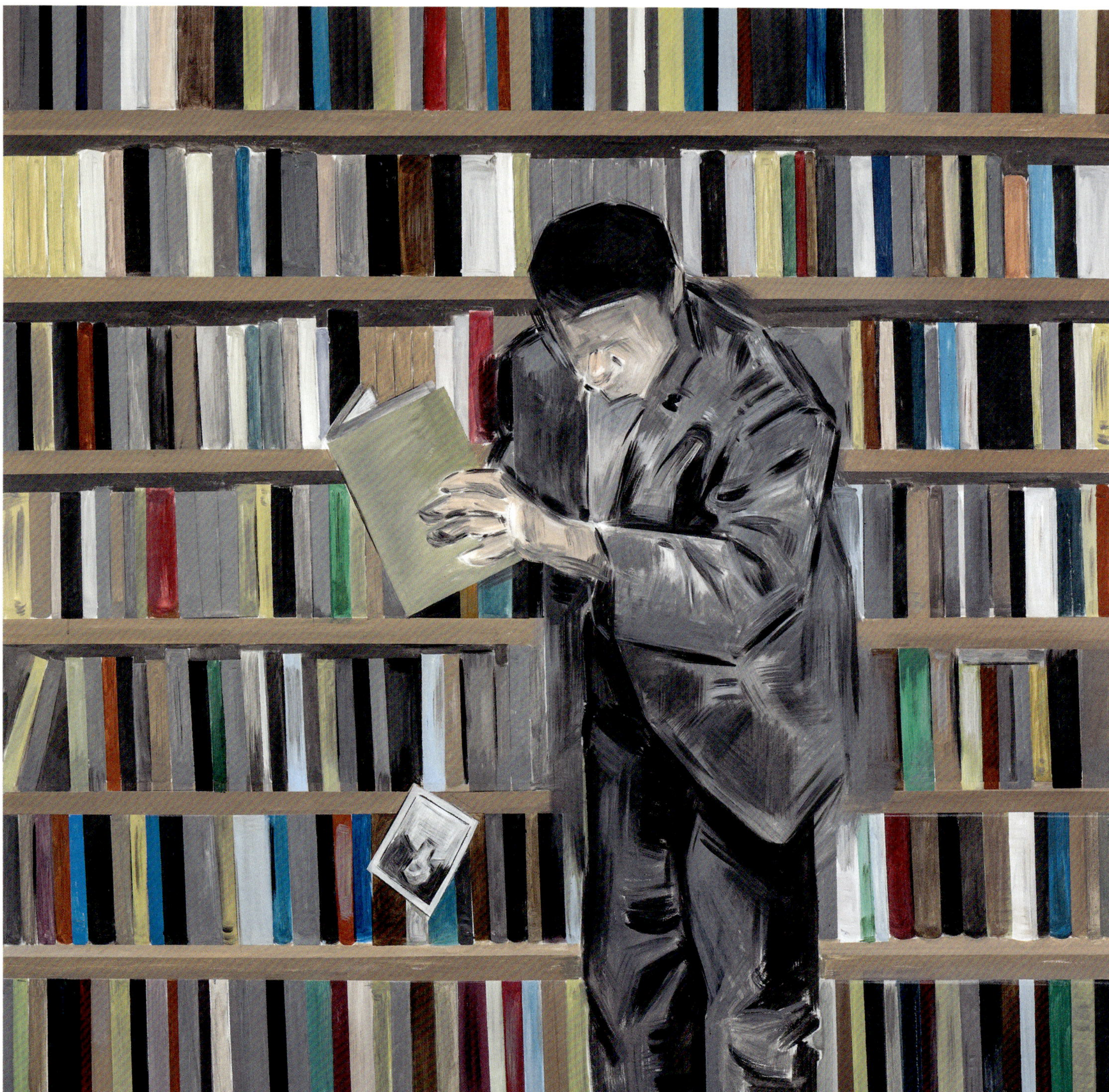

97.
Billet book with fabric token attached

Foundling 10563, a girl, admitted 22 November 1758
Open: 35 × 44.2 × 6 cm
The Foundling Hospital, which continues today as the children's charity Coram
BA/FH/A/09/001/118

98.
Billet book with fabric token attached

Foundling 14922, a boy, admitted 24 December 1759
Open: 35 × 44.2 × 6 cm
The Foundling Hospital, which continues today as the children's charity Coram
BA/FH/A/09/001/164

When mothers left their babies at the Foundling Hospital, they sometimes attached tokens and wisps of fabric to them, expressing their love for the children they had to give up, often in the hope of being reunited one day. The fabric with the large heart was attached to Foundling 10563, a girl, admitted on 22/11/1758. The fabric with playing cards came from a gown worn by Foundling 14922, a boy, admitted the following year. The Foundling Hospital continues today as the children's charity Coram.

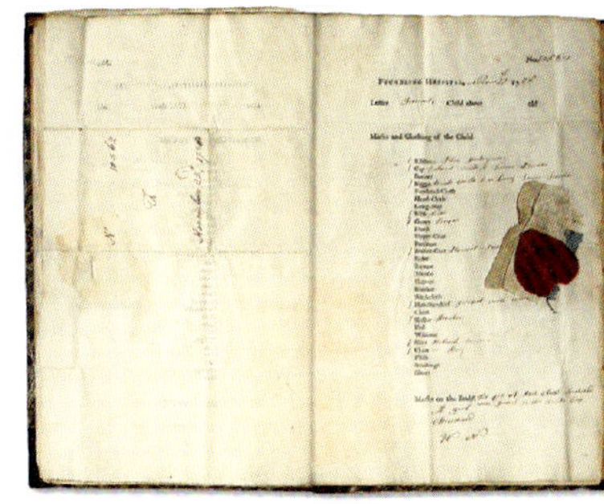

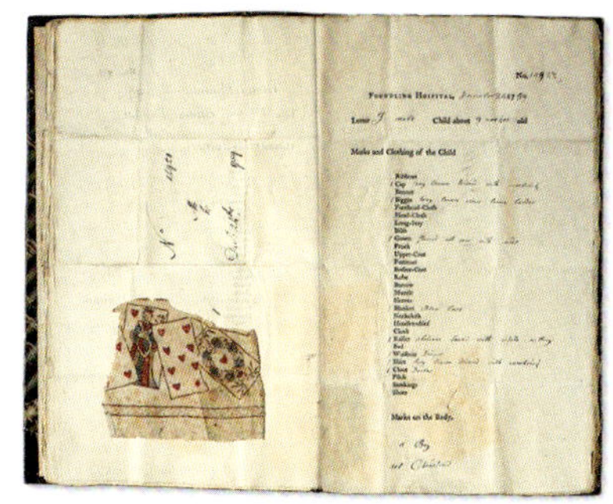

99.
Crystal beads

1700s, rock crystal, metal wire
Diameter 4.5 cm
Foundling Museum, London
2005.5.391

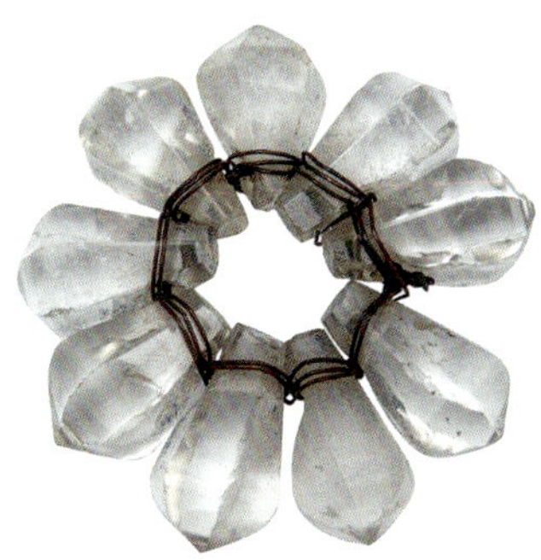

100.
Ring

1700s, metal and imitation 'stones'
Diameter 1.5 cm
Foundling Museum, London
2005.5.134

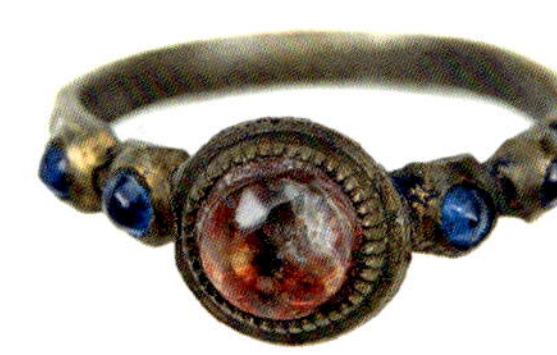

101.
Engraved King James II shilling

1685–88, smoothed and engraved about 1756, silver
Diameter 2.6 cm
Foundling Museum, London
2005.5.49

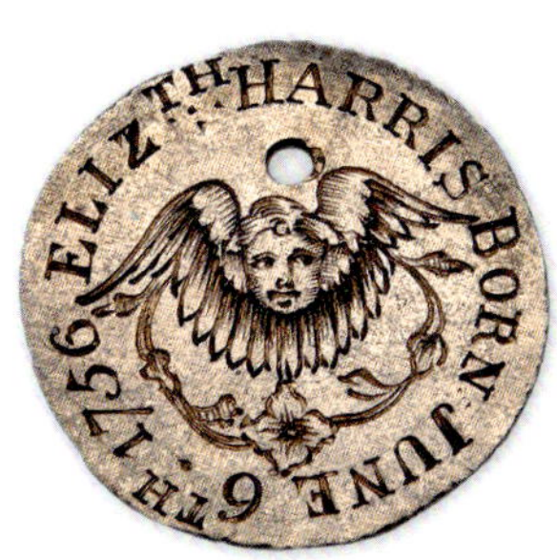

102.
Heart-shaped token

1700s, brass
2.5 × 2.7 cm
Foundling Museum, London
2005.5.63

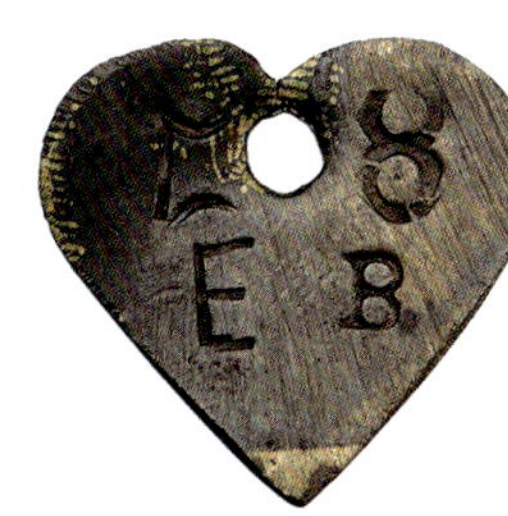

103.
Coral necklace

1700s, coral beads, cotton string, metal clasp
Diameter about 10 cm
Foundling Museum, London
2005.5.156

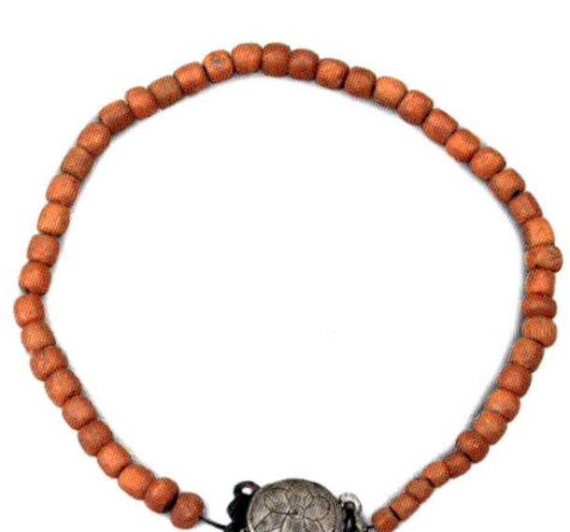

104.
Sarah Williamson
Sampler

1795, wool embroidered with coloured silks
43 × 31.2 cm
The Fitzwilliam Museum, Cambridge
Given by Miss J.D.W. Eames, 2000
T.1-2000

Sewing a sampler was a popular way to teach young women needlework skills. By including verses from the Bible and lines from books on virtuous Christian behaviour they also provided moral and religious instruction. The ten-year-old Williamson's idyllic vision of her family is accompanied by embroidered text expressing gratitude to her parents, who are 'Next unto God' as figures of authority and virtue.

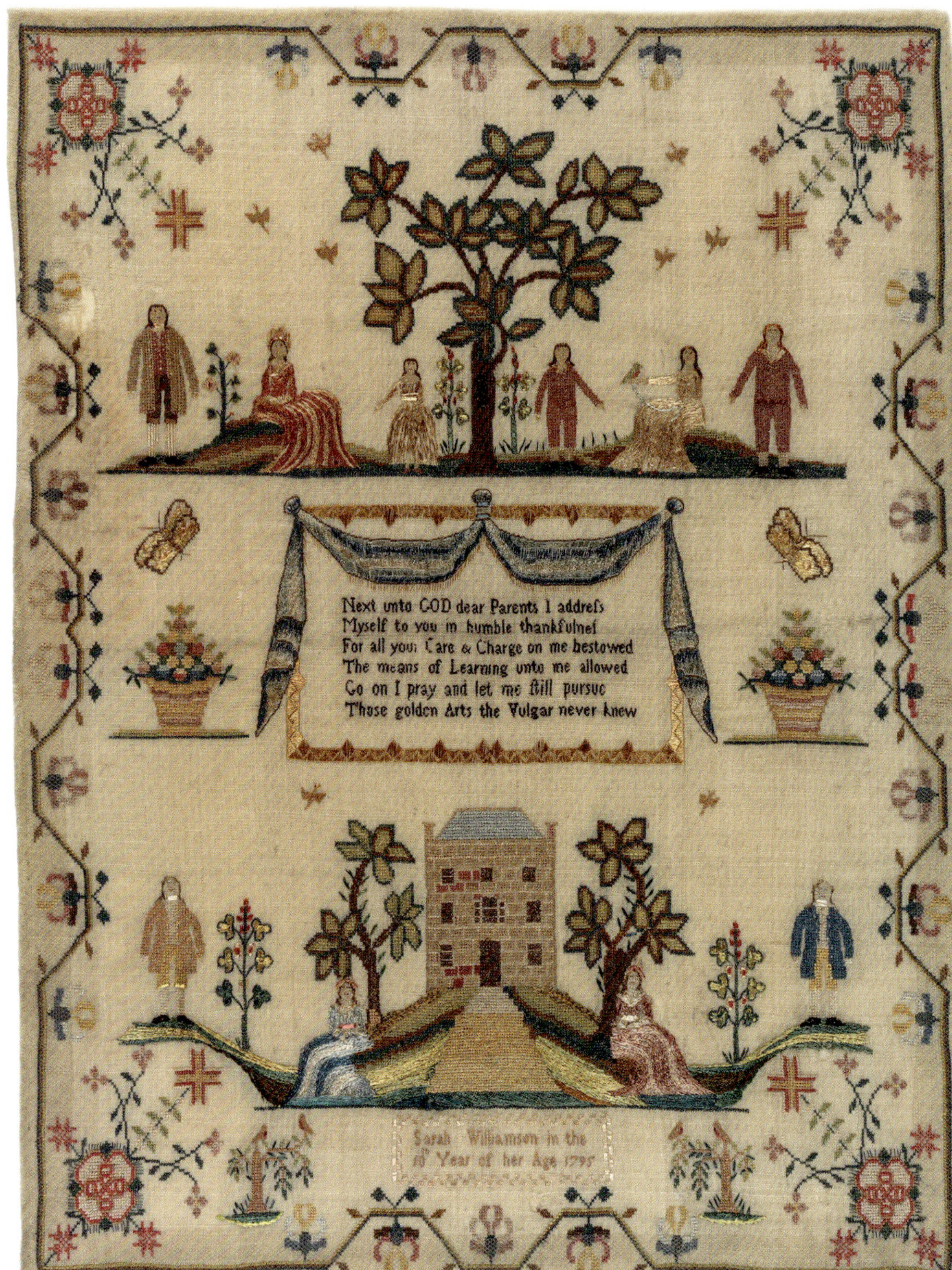

105.
Unidentified Staffordshire potter
Model cradle

1708, lead-glazed earthenware
inscribed: *HS*, *John Walker* and
HS 1708 EC
20.6 × 34.3 × 17.2 cm
The Fitzwilliam Museum, Cambridge
Bequeathed by J.W.L. Glaisher, 1928
c.256-1928

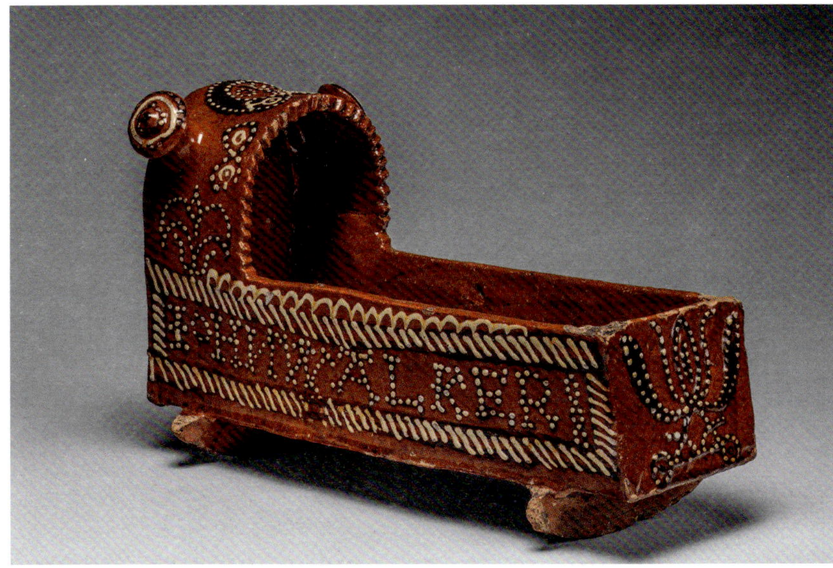

106.
Unknown maker
Model cradle

1729, lead-glazed earthenware
inscribed: *Mary / Overton /*
Her cradle, *1729*
15.6 × 24.5 cm
The Fitzwilliam Museum, Cambridge
Bequeathed by J.W.L. Glaisher, 1928
c.237–1928

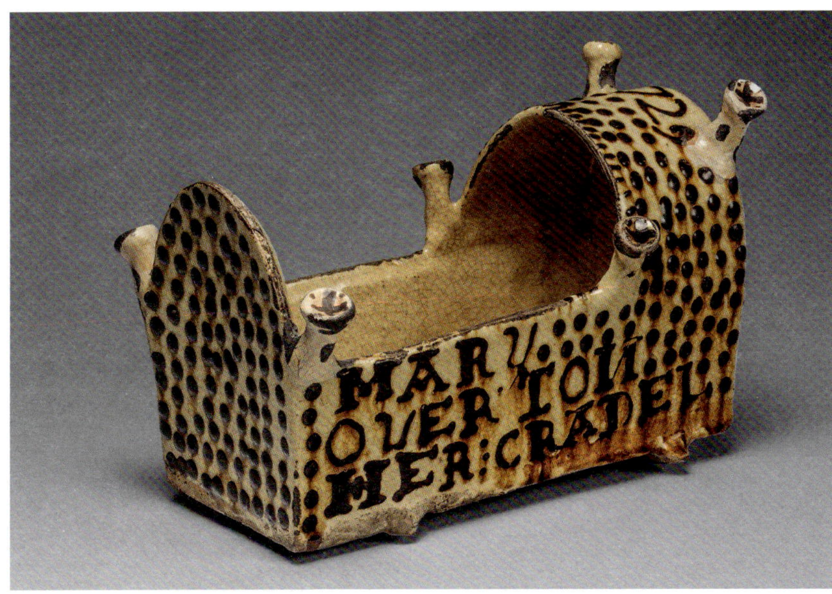

Miniature pottery cradles like these were given as gifts to newly married couples to express hope for the birth of future children, or as celebratory tokens at christenings. They were popular between the late 1600s and mid 1800s. The reasonable price of pottery made it more affordable for many than traditional gifts for new-borns, such as silver spoons.

107.
Unknown maker
Infant's bonnet

1700s, linen embroidered with
the words *Sweet Babe*
12 × 12 cm
The Fitzwilliam Museum, Cambridge.
Given by J.N. Peyton, 1981
T.19-1981

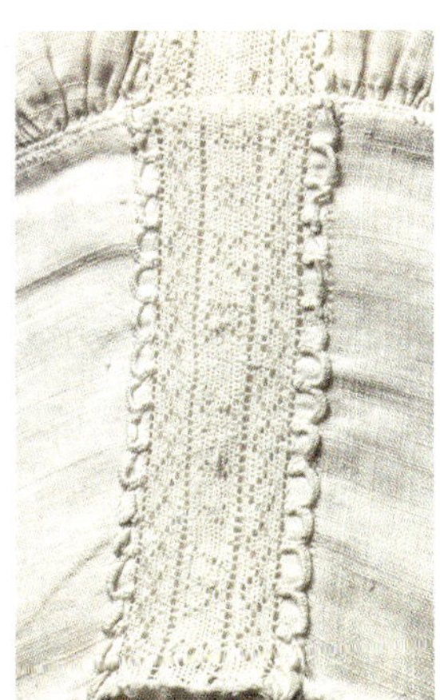

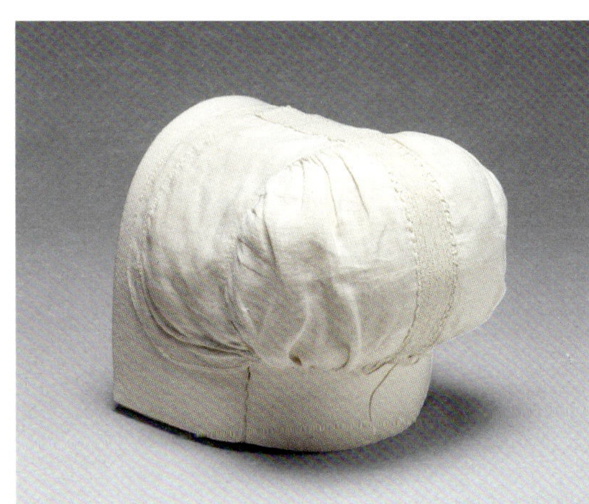

People made their own gifts for new-born babies, such as this bonnet embroidered with the words *SWEET BABE*.

108.
Unknown maker
Mourning pendant

About 1790, gold, gilt-metal, glass, hair, enamel
Inscribed: *SACRED TO THE MEMORY OF AN ADOPTED CHILD.*
2.9 × 2.4 × 3.8 cm
The Fitzwilliam Museum, Cambridge
Bequeathed by S.G. Perceval, 1922
PER.M.274-1923

The inscription on this pendant suggests that adopted children were mourned just as fiercely as other children, and were remembered by their parents through the same tokens and rituals. Mourning jewellery, like this example, were decorated as miniature funerary monuments. The motif of the urn was a common symbol of death and grief.

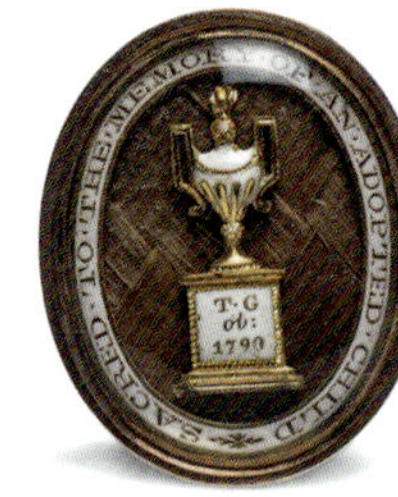

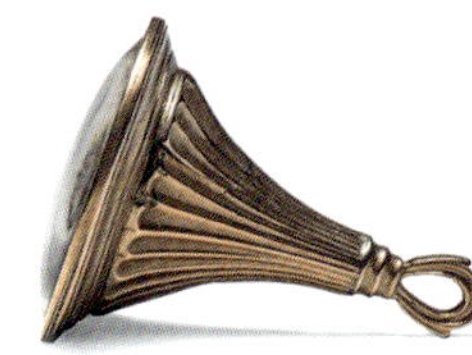

109.
Unknown maker
Mourning ring made for a child to commemorate Frances Greene, who died aged 61 years

1767, gold, amethysts and hair
Diameter 1.5 cm
The Fitzwilliam Museum, Cambridge
Given by Mrs J.C. Burkill, 1979
M.26-1979

Up until the end of the 1800s, people often left money in their will to make inscribed rings commemorating their death. Hair from the deceased was often incorporated into the design of mourning jewellery, allowing the bereaved to feel that a part of their loved one lived on. This ring, made for a child to wear, includes hair intricately arranged into a floral pattern.

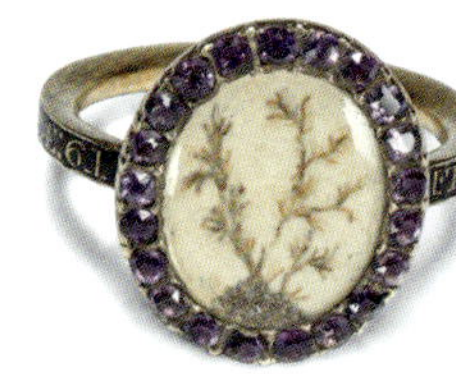

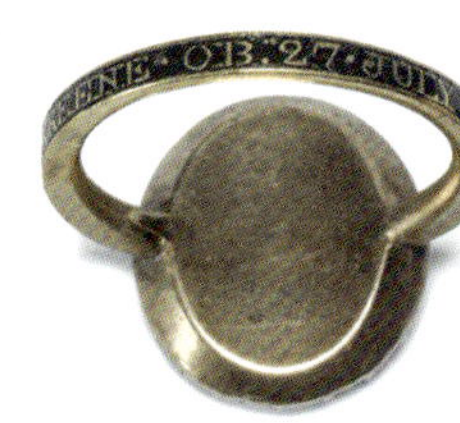

110.
Unknown maker
Mourning ring to commemorate N.B. and W. Toms, who died aged five and eleven years

1794, gilt-metal, hair from two different heads
Diameter 2.1 cm
The Fitzwilliam Museum, Cambridge
Bequeathed by S.G. Perceval, 1922
PER.M.272-1923

In this mourning ring made for grieving parents, the hair of two young brothers who died only a few years apart is interlaced and studded with stars, suggesting a togetherness in a heavenly afterlife. The inscription on the underside of the ring names the children and their dates of birth and death. Child mortality rates remained high in this period, but their losses were still deeply felt.

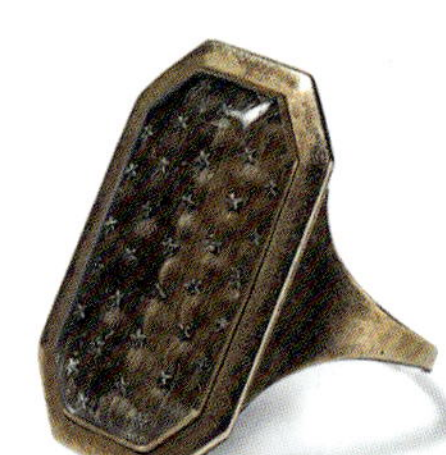

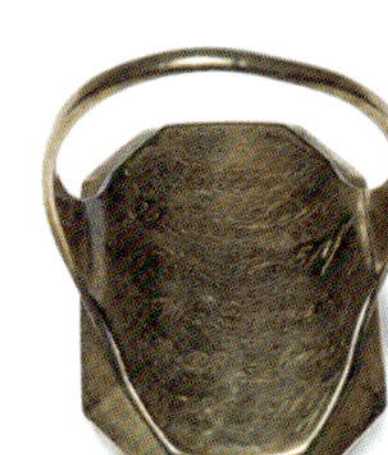

111.
Sally Mann
Three Generations

Edition, exhibition print
1991, gelatin silver print
20.3 × 25.4 cm

Family resemblances are endlessly fascinating, with conversations about who someone takes after, either in appearance or behaviour, being part of family life. A strong resemblance, as portrayed in Sally Mann's *Three Generations*, helps people feel connected to their family. A lack of resemblance, perhaps due to adoption or donor conception, can make people feel they don't belong.

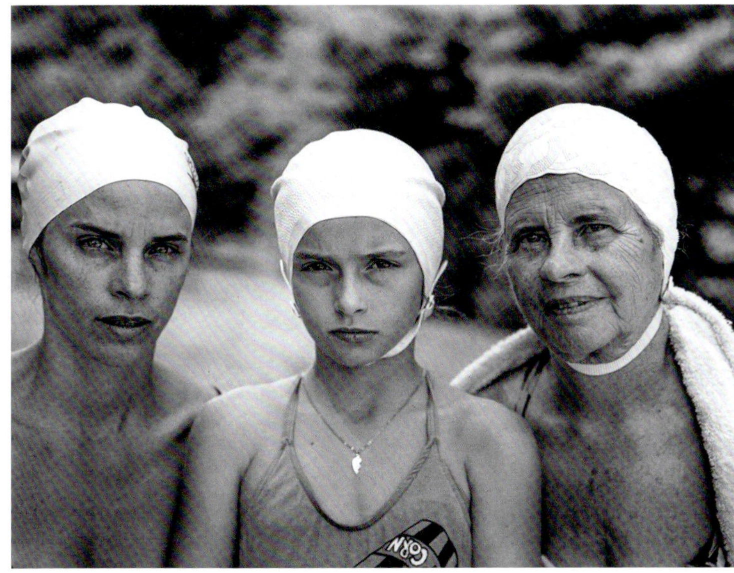

112–13.
Mary Berridge
Grayson with his Sister

From the book *Visible Spectrum: Portraits from the World of Autism*
2021, archival pigment print
43.2 × 55.9 cm
On loan from the artist

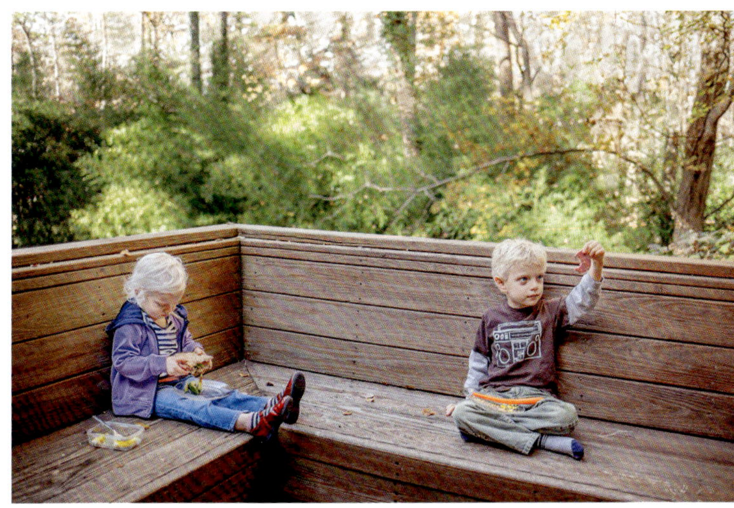

Graham at the Louvre

From the book *Visible Spectrum: Portraits from the World of Autism*
2021, archival pigment print
43.2 × 55.9 cm
On loan from the artist

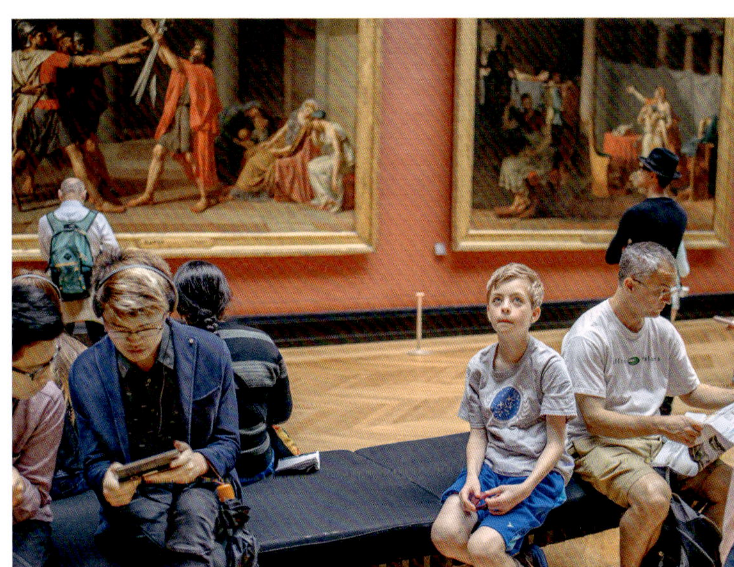

Grayson sits somewhat apart from his sister. She is pondering her sandwich as food, but he appears absorbed by the bite shape in his slice of salami. Heightened interest in form is common in autistic children and can lead to strong reactions to changes in their environment. *Graham at the Louvre* illustrates how neurodiversity produces different perspectives: everyone else is looking down, but his gaze is drawn upwards, captured by a detail that has escaped everyone else's attention.

114.

Zineb Sedira

Mother Tongue

2002, video, 3 flat screens,
colour and sound (stereo)
Duration: 5 min
Tate: Purchased 2007
T12315

Mother Tongue by Zineb Sedira is a demonstration of the impact of migration on communication between family members. On the left, the grandmother speaks to the mother, the artist, in Arabic. In the middle, the mother speaks to her daughter in English. On the right, the grandmother and granddaughter are silent as they don't speak the same language.

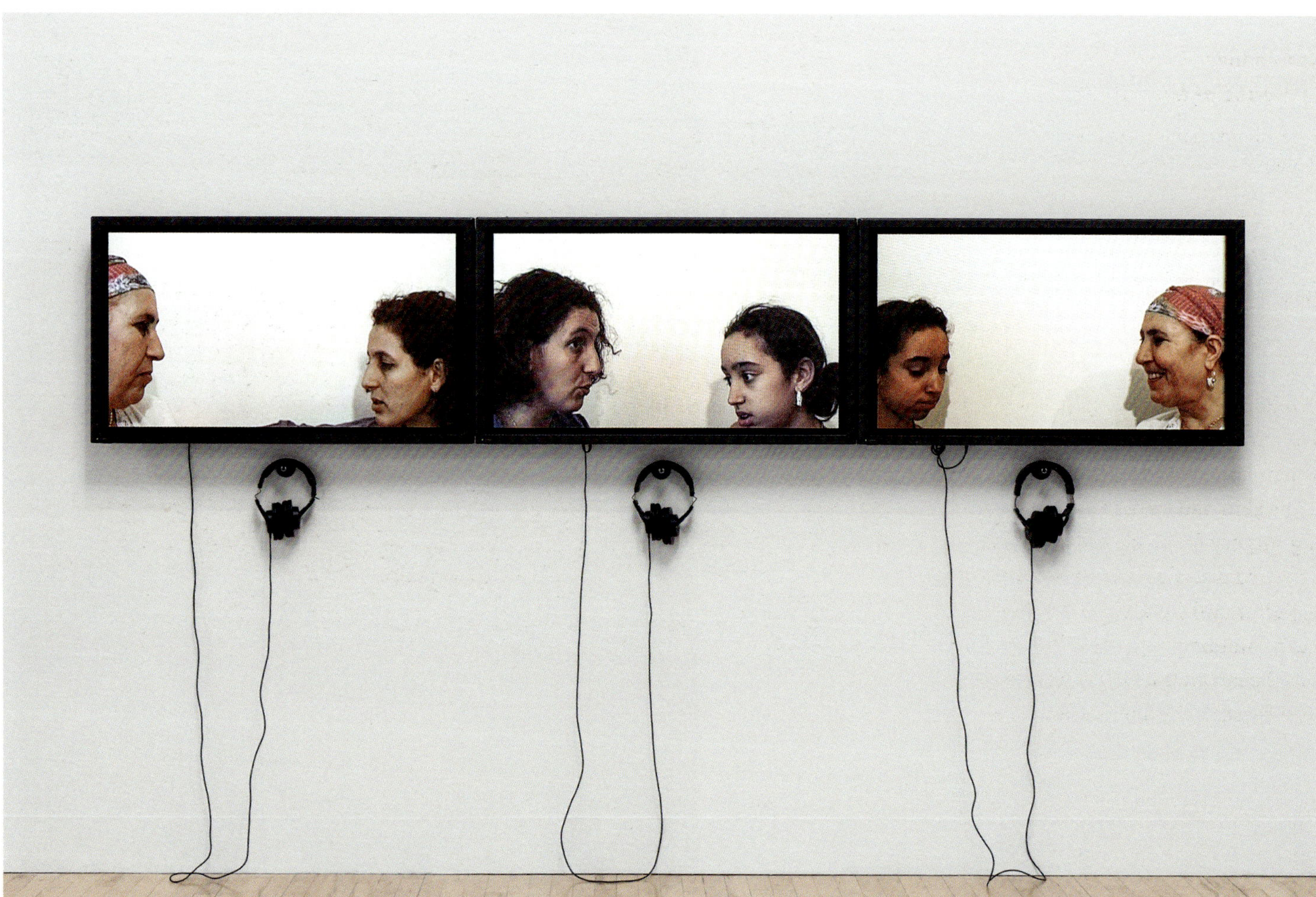

115.
Hardeep Pandhal
Baba Deep Thing By Mum

2014, synthetic wool, hanger
150 × 60 × 15 cm
Arts Council Collection
ACC41/2017

Hardeep Pandhal's piece, created in collaboration with his mother, foregrounds the connections and disconnections that arise in families as a result of migration. The mother speaks little English, while the artist speaks little Punjabi. Communication between them takes place in other ways, including the creation of joint artworks.

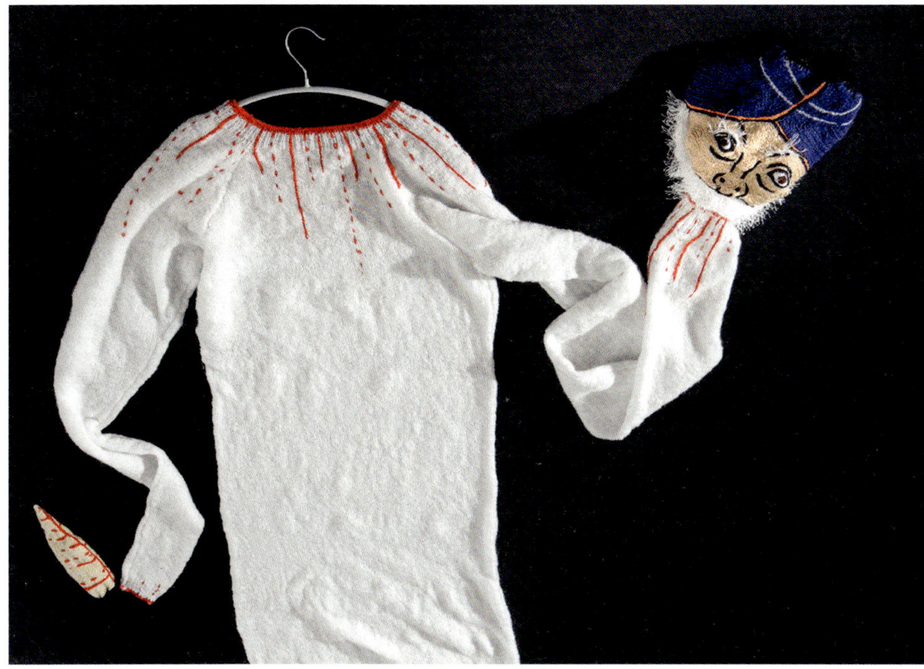

116.
Donald Rodney
In the House of My Father

1996–97, photographic print on aluminium
153 × 122 cm
Arts Council Collection
ACC59/1997
Photograph taken by Andra Nelki.
Donald Rodney © The Estate of Donald G Rodney

Donald Rodney's photograph shows a small sculpture of a house resting in his hand, made from the artist's skin. The skin had been removed during surgery for sickle cell disease, an inherited disorder that reduces life expectancy dramatically and is prevalent among people of African and Caribbean ancestry. Rodney died of the disease at the age of thirty-six.

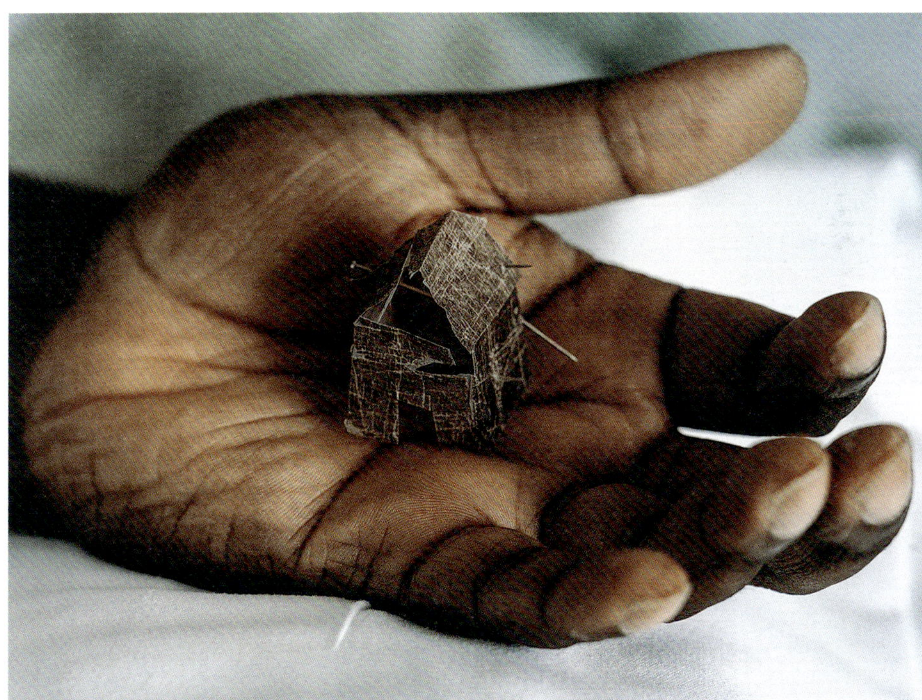

117.
Chantal Joffe
Story

2020, oil on canvas
60 × 80 cm
Private collection

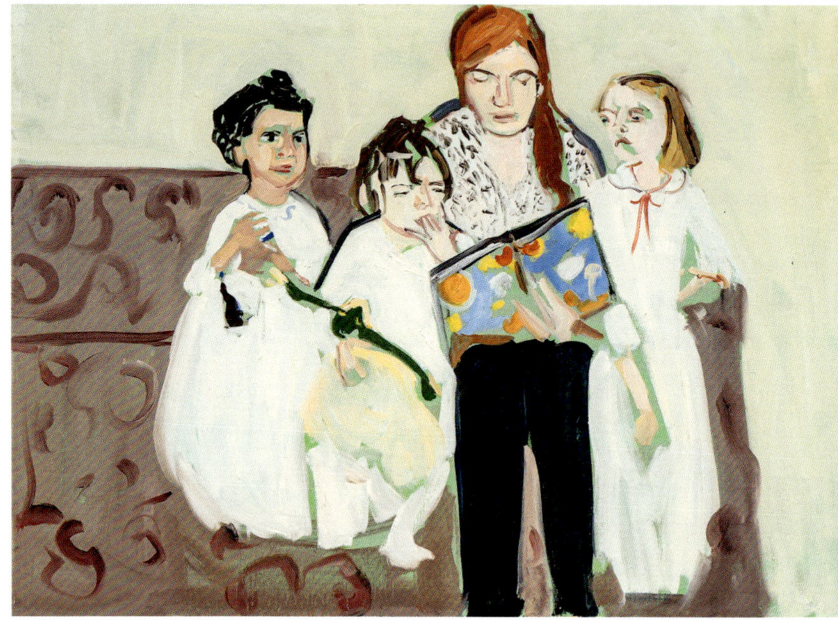

118.
Chantal Joffe
Mother and Child II

2005, oil on board
243 × 182 × 6.3 cm
Collection of Idris Khan
and Annie Morris

Chantal Joffe's captivating and deeply psychological paintings of her family illuminate the complexities and tensions, and comfort and joy, that family relationships can bring. These portraits convey what it means to feel secure in one's family as a child, the anxieties of being a new mother, the pleasures and challenges in watching one's child grow up, the mixed emotions that can accompany the relationships of adults with their parents and siblings, and the entry of a new partner into the family.

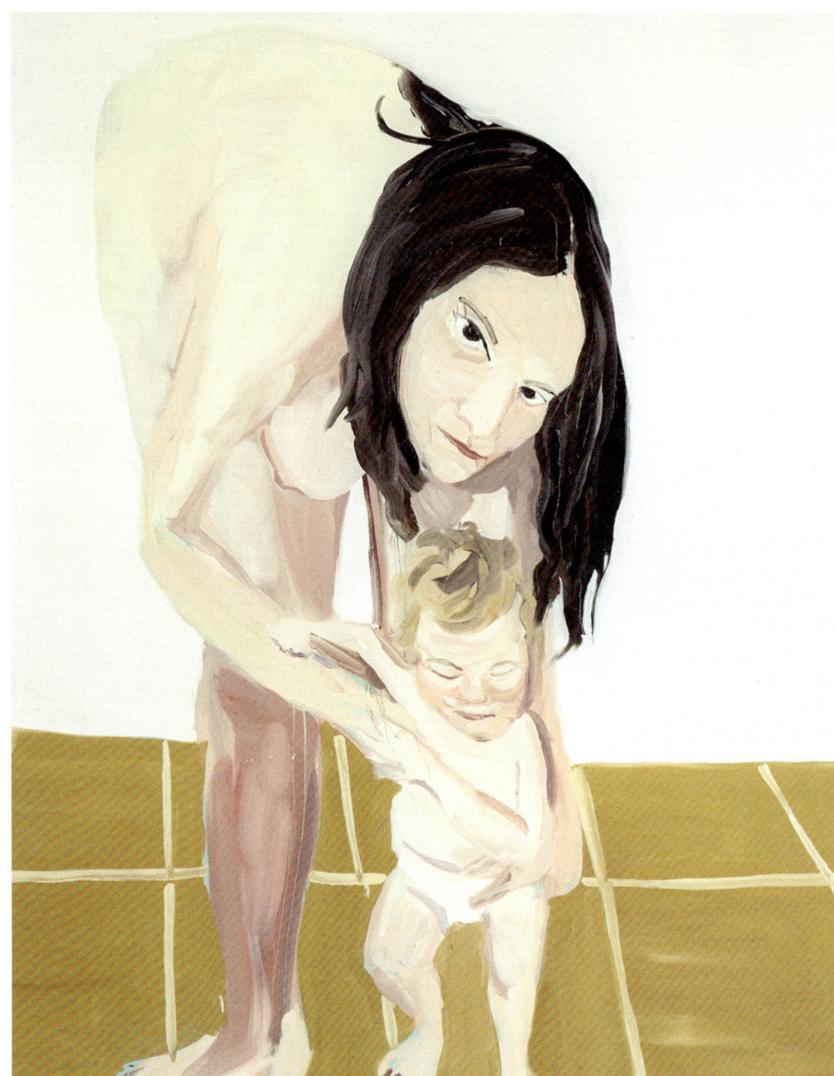

119.
Chantal Joffe
Esme with a striped blanket

2005, oil on canvas
30 × 30 cm
Courtesy the artist and
Victoria Miro

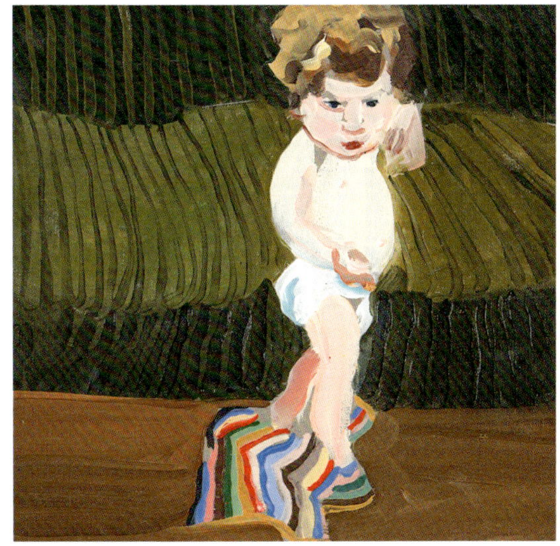

120.
Chantal Joffe
Esme at the Kitchen Table

2019, oil on canvas
39.7 × 50 cm
Courtesy the artist and
Victoria Miro

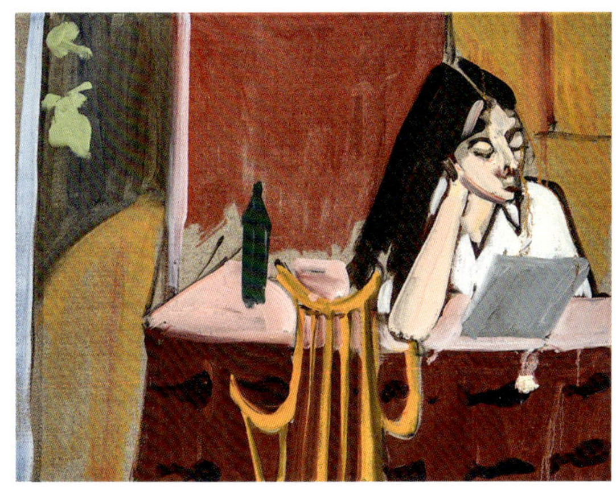

121.
Chantal Joffe
Self-portrait with Emily

2017, oil on canvas
213.5 × 152 × 3.3 cm
Courtesy the artist and
Victoria Miro

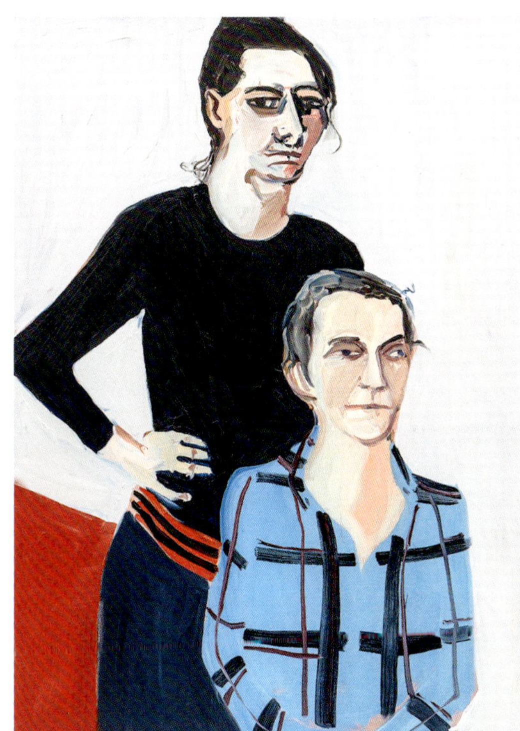

Timeline

1967 **Sexual Offences Act**
Homosexuality partially decriminalised

1969 **Divorce Reform Act**
Allowed divorce based on 'irretrievable breakdown'

1978 Public awareness of lesbian mother families in UK

1978 World's first 'test-tube' (IVF) baby born in UK

1983 World's first baby born through egg donation in Australia

1985 Birth of 'Baby Cotton' in the UK, causing a media storm about commercial surrogacy

1985 **Surrogacy Arrangements Act**
Prohibited commercial surrogacy and advertising for surrogates

1986 Around this time, the first baby was born through embryo donation

1987 **Family Law Reform Act**
Abolished status of illegitimacy for children born outside marriage

1988 **Section 28 of Local Government Act**
Prohibited 'promotion of homosexuality' and described families with same-sex parents as pretend families

1989 **Children Act**
Made children's welfare paramount in proceedings that affect them

1990 **Human Fertilisation and Embryology Act**
Required clinics to take account of child's need for a father in the decision to offer fertility treatment

1991 First UK report of single heterosexual women having children by sperm donation

2002 **Adoption and Children Act**
Allowed joint adoption by same-sex couples

2003 **Sexual Offences Act**
Homosexuality fully decriminalised

2004 **Civil Partnership Act**
Introduced institution similar to marriage for same-sex couples

2008 **Human Fertilisation and Embryology Act**
Required fertility clinics to take account of child's need for supportive parenting rather than a father, and allowed same-sex couples to be joint legal parents of children born through assisted reproduction

2010 Birth of first child to lesbian couple through shared biological motherhood where one mother carried a pregnancy created using the other mother's egg

2013 **Marriage (Same-Sex Couples) Act**
Introduced same-sex marriage

2018 **Amendment to Human Fertilisation and Embryology Act**
Permitted single parents to apply to become sole legal parents of children born through surrogacy

2019 Transgender man Freddy McConnell gives birth to child in high profile UK case in which he contested being given the legal status of mother

2020 **Divorce, Dissolution and Separation Act**
No-fault divorce permitted

2020 Around this time, attempts by adopted and donor-conceived people to trace biological relatives online through combined genetic and ancestry databases became increasingly successful

2023 First UK baby with genetic material from three people born through mitochondrial donation, a procedure developed to prevent serious inherited disorders being passed on to children

2023 The first children conceived after the removal of donor anonymity turn 18 and become legally entitled to request the identity of their sperm and/or egg donor through the Human Fertilisation and Embryology Authority Register of Information

Further reading

Stories of Change

Susan Golombok, *We Are Family: What Really Matters for Parents and Children*, Scribe, 2020

Lotte Jeffs and Stu Oakley, *The Queer Parent*, Bluebird, 2023

Dani Shapiro, *Inheritance: A Memoir of Genealogy, Paternity and Love*, Daunt Books, 2019

John Styles, *Threads of Feeling*, The Foundling Museum, 2010

A Sunday Kind of Love

Jackie Kay, *The Adoption Papers*, Bloodaxe Books, 1991

Jackie Kay, *Trumpet*, Picador, 1998

Jackie Kay, *Red Dust Road*, Picador, 2011

Jackie Kay, *Fiere*, Picador, 2011

Jackie Kay, *Bessie*, Faber, 2021

Annunciations: Three Women Talk Back to Tradition

Susanne Bosch Abele, *Annunciation*, Phaidon Press, 2004

Rebecca Birrell, *This Dark Country: Women Artists, Still Life and Intimacy in the Early Twentieth Century*, Bloomsbury, 2021

Sarah Drummond, *Divine Conception: The Art of the Annunciation*, Unicorn, 2018

Marina Warner, *Alone of All Her Sex: The Myth and the Cult of the Virgin Mary*, Oxford University Press, 1976

Everyday Madonnas

Michael Baxendall, *Painting & Experience in Fifteenth-Century Italy*, Oxford University Press, 1988

Patrick Bringley, *All The Beauty in The World*, Bodley Head, 2023

Leonardo da Vinci, *Treatise on Painting*, Dover Publications, 2005

Legitimising Motherhood

Hilton Als, *Alice Neel: Uptown*, David Zwirner Books, 2017

Phoebe Hoban, *Alice Neel: The Art of Not Sitting Pretty*, David Zwirner Books, 2021

Katy Hessel, *The Story of Art without Men*, Hutchinson Heinemann, 2022

Eleanor Nairne, *Alice Neel: Hot Off The Griddle*, Prestel, 2023

Attachment and Human Experience

John Bowlby, *A Secure Base: Clinical Applications of Attachment Theory*, Taylor & Francis, 2005

Robbie Duschinsky, *Cornerstones of Attachment Research*, Oxford University Press, 2020

Siblings: A Love-Hate Relationship

Lucy Blake, *No Family is Perfect: A Guide to Embracing the Messy Reality*, Welbeck Publishing Group, 2022

Victor Cicirelli, *Sibling Relationships across the Life Span*, Springer Science and Business Media, 2013

Dalton Conley, *The Pecking Order: Which Siblings Succeed and Why*, Pantheon Books, 2004

Judy Dunn and Robert Plomin, *Separate Lives: Why Siblings Are So Different*, Basic Books, 1990

Naomi White and Claire Hughes, *Why Siblings Matter: The Role of Brother and Sister Relationships in Development and Well-Being*, Routledge, 2017

Roman Charity

Ancient texts:

Valerius Maximus, *Facta et Dicta Memorabilia* 5, 4.7 – 4e, 1

Pliny, *Historia Naturalis* 7, 121 (translations in Loeb Classical Library, Harvard University Press)

Modern Studies:

Margherita Carucci, '*Domestica bona* on stage in the Pompeian House', *Arctos* 44 (2010), 27–44

Kristina Milnor, *Gender, Domesticity and the Age of Augustus: Inventing Private Life*, Oxford University Press, 2008, chapter 2

J.G. Sperling, *Roman Charity: Queer Lactations in Early Modern Visual Cultures*, Bielefeld Verlag, 2016

http://www.essentialvermeer.com/catalogue/music_lesson.html

Much to Give Thanks For

Michel Foucault, *The History of Sexuality*, Vintage Books, 1990

Alexia Pauline Gumbs, China Martens and Mai'a Willimas (eds), *Revolutionary Mothering*, PM Press, 2016

Andrew Solomon, *Far from the Tree: Parents, Children and the Search for Identity*, Vintage, 2014

Susan Sontag, *On Photography*, Penguin, 1979

Justin Richardson and Peter Parnell, *And Tango Makes Three*, Simon and Schuster Children's UK, 2007

The Visitation

Miri Rubin, *Mother of God: A History of the Virgin Mary*, Penguin, 2010

There Will Be Blood

Ivy Compton-Burnett, *A House and its Head*, New York Review of Books, 2001

Stella Gibbons, *Cold Comfort Farm*, Penguin Classics, 2006

Melanie Klein, *Envy and Gratitude and Other Works 1946–1963*, Vintage Classics, 1997

Toni Morrison, *Beloved*, Vintage Classics, 2007

Gwendoline Riley, *My Phantoms*, Granta Books, 2022

Acknowledgements

This exhibition would not have happened without the vision, intellectual engagement and support of Luke Syson and his outstanding team at the Fitzwilliam Museum. It has been such a privilege to work with you, Luke. Thank you for having the courage to work with an academic department in the university that is not a typical partner for a distinguished museum, for trusting us, and for making the whole enterprise so enjoyable. I have heard it said that truly creative things happen when disciplines that don't usually communicate work together. *Real Families: Stories of Change* reflects a unique perspective on the family that has resulted from a genuine collaboration between the Fitzwilliam Museum and the Centre for Family Research.

My thanks are also due to Barnaby Wright, Deputy Director of the Courtauld Gallery, who gave me the confidence to pursue the idea of an exhibition on the family back in 2016, and to the writer and psychologist Andrew Solomon for introducing Luke and me in 2019. The art historian and a co-curator of this exhibition, Coralie Malissard, provided expert guidance on the selection of many of the artworks from 2018 to 2021, as did Capucine Poncet, who was a research assistant on the project from 2019 to 2022. Thank you both for your significant contribution to the shape and content of this show.

At the Fitzwilliam, it has been an honour and a pleasure to work with Deputy Directors Karen Livingstone and Neal Spencer, both of whom have welcomed me into the museum family. I would particularly like to thank Rebecca Birrell, also a co-curator of the exhibition, for her expertise on the historical works which have enriched the show. Over the past year, I have worked most closely with Rebecca Virag. Thank you, Rebecca, for your insight and extensive knowledge of the artworks, your patience in putting up with a novice to the world of museums, and for being an absolute delight to work with. I am extremely grateful to Alex Fairhead, Jennifer Grindley, Elena Saggers, Nadine Langford, Emma Shaw, Tracy Hall, Carey Robinson, Richard Farleigh, Jane Ison, Vicky Sutcliffe, Katie Young and Len Dunne for their vital roles in the creation of this show. I will never again visit an exhibition without thinking of all of you and the incredible work that you do. It has also been a great pleasure working with Shaun Ihejetoh from West Port Architects and Carolyne Hill from ChillCreate on the superb 3D and 2D design, with Kitty Malton and Sam Talbot, and everyone at POCC.

I have very much enjoyed working with Susannah Lawson on the exhibition catalogue and hugely appreciate her dedication to producing this lovely book. Thank you also to Sophie Hartley for collecting all the images. I am grateful to Sarah Williams, Natalie Gamble, Mavis Maclean, Professor John Eekelaar and Professor Jens Scherpe for their advice on the timeline. I am grateful to Paul Sloman for the beautiful design of this book, and to Paul Holberton and his team for making the production process run so smoothly. A very big thank you goes to the wonderful authors for their illuminating, and often very personal, essays. It has been delightful working with you all. I feel truly honoured that such an acclaimed group of writers contributed to this book. I would also like to convey my heartfelt thanks to the remarkable artists who spoke to me about their families and their work, and their galleries for their support. Special thanks are due to Victoria Miro in London and the Kasmin Gallery in New York.

My sincere thanks are due to the Wellcome Trust for funding my research since the 1980s and for supporting this exhibition. I would also like to thank everyone, past and present, at the Centre for Family Research for their exceptional work that makes a real difference to real families.

Susan Golombok
Centre for Family Research
University of Cambridge
May 2023

Index

References are to page numbers, with catalogue numbers of the illustrations in **bold**.

Abbassy, Samira, *Reincarnated Fears*, 136 (**79**)
adolescence, 85, 91–92; 106–07 (**56–57**)
adoption, 18–23, 31; 19–20 (**6–9**), 58 (**28**)
Adoption and Children Act (2015), 10
adult-parent relationships, 96–103; 101 (**50**), 113–15 (**68–73**)
attachment theory, 74–79; 76 (**43**), 105 (**54**)
autism, 167 (**112–13**)
Barney, Tina
Andrew, John and George, 118–19; 122 (**74**)
Thanksgiving, 121, 124–26; 123 (**75**)
Barraclough, Jon, and Tabitha Moses, *Investment: Tabitha*, **59** (**32**)
Bellavia, Marcantonio, *Romulus and Remus Discovered by Faustulus and his Wife, Louva*, 58 (**28**)
Berridge, Mary
Graham at the Louvre, 167 (**113**)
Grayson with his Sister, 167 (**112**)
billet books, 163 (**97–98**)
Billingham, Richard, *Untitled*, 136 (**78**)
bonnets, 165 (**107**)
Borden, Harry
Florian (the Photographer's Son), 56 (**25**)
Jonathan with Xavier, 55 (**23**)
Tony, Emma and Louise, 56 (**24**)
Brotherus, Elina, 41–43
Annonciation 7, Jour de l'Annonciation, 41–42, 44–47; 59 (**30**)
My Dog is Cuter than Your Ugly Baby, 62 (**38**)
Buckman, Zoë, *When She Had a Black Eye*, 137 (**80**)
Calle, Sophie, *Today My Mother Died (Aujourd'hui ma mère est morte)*, 63 (**41**)
Carrington, Dora, 40
childlessness, 61–62 (**34–38**)
see also infertility; miscarriage
children without siblings, 93–94
chosen families, 155; 62 (**39**)
coins, 163 (**101**)
Cole, Caleb
Big Day, The, 140 (**87**)
Stripes, 140 (**86**)
comfort, 74–76, 81, 89–90
conflict, 83; 136 (**78**)
Cornet, Jean-Loup, *Michael Andrews and his Daughter Melanie Swimming in Glenartney, Scotland*, 109 (**63**)
cradles, 165 (**105–06**)
Cronqvist, Lena, *The Madonna*, 105 (**53**)
d'Aki, Loulou, *Sandra and Lilje*, 24; 55 (**22**)
divorce, 56 (**25**)
donor conception, 10, 14–18; 16–17 (**4–5**)
Dürer, Albrecht, *The Visitation*, 129–32; 129 (**76**)
Emin, Tracey
May Dodge, My Nan, 112 (**67**)
Me and Paul – The Twins, 92; 91 (**48**)
Evening News reports, 9–10; 11 (**2–3**)
family dynamics, 156–61
father-child relationships, 38, 40; 39 (**13**), 108–10 (**59–64**)
fathers, 57 (**26–27**)
black fathers, 59–62
gay fathers, 118–24, 126–27; 53 (**18**), 122 (**74**)
single fathers, 55–56 (**23–24**)
Foundling Hospital, London, 163 (**97–103**)
Freud, Lucian, *The Painter's Mother Resting*, 113 (**69**)
genealogy, 145, 147–51
Georgiou, Apostolos, *Untitled*, 144–46, 150–51; 162 (**96**)
Goldberg, Jim, *Untitled*, 116; 138–39 (**82–85**)
Goldin, Nan, 68–69
Lil Laughing, Swampscott, MA, 115 (**72**)
My Father Shaving, Swampscott, MA, 115 (**73**)
grandparents, 111–12 (**66–67**)
Gupta, Sunil, *Shalini, Rudi, Sunil, Léo, 3425 Stanley*, 62 (**39**)
Hepworth, Barbara, *Group of Three Magic Stones*, 84–85 (**45**)
Heynen, Bart, *Milo with her fathers and sister. New York City*, 53 (**18**)
Holton, Thomas, *Bored, 2011*, 106 (**56**)
Human Fertilisation and Embryology Act (2008), 10
Husted, Mary, 13, 18–19, 21–23
Dreams, Oracles, Icons . . ., 21; 20 (**9**)
Luke [at 3 Days Old] 31 January 1963, 19 (**6**)
Luke at 8 Days Old, Born 28 January 1963, 19 (**7**)
Luke at 10 Days Old, Born 28 January 1963, 19 (**8**)
infertility, 41–42, 44; 59 (**30**)
inheritance, 51 (**15**), 53 (**17**)
intergenerational transmission, 136 (**79**)
IVF (*in vitro* fertilisation), 10, 41–42, 47; 11 (**2–3**), 58–59 (**29–32**)
jewellery
coral necklace, 163 (**103**)
crystal beads, 163 (**99**)
mourning pendant, 166 (**108**)
mourning rings, 166 (**109–10**)
ring, 163 (**100**)
Joffe, Chantal, 13, 67, 153–55
Beach Hut, 154 (**91**)
Esme at the Kitchen Table, 171 (**120**)
Esme on the Sofa 1, 156–57 (**92**)
Esme with a striped blanket, 171 (**119**)
Living Room 2, The, 159–61 (**95**)
Me, Em and Nat, 156, 159; 158 (**93**)
Mother and Child II, 170 (**118**)
Self-portrait combing Esme's hair, 152, 159; 160 (**94**)
Self-portrait with Emily, 171 (**121**)
Story, 142; 170 (**117**)
John, Gwen, 38
Labinjo, Joy, *Having the Conversation*, 111 (**66**)
Lee, Zun
Bedtime shenanigans with Carlos Richardson and his daughter, Selah, Harlem, NY, August 2012, 108 (**60**)
Billy Garcia and daughter Esmeralda sharing a tender moment at a gas station, Bronx, NY, September 2012, 108 (**59**)
Guy Miller keeping an eye on all of his four children, Bronx, NY, December 2012, 109 (**62**)
Guy Miller surveying the playground whilst bandaging son Nijel's injured arm, Harlem, NY, July 2013, 108 (**61**)
Levine, JJ
Alone Time 19, 52 (**16**)
Harry, Joah and JJ, 2018, 54 (**21**)
Harry and Joah, 2016, 54 (**20**)
Harry Pregnant, 2015, 54 (**19**)
LGBTQ+ families, 12, 119–27; 63 (**40**)
gay fathers, 118–24, 126–27; 53 (**18**), 122 (**74**)
lesbian mothers, 9–10, 28–30, 32; 11 (**2–3**), 30 (**10**), 104 (**51**)
Li, Tianbing, *Autoportrait sur neige (Self-Portrait on Snow)*, 93–94; 93 (**49**)
Mann, Sally, *Three Generations*, 167 (**111**)
Markosian, Diana, *Not too long ago, my father had another child. I should be happy for him, but watching him play with her, feels like a bruise someone keeps pressing*, 57 (**26**)
mental health, 140–41 (**86–90**)
migration, 168–69 (**114–16**)
miscarriage, 60 (**33**)
Moffatt, Tracey
Birth Certificate, 1962, 141 (**88**)
Useless, 1974, 141 (**90**)
Wizard of Oz, 1956, The, 141 (**89**)
Morisot, Berthe, 69
Moses, Tabitha
Investment: Emma's Gown, 59 (**31**)
Investment: Tabitha (with Jon Barraclough), 59 (**32**)
mother-child relationships, 39–41, 43, 67–68, 71; 63 (**41**), 104–05 (**52–55**)
motherhood, 37–43, 67–71, 133–34
mothers
lesbian mothers, 9–10, 28–30, 32; 11 (**2–3**), 30 (**10**), 104 (**51**)
single mothers, 11, 18–19, 21–23; 19 (**6–8**), 55 (**22**)
Myerscough, Ishbel, *All*, 107 (**57**)
Neel, Alice, 28, 30, 67–69
De Vegh Twins, The, 90; 70 (**42**)
Nancy and Olivia, 66, 70–71; 104 (**52**)
Nicholson, Winifred, 38–41
Father and Son, 38–39; 39 (**13**)
Kate and Jake, Isle of Wight, 107 (**58**)
Nisenbaum, Aliza, *Susan, Aarti, Keerthana and Princess, Sunday in Brooklyn*, 26–30, 33; 30 (**10**)
Nixon, Nicholas
Bebe and Clementine, Cambridge, Massachusetts, 106 (**55**)
Clementine and Sam, Cambridge, Massachusetts, 80–81; 111 (**65**)
Sam et Clementine, Cambridge, Massachusetts, 81; 82 (**44**)

Opie, Catherine, *Self-portrait / Nursing*, 104 (**51**)
Pandhal, Hardeep, *Baba Deep Thing by Mum*, 169 (**115**)
parental favouritism, 85–87; 86 (**46**)
Paul, Celia, *My Mother with a Rose*, 113 (**68**)
Perry, Grayson, *Vase Using My Family*, 110 (**64**)
Poussin, Nicolas, *The Annunciation*, 35; 34 (**12**)
Rego, Paula, 27
 Split, 137 (**81**)
rejection, 141 (**88–90**)
resemblance, 167 (**111**)
resilience, 138–39 (**82–85**)
Reynolds, Joshua, *The Braddyll Family*, 51 (**15**)
Rodermondt, Pieter (after Rembrandt), *Esau Selling his Birthright to Jacob*, 86 (**46**)
Rodney, Donald, *In the House of My Father*, 169 (**116**)
Sadeler I, Jan (after Maarten de Vos), *The Visitation*, 130, 132; 131 (**77**)
samplers (Sarah Williamson, 1795), 164 (**104**)
Sassoferrato, *The Holy Family*, 57 (**27**)
Schaer, Miriam
 Untitled #1 ('Your not having children was the biggest disappointment of our life'), 61 (**34**)
 Untitled #11 ('Children are what makes a real family'), 61 (**35**)
 Untitled #13 ('You are not a real parent if you have only one child'), 61 (**37**)
 Untitled #15 ('Yes, you're married...'), 61 (**36**)
secrecy, 162
Sedira, Zineb, *Mother Tongue*, 168 (**114**)
Shah, Tejal, *You too can touch the moon – Yashoda with Krishna*, 63 (**40**)
Showering, Antonia, 71
sibling relationships, 81–85, 89–90, 94–95; 82 (**44**), 106 (**55**), 111 (**65**), 137 (**81**)
 see also, children without siblings; twins
Sorgini, Lisa, *Lise (36 weeks) and Lulu*, 78; 76 (**43**)
Spare Rib magazine, 9; 32 (**11**)
Sultan, Larry
 Business Page, 114 (**71**)
 My Mother Posing, 114 (**70**)
surrogacy, 10; 53 (**17**)
Thomas, Britt, *No Heartbeat/Little Rainbow*, 60 (**33**)
tokens, 163 (**102**)
traditional families, 51–52 (**15–16**)
transgender parents, 12; 54 (**19–21**)
twins, 90–93; 58 (**28**), 70 (**42**), 91 (**48**)
Vacuum desiccator bell jar, 58 (**29**)
Van Baburen, Dirck, *Roman Charity, Cimon and Pero*, 96–98; 101 (**50**)
Van Cleve, Joos, *Virgin and Child*, 45, 47–50; 48 (**14**)
Van Meyer, Jan, *The Daughters of Sir Matthew Decker, Bart.*, 89; 88 (**47**)
Vien, Joseph-Marie, *Sarah Presents Hagar to Abraham*, 53 (**17**)
violence, 86–87; 137 (**80–81**)
virginity, 133–35
Virgin Mary, The 35–37, 47–50, 129–32; 34 (**12**), 48 (**14**), 57 (**27**), 128 (**76**), 131 (**77**)
Walker, Caroline, Study for *Refreshments*, 72; 105 (**54**)
Wilkes, Cathy, *Untitled (Possil, At Last)*, 9; 9 (**1**)
Wright, Stuart Pearson, 13–18, 22–23
 Halfboy and Halfsister, 16; 17 (**5**)
 Stepdad, 15; 16 (**4**)

Picture credits

References below are to catalogue numbers:

Installation view 'The Encyclopedic Palace', Venice Biennale, Venice, 2013. Courtesy of The Artist and The Modern Institute/Toby Webster Ltd., Glasgow. Photo: Cristiano Corte 1; dmg media licensing 2, 3; Stuart Pearson Wright 4, 5; Courtesy Mary Husted, photo courtesy Ian Verge 6, 7 and 8; The Women's Art Collection, Murray Edwards College, Courtesy Mary Husted 9; © Aliza Nisenbaum. Photo courtesy the Artist and Anton Kern Gallery, New York 10 and p. 26; Courtesy Rosie Boycott, Marsha Rowe and photograph by Angela Phillips 11; © The National Gallery, London 12; © Trustees of Winifred Nicholson 13; © Trustees of Winifred Nicholson, Courtesy of Bristol Museums: Bristol Museum & Art Gallery 58; © Fitzwilliam Museum, Cambridge 14, 15, 27, 28, 46, 47, 76, 77, 104, 105, 106, 107, 108, 109, 110; Courtesy JJ Levine/ELLEPHANT Gallery 16, 19, 20, 21; © Musée Fabre de Montpellier Méditerranée Métropole/ photography Frédéric Jaulmes – Reproduction prohibited without authorisation 17; Bart Heynen 18; Loulou d'Aki www.dakiloulou.com 22 and p. 24; Harry Borden 23, 24, 25; Diana Markosian/Galerie les filles du Calvaire 26; Bourn Hall Fertility Clinic 29; © DACS 2023 30, 38 and p. 44; Photo: Jon Barraclough 31; Jon Barraclough and Tabitha Moses 32; Britt Thomas, Lullabies for Loss installation, 2018. Photo by Alex Barber, courtesy of Art League Houston 33; Artist: Miriam Schaer, photo: Stephen DeSantis 34, 35, 36, 37; © Sunil Gupta. All rights reserved, DACS 2023. Courtesy of the Harris Museum, Art Gallery & Library, Preston, and Hales Gallery 39; Image courtesy of the artist and Project 88 40; © ADAGP, Paris and DACS, London 2023. Courtesy of the artist and Perrotin. Photographer: Claire Dorn 41; © The Estate of Alice Neel, Courtesy The Estate of Alice Neel and David Zwirner, photo by Malcom Varon 42 and p. 66; Lisa Sorgini 43; © Nicholas Nixon, courtesy Fraenkel Gallery, San Francisco 44, 55, 65 and p. 2, p. 80; Barbara Hepworth © Bowness, photo © Kettle's Yard, University of Cambridge 45; © Tracey Emin. All rights reserved, DACS/Artimage 2023. Image courtesy White Cube. Photo: Stephen White & Co. 48; © ADAGP, Paris and DACS, London 2023. Courtesy of the artist and Opera Gallery 49; Image courtesy of York Museums Trust, https://yorkmuseumstrust.org.uk, Public Domain 50 and p. 96; © Catherine Opie, Courtesy Regen Projects, Los Angeles, and Thomas Dane Gallery, London 51; © The Estate of Alice Neel, Courtesy The Estate of Alice Neel and David Zwirner 52; © DACS 2023. Photo: Moderna Museet/ Stockholm 53; © Caroline Walker. Courtesy the artist; Stephen Friedman Gallery, London; GRIMM Gallery and Ingleby Gallery, Edinburgh. All rights reserved, DACS 2023. Photo: Peter Mallet 54 and p. 72; © Ishbel Myerscough, Flowers Gallery, London 57; Copyright Zun Lee. All rights reserved 59, 60, 61, 62 and p. 64; Photographer: Jean-Loup Cornet. Photo © The Estate of Michael Andrews/ Tate, © Photo Tate 63; © Grayson Perry. Courtesy the artist, Stedelijk Museum, Amsterdam and Victoria Miro. Photo Stephen Brayne 64; Courtesy of the artist and Tiwani Contemporary 66; © Tracey Emin. All rights reserved, DACS/ Artimage 2023. Image courtesy White Cube. Photo: Antonia Reeve 67; © Celia Paul. Courtesy the artist and Victoria Miro 68; © The Lucian Freud Archive. All rights reserved 2023/Bridgeman Images 69; © Estate of Larry Sultan. Courtesy of Casemore Gallery, San Francisco; Yancey Richardson Gallery, New York; Galerie Thomas Zander, Köln; and the Estate of Larry Sultan 70, 71; Courtesy the artist; © Nan Goldin/Gagosian 72, 73; © Tina Barney. Courtesy Kasmin, New York 74, 75 and p. 118; © Richard Billingham. All rights reserved, DACS 2023. Courtesy of Anthony Reynolds, London 78; Courtesy of Samira Abbassy. Photo by Jeanette May 79 and p. 116; Courtesy Pippy Houldsworth Gallery, London. © Zoë Buckman 2023 80; © Ostrich Arts Ltd. Courtesy Ostrich Arts Ltd and Victoria Miro 81; © Jim Goldberg. Courtesy of the artist 82, 83, 84, 85; Courtesy of the artist and Gallery Kayafas 86, 87; © Tracey Moffatt/Copyright Agency. Licensed by DACS 2023, © Photo Tate 88, 89, 90; © Chantal Joffe. Courtesy the artist and Victoria Miro. Photo: Angus Mill 91, 117 and p. 142; © Chantal Joffe. Courtesy the artist and Victoria Miro front cover, 92, 93, 94, 95, 118, 119, 120, 121 and p. 152; Haidas Collection 96 and p. 144; Courtesy Coram 97, 98; © The Foundling Museum, London 99, 100, 101, 102, 103; © Sally Mann. Courtesy Gagosian 111; Mary Berridge 112, 113; Courtesy the artist and Goodman Gallery, London and Mennour, Paris, © Photo Tate 114; Hardeep Pandhal, photo Joel Chester Fildes 115; Arts Council Collection, Southbank Centre, London. Photograph taken by Andra Nelki © The Estate of Donald G. Rodney 116